LETTERS & PAPERS OF
JOHN SINGLETON COPLEY
AND HENRY PELHAM
1739—1776

Library of American Art

LETTERS & PAPERS OF
JOHN SINGLETON COPLEY
AND HENRY PELHAM
1739–1776

Kennedy Graphics, Inc. • *Da Capo Press*
New York • *1970*

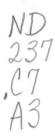
This edition of the *Letters & Papers of John Singleton Copley
and Henry Pelham, 1739–1776,* is an unabridged republication
of the first edition published in Boston in 1914 as Volume 71 of the
Collections of the Massachusetts Historical Society.

Library of Congress Catalog Card Number 78-100615

SBN 306-71406-X

Published by Kennedy Graphics, Inc.
A Division of Kennedy Galleries, Inc.
20 East 56th Street, New York, N.Y. 10022

and

Da Capo Press
A Division of Plenum Publishing Corporation
227 West 17th Street, New York, N.Y. 10011

LETTERS & PAPERS OF
JOHN SINGLETON COPLEY
AND HENRY PELHAM
1739–1776

John Singleton Copley
From the original painting by Copley
in the New York Historical Society.

LETTERS & PAPERS

OF

John Singleton Copley

AND

Henry Pelham

1739~1776

THE MASSACHUSETTS HISTORICAL SOCIETY

1914

Contents

Contents

Contents

Contents

Contents

Illustrations

Prefatory Note

THE letters and documents printed in this volume are in the Public Record Office, London.[1] They appear to have been drawn in part from the Domestic State Papers, but no note shows the history of the papers and how or when they reached the Record Office. For a long period of time they were among the papers intercepted by the British Government during the first months of the American rebellion; but they could hardly have actually been intercepted, as so many never passed through the English post-office or even crossed the ocean. Mr. Paul Leicester Ford, to whom one bundle of the papers was known, and who printed a few of the papers in the *Atlantic Monthly*, LXXI. 499, states, but without giving his authority, that Copley and Pelham fell under the suspicion of the Government. "To what extent suspicion was attached to them it is now impossible to say; but it certainly went so far as to lead these two men to turn over their private papers to the government; and these, instead of being returned, drifted into this great depository of manuscripts."

Since Mr. Ford wrote, the collection has been much increased by newly discovered material, and in a rearrangement it had been assorted into four bundles. Three of those were discovered quite by accident by Professor Guernsey Jones, of the University of Nebraska. Becoming interested, he began to make copies, and while thus engaged, his attention was called by Professor Charles M. Andrews, whose *Guide* had not then been printed, to a fourth bundle, containing the earliest Pelham letters. The transcripts and the notes upon them[2] were offered by Professor Jones to this Society for publication. Of the collection he writes:

"All of Pelham's letters and all of Copley's, except those to Pelham and his mother (and the one to his wife from the Chamberlain Collection), are in the form of rough drafts, sometimes in duplicate or even in triplicate with slight variations. The others are the letters actually received, with

---

[1] Designated in Andrews's *Guide* as C. O. 5/38, 39. The arrangement in two bundles was made at the suggestion of Professor Jones.

[2] It has not been thought necessary to locate the portraits by Copley mentioned in these letters, as Mr. Frank W. Bayley, of Boston, is preparing an exhaustive list of Copley's paintings.

trifling exceptions, which may be readily inferred from the letters themselves. The entire correspondence was once carefully sorted and arranged by Pelham, but is now in the utmost confusion. The less important letters, together with Pelham's memoranda and household bills, are omitted in this volume.

"It has been impossible to discover how these private letters of a provincial family came to be incorporated into the great collection of British State Papers. When Copley started on his Italian tour in the summer of 1774, he left his letters and papers with Pelham, who kept them with his own. In less than two years, Pelham in turn left Boston — a Tory refugee upon the British evacuation of that place. He presumably took his papers with him, for upon one of the wrappers he has written, 'Letters from Mr. Copley, rec'd at Halifax.' On May 12, 1776, more than eleven hundred New England refugees embarked at Halifax for England. Among them was Pelham on the Brigantine *Unity*, Captain Hill.[1] He reached Dover after a short passage on June 5.[2] What happened to his papers is a matter of conjecture. We only know that, fortunately for us, they are now preserved in the British archives."

The correspondence concerns Massachusetts before the date of Independence, and throws valuable light upon Copley and his early paintings. Mention is made of a number of his portraits, hitherto unknown, and his impressions of the work of other painters and methods of painting are detailed in his letters from France and Italy. The papers are thus both historical and technical.

Professor Jones makes acknowledgment to Lord Aberdare, the Honorable Lady Du Cane, and the officials of the Public Record Office for courtesies received. The Society adds its acknowledgment for assistance to Mr. Frederic Amory, Mr. Charles Pelham Curtis, Mr. Henry Copley Greene, Mr. Copley Amory, the late Mr. Denison R. Slade, and the New York Historical Society.

CHARLES FRANCIS ADAMS.
GUERNSEY JONES.
WORTHINGTON CHAUNCEY FORD.

BOSTON, *September* 15, 1914.

---

[1] C. O. 5/93, p. 333. Pelham, known to be an artist, was listed as a "reputable tradesman." See Copley's objection to the word "trade" as applied to art (p. 65, *infra*).
[2] *Morning Post*, June 8, 1776. Governor Hutchinson heard of Pelham's arrival on June 7. *Diary and Letters*, II. 61.

LETTERS & PAPERS

OF

John Singleton Copley

AND

Henry Pelham

1739–1776

The Copley-Pelham Letters
1739-1776

Peter Pelham, Sr. to Peter Pelham, Jr.

I was indeed somthing surpris:d on the 6th of May last on the Receiveing a Letter from an almost an unknown Person which Referd me to Captain woodside for a Pirtickuler account of you and your affairs, who gave me but a short and unsatisfactory Relation as I found in your Letter which was that you was married to a second wife [1] with a Prospect of an Increase of your famely without any fortune which makes me Concernd at your being too near Re[l]ated to me by being forst to labour under Deficultys as I my self am and have been many years; but of all afflictions being slighted and forsaken by my owne flesh and Blood gives me more trouble and vexation than all other Crosses and Disapointments; but as their is a time for all things and when are at a Crises it is sure that a turne is to be Expected. and as it is my nature to putt the best Constructions in most things Relating to my self from my Children, Espesialy for your so long silence and neglect of me. but since you make me beleive you are sorry for what is Past I Cannot be of that stuborn and unforgiveing Disposition as not to Pardon and wipe of all Misdemeaners, and do heartily forgive what Ever has been amiss in you on my account, and never for the future I hope shall have any more Cause of Complaint.

I had another Letter on the 12th of June last Dated April the 5th by Mr. Hilhouse who Pleasd me by saying you Lin:d very

[1] Margaret Lowrey, whom he married, October 15, 1734.

well and in a handsome manner which I am heartily Glad of. I Prest him very much to lett me know where he Lodg'd that I might waite on him, but Could not Prevail. so have not seen him since. I was at Chelsea to see Captain woodside once, who was att his fathers house, a Decenting Minester but was not at home at that time. he has been to see me severall times since, but the last time he was with me is above two months, and what is become of him I know nott, whether in England still or gone. I am but latly Recoverd of a feavor since then but am very well at this time; your sister Messenger, thank god, is very well and shed tears of Joy at my haveing a letter from you, and sends her kind Love and servis to you, and her sister in law, and Blessing to all your great and litle ones. your sister heley [1] is in the Country and was very well when the other day I had a letter from her. She writt to you some time ago but haveing no answer soposd might miscarry. and now once more my Dear son since the Ice is Broake Between us, I hope for a great deale of Pleasure by Renewing our Corispondence, and shall heartily Prey god to Bless and Prosper you in all your honest undertakeing has been my Constant and Daly Prayers; and were I in any Circumstance of shewing my love to you other than my hearty wishes for you, you should soon find how sincearly my Dear son I am Intirely your Most Affectionate father

P: PELHAM.

Pray give my Blessing and servis to my Daughter in law, and I wish all health and happyness to attend her and hers. I was mightily Pleas:d with Charles:s [2] Prety Letter to whome I send

[1] Helena.

[2] Charles Pelham, born in London, and baptized at St. Paul's, December 9, 1722, became a schoolmaster at Medford and elsewhere, and married Mary Tyler, niece of Sir William Pepperell.

Peter Pelham
From the original painting by Copley
in the possession of Mr. Charles Pelham Curtis

my Blessing and thankes for the same and when you write to Poor Peter [1] my Blessing to him and am heartily glad he is like to do so well. your sister Messenger gos to see Mr. and Mrs. Simons some times but I have not been so farr this half year for I very seldom go abroad so have not seen them but they are very well.

Pray Derect your next to me att the Right Honble the Lady Isabella Scotts, in Grosvenor Street, Grosvenor Square London. my Blessing to all the Rest of your famely and God Bless you

good night

[L]ONDON, September the 12th, 1739.

[Addressed:] To Mr. Pelham att his house att Boston in New England. [2]

Bofton, *March* the 19 172*7/8*

REceived of Mr. *the Revd. Benj: Coleman* the Sum of 3 *shillings* being the firft Payment of the Subfcription for a *Print in Metzotinto* of the late Rev. Dr. **Cotton Mather**, by which the Bearer is Entitled to the faid *Print* Paying 2 *shillings* at the Delivery of the fame, By me *Peter Pelham*

RECEIPT BY PETER PELHAM, JR.

[1] The brother of Charles, born in England, and baptized at St. Paul's, December 17, 1721, later removed to South Carolina, and thence to Virginia.

[2] In February, 1738, Pelham occupied a house on Summer Street, next to that of Philip Dumaresque, and taught "Dancing, Writing, Reading, painting upon Glass, and all kinds of needle work." *Boston Gazette*, February 6, 1738.

Peter Pelham, Sr. to Peter Pelham, Jr.

MY DEAR SON,

I will assure you that I have not faild answering all the Letters I had the Joy and Pleasure of Receiveing from you in answer to one Dated April the 5th, 1739 and Recd June 12th, Answerd September 12th following: another I had Dated october 30th, Recd November 26th, 1739, and likewise Answerd February 19th, 1739–40 so that I hope my Dear Son will not Imput any thing wanting in me or Neglect in giveing you all the satisfaction you so Earnestly Desire in hearing from me as I am the same of you. but as the times are at Present it Cannot be much wonderd at our Letters being intercepted when it is so haserdus for all English ships to go any where abroad, who are very frequently taken by the spaniards. however I have the Pleasure of Receiveing your Last Dated March 14th I had the 1st of July by the Boston Trader who says [he] is to Return very soon, so [I] would not lose the opertunity of Writeing by him. tho you Referd me to the *Britania* Captaine Fores,[1] I have venturd to send this answer by the same hands that Brought me your Letter. I am heartily Pleasd to hear, by Lady D: Lorain [2] that Came from Charlestowne in Carolina about a year ago, that my Grandson Peter was a very Genteel Clever young man being very well acquainted with him by teaching Miss Fenwick her sister to play on the Harpsicord which he Performs very well.

---

[1] A Captain Fones cleared from Boston to London before March 17. *New England Weekly Journal*, March 17, 1741.

[2] Elizabeth, daughter of John Fenwick, of South Carolina, married Henry Scott, a son of Henry Scott, Earl of Deloraine. Captain Scott was grandson of James Scott, Duke of Monmouth, and Anne, Duchess of Buccleugh. Fenwick removed to England, and died there in 1747. His will is printed in *South Carolina Historical and Genealogical Magazine*, VII. 27.

Lady D: Lorain was Married to Mr. Scott Captain of a man of Warr that was stationd att Carrolina whose Brother[1] died a litle before he left that Contry with out Children so he Came to the title and he died that very night he Came to London. so she is now a widdow has one son about four years old now Lord D: Loraine, and another younger with her father and mother in Charlestowne. I Pray god give you Comfort and happyness with all your Children. I am heartily Pleasd at the Charicter you give of Dear Charles and I hope he will Continue to be a Blessing to you. I hope you will make my Blessing and kind affections Acceptable to your Dear Spoues and I wish all health and happyness to attend you all. Dear Son as to your Sister Messengers sending Cloaths that was the Dutchess of Monmouths,[2] it is now about Nine years since she Died and Left the Poorest Wardrobe that Ever Dutchess did that had twenty thousand Pounds a year, and those Devided amongst three Women. and your Poor sister has been out of Place Ever since, so that you may Imagin she Cannott have where with to assist you. and your sister heley is as much Concernd. she has not any thing worth sending at Present her Lady has Lived in the Country alltogather, till now very Lately she is Come to towne, and has taken a house very near me, which will give me opertunitys to see her oftener than I have done these 14 years. your sister heley did in your first wives time gave a Captain of a ship a litle Box with a few things for her, which he Promist to deliver, who gave his man a great Charge to Put them up but the Captain saild and his man forgott the Box that he Put in the Clos-

[1] Francis Scott, second Earl of Deloraine.

[2] Charles Mordaunt (1658–1735), third Earl of Peterborough, took the title of Duke of Monmouth in 1689. His wife was Carey, or Carry, daughter of Sir Alexander Fraser, of Durris in Kincardineshire. She is said to have survived her husband, so "about nine years since" may be an error.

sett, so she never had another opertunity of sending it. but she hopes in some time to have some little matter to send they both Desires their Best kindest Love and Affections and kind Rispect to you both and Blessing to all the Rest.

I hope my Dear son will Consider my near Aproach to 70 and Excuse the failing of my Eyes and a shakeing hand, which I fear will give you some troble to Read. I have no Ailment on me at Present but a Thorough Concern I am not in a Condition to assist my Dear Children according to my unfined love and affections which I Ever bore for them. I am very much putt to it to find my self in nesesarys in outward apparrell, for which I Cannot free my self from Debt theirfore [am] farr from assisting those I have so much att heart and I Can find no other Remedy but to Consider that all Events are from god and as his Providence orders all things according to his will and Pleasure, who shall say why is it so; I fear you will be out of Patiance with this Dull subject, but I beg you will take the sincearity of my good meaning, and with my Blessing to you your spoues and all the Litle ones, I will give you now no further troble, but my Desire and beg I may hear from you as soon and as offten as you Can, and that you will beleive me to be my Dear Son your most Intire and Ever Most Affectionate father

PETER PELHAM.

LONDON, July 4th, 1741.

I so seldom go abroad that I have nott seen Mr. or Mrs. Simons above these twelve months, so Can give no account of them but by your sisters who gos to see them some times. so god bless you.

[Addressed:] To Mr. Pelham att his house att Boston in New England.

Helena Pelham [1] to Peter Pelham, Jr.

Maby my Dear Brother will be a little surprisd at haveing a
letter from me, but I do asure you I have greate pleasure in
wrighting to you and in hearing of your wellfair. but I have
not allway the opportunity for some times I am in Irland and
sometimes in England, and have been settled noware tell now,
and now I hope I am, for my lady [2] has taken a house in london. my Dear brother I have been four times in Irland, and
the sickest sole all ways at sea that ever was. I hope to god I
have dun going to sea now. I live with the same lady that I
went over to. o my Dear Brother I long to see you but I am
sure I never shall. since you are marrid a gaine to be sure you
will not leave that place. poor mrs Guy is verey olde and
verey poor. wee are all kind to her, or I dont know what she
would have dun. she desierd when I wrote, her blessing to the
children and kind love to you. thanke god my Dear father is
verey well and looks most charmingly. my sister has been ill a
long time and is but in diferant. now boath my father and she
desiers to be kindley remembert to you. I must tell you that a
long time a go when Patty [3] was a live, hear was some gentleman
in town who came from ware you are and was takeing his familey over to settle thare. I heard this at mr Simons so I desierd that he would take a small parcel and a letter to you from
me and he promisd he would. So I left at mr Simons, for the
gentle man would send thare for it, a letter and a short apron
and a fann for dear Patty. accordingley the gentle man sent his

[1] She was living in Chichester, England, in 1774.

[2] Henrietta, Lady Conway, daughter of Lord Conway and Lady Mary
Hyde. Edward Solly in 4 *Notes and Queries*, XII. 179.

[3] Martha, Pelham's first wife, whom he married in England. By her he
had three sons, Peter, Charles and William.

man for them and had them and be holde the man never packd
them up but left them on a shelf in his masters closet. so some
days after I had them a gaine which I was verey sorey for. I
now in tend makeing the second trial. the gentle man who
brings this is one I have some little knowledge of. he lived with
a lady and gentle[man] who my lady made a viset to in the
countrey. wee was thare six weeks. I heard he was going to
leave his place and go to new England, so I asked the favour
of him to carrey a letter for me to you, and when he Calls for
my letter I will aske him to take a little parcel for me, which is
a drest cap I send your little girl, who you say is a charming
girl and her name Penelope.[1] poor thing, I shall never see her,
nor my Dear old acquiantence Petter and Charls, who I hope
is verey well. a lady hear told my father she knew Petter, for
that he taught her sister on the harpsycord at South Carrolina,
and that he was a verey agreable entertaining young man. you
may be sure that account of him pleasd my father as well as
me. I send my love and blessing to them all. I have sent your
wife a preasent of a fann and a short apron, with my service and
respects to her. I am glad since you marrid againe you have so
prudend and good a wife as you say she is, and I have sent a
pair of glove tops for penny as well as a cap. mr and mrs
Simons was hear to see me the other day, when I was a wrighting to you in the beginning of this letter. thay desierd thare
Service to you. I have been three or four times at this letter
and hope now I shall finish. my father has wrote ofen to you,
and you complain that you sildom hear from him. so he fanceys
thay must miscarrey. my dear brother I hop you will write to
me by the first opportunity, and let me know if you have re-

---

[1] Penelope (1735-1756). She is said to have died, unmarried, at Boothbay,
Maine.

ceved my small poor present. I shall be rejoyced at a letter
from you. I would have sent petter and charls each of them a
little bit of gold but am a fraid to venture. if you git these safe
and when ever you send me a letter by aney ship, if you know
aney one in it that I may trust, I will not forgit my two dear
boys. I now conclude with wishing my Dear Brother health
and prosperity. my prayers and best wishes allways atend you
and yours. so god bless you my Dear Brother and beleave me
to be your ever loveing sister

H. PELHAM.

Diret for me at the Honble mrs Conways in Green Street
by Grosvenor Square

Sept. the 1, 1741.

[Endorsed:] Boston Decr. the 9th: 1741. Rec:d this with the
Banbox, with the Cap, fan, Apron, and knott, by the hands
of Mr. Rello.

[Addressed:] To Mr. Petter Pelham at Boston in New England.

Peter Pelham, Sr. to William Pelham [1]

MY DEAR WILLIAM,

I Return you my hearty thankes for your kind and Prety
Letter which gave me a great deale of Pleasure and satisfaction
at your tender years to Perform so good and Dutifull a Letter
to me, your Poor old Grandfather, which I hope you will Continue to do as offten as you have an opertunity. for their Can
be nothing so Pleaseing to me as to hear of the wellfair of my
Dear Children, which you all are, and shall all Pertake of my

---

[1] Son of Peter Pelham, Jr., by his first wife, Martha. He was born in Boston,
February 22, 1729, and buried January 28, 1761.

Blessing and hearty Prayers to god that you may live to be a Comfort to your Dear father and mother, which will indear me to value so obeideant a son, and I hope a good man as well as a good Christian, which will be the greatest happyness to your Parent yourself, but more Espsilarly to your Ever Tender and Affectionate Grandfather

P: PELHAM.

My kind Blessing to Thomas and thank him for his Rememberance of me in your Letter.

LONDON, February the 19th, 1741:2

Helena Pelham to Peter Pelham, Jr.

LONDON, febury:the:19:1741 [1742.]

MY DEAR BROTHER,

you may be sure it gives us a greate pleasure to hear from you. I never was more pleasd with aney thing then with your little girls letter. I dare say she is a charming childe, and I was glad to hear from my own dear boy charls, who I hope is still handsome. he was the preteyest boy when he went over that ever was. my father heard that Petter was a sencable young man, and verey chomical and entertaining. Lady Delleraine knows him. he teaches her sister at South carrolina. She came from thence. my father intends wrighting to him when her Ladyship writs to her father, and she will send it. I am sorrey you never got those things I sent over to penny [Penelope]. it was a cap I drest her up and pink and silver ribbon in it and a pair of silver glove tops and a tippet I thinke. I sent the banbox by one mr Rello, a swiss. he sayde he went to boston to be gunner of a ship thare at boston, so pray in quire for him and aske him what he did with a little banbox which I gave him directed for you at Boston. I hope the poor childe will git her cap yet. it is a verey pretey one. I thinke it is runing a hased [hazard] to send things so far of. I knew this mr Rello. he lived with a familey ware my lady visets, and tolde me he was going a broad. I asked ware he sayde to boston, so I tolde him I had a brother thare, if he would be so good as to Carrey a letter and a little parcel for me. he sayde aney thing he would take care of it. so I got these things dun up for the childe, and gave the box into his own hand, and desierd him to deliver it to you. he promisde me he would I made no Doubt but thay would have [reached] you Safe. I hope these will git Safe to you how ever that the poor child ma not loos all her fine things. I sopose my father tolde you my sister was married a gaine.[1] She was marrid last michelmus, and lives in the countrey by Barnet. She is verey ill. I question if she can live long, she is in so bad a way. my Dear Brother I am still with the same good Lady that I went over to Irland to. I have been three times since, so in all I have crost the Irish seas eight times, and allways the sickest sole at sea that ever was. I wonder if ever you will cross the sea to come to olde England a gaine. I fear not. I shall never be so happey as [to] see you mor or aney of yours. all the pleasure I can expect is to hear from you, which I hope you will never fail of doing as ofen as opportunity will sarve. I live Just by my father, which is to me a greate happeyness, for I have ofen the pleasure of seeing him. my Lady has taken a leas of her house for five year, so I thinke now I am settled. pray let me hear from you as soon as you can. Direct for mrs Pelham at the Honble Mrs Conways in Green Stre[et] by Grosvenor Square. poor mrs Guy is yet a live but verey poor. wee are all kind to her, or I dont know what she would do. I tolde you

---

[1] The name of her husband, Baker, is given on p. 15, *infra*.

this in my letter you never got, and that she desierd her service to you and blessing to the children. I now must conclude
my Dearest Brother your ever faithfull frind and Loveing Sister.

H. PELHAM.

Pray make my compleyments to your Wife

Helena Pelham to Penelope Pelham [1]

febury the 19: 1741 [1742.]

DEAR LITTLE UNKNOWN PENELOPE,

I must love you childe for your name. you are the preteyest
little wrighter I ever knew. I hope to convirce with you by letter
as ofen as you have an opportunity, that I may see how
finley you improve. you have all your requests granted. See
what it is to be a pretey little begger. a baby a red trunke and
a lock and key. and I my little childe have sent you a blue
Ring and a necklace, and a Pelerin to wair a bought you neck,
such a one as your baby has on. I should be mightley pleasd
to see you at the opening of the trunke, for I am sure you will
be in greate Joy. pray let me hear how you like all your things
and give my service to your mama. so a Due my little unknown
girl I shall be allways your loveing Aunt

H. PELHAM.

Peter Pelham, Sr. to Peter Pelham, Jr.

MY DEAR SON,

haveing no Answer of mine to you since I Writt, which was
Dated February 19th 1741:2, which was an Answer to yours I
Recd February 4th, Dated November 30th 1741, and haveing

[1] Her niece.

Recd the inclosd from Mr. Lowrey Directed in a Blank Paper
to me Directed, tooke the first opertunity to send it, and withall
to Acquaint you that your Poor Sister Baker Dyde on Sunday
the 29th of August Last after a Long and tedious Illness. your
Sister Heley Desires her kindest Love Affections Blessing and
Servis to you and all yours, and is much Concernd to know if
you Ever Recd her Litle Presents to her Dear Neice Penelope,
she sent by Mr. Cahill, who Promist to take great Care to Deliver them with his owne hands; I had the Pleasure of a Letter
from Dear Peter from Charlestowne, Carolina, the 15th of May
last. which I Designe to Answer very soone. it Reioices me
Extreamly to hear by the Countess of Deloraine that Came
from thence that he is Extreamly Likd, and behaves himself
mighty well, and teaches her sister to play on the spinett and
has a very good Charicter which is a great Comfort to me to
hear.

I Cannot give you any Account by what Ship or Captain
this Comes to you, not being able to go so farr as the new England Coffee house [1] to putt my letter in my self; but am forst to
send it to a friend to put it in for me, who lives Just by and hope
it will Come safe to you, and shall be Extream Glad to hear
from you. this with my Blessing to you, my Daughter Pelham, William, Charles I should have said first, Tho: and my
Little Dear Penelope, and Chiefly to your Self, who am in Con-
tinuall Prayers to god to send his Blessing on [you] and all
yours from a sincear Most Affectionate and Ever Indulgent
father

PETER PELHAM.

LONDON, october 12th, 1742.

[1] This was in Threadneedle Street, behind the Royal Exchange, and facing
the favorite Coffee House known as "Grigsby's."

Peter Pelham, Sr. to Peter Pelham, Jr.

MY DEAR SON,

I take this opertunity of a Gentleman that is Designd for Boston, who is to Call in me this morning. theirfore am very scanty of time, and to acquaint you that I have not heard from you since october the 12 Dated November 30th 1741. but as my grandson has writ severall to me I Impute the miscarridge by the Spaniards Intersepting them, which I hope is the Case with you, which makes me very Ready to Judge it not want of Duty or Love and affections, which you so much Exprest in your Last to me. your Poor sister Baker Died Last August on the 29th after a very Tedious indisposition. your sister Helena thank god is very well. I hope in the Lord this will find you all the same. my kind Rispects to my Daughter Pelham. with my hearty Blessing to her to you and to all my Dear Grand Children I am in great hast. Expect the Gentleman and my Ladys Call, and am my Dear son your Ever Most Affectionate father

P: PELHAM.

LONDON, July 20th, 1743.

[Endorsed] Rec'd this Letter Octo'r the 14, 1743, per Mr. Wakefield [1]

Helena Pelham to Peter Pelham, Jr.[2]

Oct. 3, 1748.

MY DEAR BROTHER,

I begin writing to you without knowing whether it will ever come to your hands or not, but I am determined to write, and hope you will get some of my letters if not all. This is the third

---

[1] Pelham married for his third wife, Mary Copley, widow of Richard Copley and daughter of John Singleton, of Quinville Abbey, County Clare. The marriage took place in Boston, in 1748. [2] From *Mass. Hist. Soc. Proceedings*, IX. 202.

My Dear Lady. Boston Sep. 22. 1784.

I duely not'd your kind and agreeable
Fav.r of the 6th Ins.t which believe me I should
have sooner answer'd but you well know my ina-
bility, and have not till now had an oportunity of
doing it by means of a friend. I greatly regret
your indisposition which prevented me the pleasure
of seeing you, but hope the pleasure of hearing you
are better. I thank you for your kind intelligence
from London, and in return have the pleasure to
inform you that I have since Rec.d a Letter from
Mr Copley of June 7. wherein he informs me that
himself and Family are well, as also Mrs Rogers
and Mrs Clarke who all desire a tender remembrance to their
conections here. Inclos'd is a Copy of the In-
scription on my dear Harry's Wifes Tomb, which
I have got Copied on purpose for you, that you
need not be at the trouble of returning it. My
best respects wait on your good Parents, your
self and Sister, and remain
                your affectionate
                    Mary Pelham

time I have wrote since February; in my last I told you that my father was very well, and so he is now, thank God Almighty for it. I am in the country, but hear frequently from my dear father. We have been out of town ever since the second of May. I long to have a letter from you to know how you and all your family does. In your last you were so good as to tell my father how your sons was disposed of. I hope Peter is happily married. As Charles is brought up a merchant I flatter myself that some time or an other he will come to England. O my dear soul how glad I shall be to see him; if please God I should be alive then. I shall here send you a direction how to write to me, which I did in my two last letters, but till I hear from you I am not sure you got them. I hope you will never fail to write when any ships come to London, for it is the greatest pleasure in the world to my dear father and me to hear of your welfare. I am sure my letters must be very stupid to my dear brother, as I have nothing entertaining to tell you, for as you know none of my acquaintance, nor I any of yours, must make my letters very stupid; for after I have inquired how you, your wife, and the dear children are, and tell you my father and self are well, I have nothing more to say. As for news I can never write of that you have in a better manner than what I can express it. So will conclude with my best wishes and love to your self and to your wife, and to all your family and hope you will believe me to be,

Your ever loving sister

HELENA PELHAM.

I send this to town to my father & get him to send it to the New England Coffee house.

Direct for me at the Honble Mrs. Conways in Green St, near Grosvenor Square.

To Mr Peter Pelham, Sr at Boston in New England.

Peter Pelham, Sr. to Peter Pelham, Jr.

MY DEAR SON,

I had the Pleasure and happiness to see your Letter to your sister, which she Recd on Monday the 23d of october, Dated August 10th last Past, where in I find you are Concernd in not hearing from me. But Could you but Imagin what a fateague it is to me in makeing so many Pott hooks and hangers you would be good Enough to Excuse me. since I have the Blessing of a Most Dutifull Daughter to do that office for me, I Cannot speake half her worth in Duty love and Affections she dos and has show'd to me for many years, in assisting me many times with Money Cloaths and linin in which I was Reduc:d in the later Part of my Poor Dear Ladys life; you seem to take it ill of your sister for not Letting you know the Place of my aboade, which is at one Mr. Comptons a grocer in South Audley Street Grocevenor Square: I am Extreamly well Pleasd that god has blest you with so Choice[?] a Companion, which is the greatest Pleasure and Comfort of life. I Pray god Bless you all with health and Prosperity and grant you Patiance till I am call[ed] home, at which time I shall not forgett my Dearest son, and asure you all that I am blest with at Present shall not go from you or yours. your sister is to inclose this so can say no more at Present but Remain My Dear son your Ever Most Affection-ate father

P: PELHAM.

SOUTH AUDLEY STREET, GROSVENOR SQUARE
LONDON, November 30, 1749.[1]

[1] Received February 12, 1749–50.

Charles Pelham[1] to Peter Pelham, Jr.

NEWPORT, Sepr. 10, 1750.

HON'D SIR!

On Saturday Evening I Arriv'd here after a very pleasant Ride of almost Two Days, and as I immagine I shall not set out from hence before the beginning of next Week I thought it proper to present you and my Mother my humble Duty and Love, which I flatter my Self will not be unacceptable to you; and I hope when I return to meet with your Blessing and Continuance of your Regard and Love.

I met with Mr. Rob't. Jenkins upon the Road on Fryday Night where I Lodg'd at 11 oClock at Night, who Wak'd me after I had been an hour in Bed, so I did not Speak to him with Regard to your Receipts, as it was an improper time, and as you will see him In Boston, what he has done with them I cannot say; But Bro'r Phillips Informs me, if you will send him Receipts, he will Engage to procure 20. or 30 Subscribers without fail, so if you see cause you may do it Writing him a Line informing him I had acquainted you of his proposition, which he says he would be glad to do to serve you.[2] whether or not he can do it I am no Judge at present, so you are to do as you Please. pray present my Love to my Brethren and Accept me as Hon'd and Dear Sir Your Dutiful and Affect'e Son, and hum. Serv't

CHAS. PELHAM.

This I Write under several Disadvantages, so hope you'l Excuse the Roughness of it. Mr. Rowand and Mr. Logan present you their kind Service.

[1] Son of Peter Pelham, Jr.

[2] In 1750 Pelham engraved a portrait of Rev. Thomas Prince, painted by John Greenwood.

Will of Peter Pelham, Sr.,[1] 1755

IN THE NAME OF GOD AMEN. This is the last Will and Testament of me Peter Pelham now of the parish of Saint George Hanover Square in the County of Middlesex Gentleman which I now make whilst I am in perfect Health in order to prevent any Disputes that might arise after my Death touching or Concerning the Disposition of my Estate and Effects in Manner following (that is to say) first and principally I recommend my Soul into the hands of Almighty God my Creator hoping for the Salvation of it through the Merits and Intercession of my Saviour Jesus Christ and my Body I Commit to the Earth to be Buried in such Decent but private manner as to my Executors hereinafter Named shall seem meet And as to such Worldly Estate as it hath Pleased God to Bless me with I Give and Dispose thereof as follows, First I Give and Bequeath unto Henry Compton and John Compton Sons of Thomas Compton of the said parish of Saint George Hanover Square Grocer the Sum of Twenty pounds apiece to be paid them as soon after my decease as possible and it is my Will and Desire that all my Wearing Apparel be sold and disposed of as soon after my Deacease as Conveniently may be and the money Arising by sale thereof shall go Into and be taken as part of the Residūm of my Estate and Effects ITEM I Give and Bequeath unto the said Thomas Compton and John Tiso of Bloomsbury in the said County of Middlesex Oylman the sum of Ten pounds apiece hoping they will take upon them the Execution of the Trusts hereby Reposed in them ITEM I Give and bequeath unto my Loving son Peter Pelham now at Boston in New England the sum of Two Hundred pounds of lawfull money of Great Britain to be paid him as soon after my decease as Conveniently may be but In Case I shall survive my said Son then the said sum of Two Hundred pounds shall go into and be taken as part of the Residuum of my Estate and Effects ITEM I Give and Bequeath unto my Loving Daughter Helena Pelham my Two Handled Silver Cup And

---

[1] From the records of the Prerogative Court of Canterbury, Somerset House.

it is my will meaning and desire that my said Daughter Helena Pelham shall have the use of all the Remainder of my plate and Rings for and during the Term of her Natural life and from and imediately after her Decease then my will and desire is that the same shall be sold by my Executors herein after named and the money arising by sale thereof shall also go into and be taken as part of the Residuum of my Estate and Effects AND all the Rest Residue and Remainder of my Estate and Effects both Real and personal of what Nature Kind or Quality soever whereof I shall Dye Possessed or whereunto I shall be Intitled at the time of my Death either in Possession Reversion Remainder or Expectancy (after payment of my Just Debts Legacys and funeral Expences which I hereby Charge with the payments thereof) I Give Devise and Bequeath the same unto the said Thomas Compton and John Tiso their Executors and Administrators Upon this special Trust and Confidence nevertheless to pay and apply the Interest and produce thereof unto my said Daughter Helena Pelham and her Assigns for and during the Term of her Natural life and from and Imediately after her Death then I Give Devise and bequeath the whole of the Residuum of my Estate and Effects unto my said Son Peter Pelham his heirs and Assigns forever but in Case my said Daughter shall happen to Survive my said son then I Give Devise and Bequeath the same (after the Death of my said Daughter as aforesaid) unto and amongst all and every the Child and Children of my said son Peter Pelham Lawfully begotten to be Equally Divided amongst them share and share alike And In Case any of the Children of my said son Peter Pelham shall happen to Dye before the Bequest hereinbefore mentioned can take Effect leaving (or is now Dead and has Left) any Child or Children behind him her or them then I Give the share of him her or them so Dying unto such Child or Children in Equal shares and proportions And I do hereby Nominate Constitute and Appoint the said Thomas Compton and John Tiso Joint Executors of this my last Will and Testament And I do hereby Revoke and make Void all former and other Wills by me at any time heretofore made And I do Declare this only to be my Last Will and Testament In Witness Whereof

I the said Peter Pelham have to this my last Will and Testament Written upon Two sheets of Paper to the first whereof I have set my hand and to the last Sheet my Hand and Seal this Thirtieth Day of June in the year of our Lord one Thousand Seven Hundred and fifty five.

PETER PELHAM. (L.S.)

SIGNED SEALED Published and declared by the said Peter Pelham the Testator as and for his last will and Testament in the presence of us who at his Request and in his Sight and in the Sight of each other have Subscribed our Names as Witnesses hereto — THOS WILLIAMS — JOSEPH KAYE South Audley Street Grosvenor Square London — JOHN MITTON his clerk.

Proved 22nd July 1756.

July 22d 1756.

Thomas Compton one of the Executors within named was sworn before me

Taverner AND: COLTER DUCAREL

Surrogate

PROVED at London the twenty second day of July 1756 before the Worshipfull Andrew Colter Ducarel Doctor of Laws Surrogate by the Oath of Thomas Compton one of the Executors to whom Administration was granted having been first sworn duly to administer (John Tiso the other Executor also one of the residuary Legatees in the Trust named in the said Will having renounced as well the Execution thereof as also the said Trust).

The Testator was formerly of the parish within mentioned but died late of the City of Chichester in the County of Sussex on the 2d day of July last a Widower.[1]

---

[1] See *Mass. Col. Soc. Transactions*, v. 194.

Thomas Ainslie[1] to Copley

D'R S'R,

I am favour'd with Yours, and the picture came very safe, and gives me great Satisfaction. I am just going to send it to Scotland to please a fond Parent, and as it goes in a Man of War, I hope She will receive it Safe.

I belive You may find it worth Your while to take a trip down here in the Spring, there are several people who would be glad to employ You, I belive so because I have heard it mentiond, if you should stay never so little while with us should You come my Assistance in any thing in my power should not be wanting, I am D'r S'r Your Oblid: hum'l Ser't

THOS. AINSLIE.

HALIFAX, 8 Oct: 1757.

Helena Pelham to Charles Pelham [2]

CHICHESTER, Feby 15th, 1762.

MY DEAR NEPHEW,

The third of this month brought me the confort and pleasure of a letter from you dated Nov. 2. 1761. Indeed I was rejoiced to see one, for I have been vastly uneasy as I have never heard from you since Oct. 27, 1759 and I have written you three letters since that. My dear I have never heard from you since that dreadful fire happened at Boston,[3] therefore judge of my uneasiness. But, thank God, I have now heard that you are

---

[1] Collector of the port of Quebec and a captain in the city's militia. His diary during the defence of Quebec against the Americans in 1775–1776 was printed by the Literary and Historical Society of Quebec, VII. 9. The manuscript is in the Sparks Mss. in Harvard College Library.

[2] From *Mass. Hist. Soc. Proceedings*, IX. 206.

[3] That of March 20, 1760. See *N. E. Hist. Gen. Reg.*, XXXIV. 288.

well, as for your brother Peter, I have not heard from him this age — poor William you mentioned to me and said he was but of a poor constitution,[1] and till then I did not know that there was any children of your mother's, but Peter and you; or if I did I had forgot it. So your brother has five children, poor man I pity him.[2] You have never seen Capt. Parker I suppose since you told me of him, I know him perfectly well.

Now Charles as to my picture, how can you think I would sit for it. Your grandfather sat for his at 80, 't is true, but there never was so handsome, so charming a man at that age as he was — it was with much ado that I got him to have it done. I told him I would not be without it for any thing in the world, nor indeed no more I would, and as there was a tolerable good painter upon the place, I insisted on it — but as to miniature there is not one nearer than London, and it would cost above half a year's income to have it done, were I even there, and most likely I shall never go there again, for tho' my dear father was older than I, yet in constitution I was always older than him. So desire never to hear any more on that subject, for I shall never come into it.

I am much obliged to Mr. Parsons who sent me your letter directly, and I send this to him and beg the favour of him to send it. I desire you will send yours to him when you write, which I hope will not be long before I shall be made so happy. Now I must tell the dates of my letters which I wrote — Yours of Oct 27, I recd Jany 2. 60 — and I answered that Apr 18 — I wrote again Aug 15, and in Mch 13 61 — so you see how often I have wrote to you — 3 letters for one. I hope this will come

---

[1] William was buried January 28, 1761.

[2] Probably Peter, who "left many descendants" in Virginia, but nothing is known of them. The name of Peter Pelham was in the militia rolls of the Revolution.

safe, for indeed my dear, writing is not the agreeablest thing in the world, unless I could write as well as you do — but my writing and spelling is so bad that I can take no pleasure in it — but it is the only way that any one can have the pleasure of conversing with their friends and I hope so near and dear as you are to me that you will be good enough to make allowances for an old woman.

I saw in the papers you had a fine burial at Boston — poor General Whitmore,[1] some of his troops are here. I think it was a sad accident he met with. My dear child I cannot possibly make my letter agreeable to you by telling you all the chit-chat, as you know not a soul here, so will conclude with assuring you how much I am Your affectionate aunt and humble servant,

HELENA PELHAM.

P.S. My dear nephew. I do not remember any thing about your ever having the small pox, but think it most likely you never had it, by your brother having so lately got it — so hope you will always avoid it, as you say you have done. I cannot tell what to say in regard to your coming to England, as it is not in my power to give you the assistance I could wish, therefore must say you are right in staying in a place where you are known and settled — and dont doubt but God will give a blessing to your honest endeavours, and shall think myself happy in hearing from you and of your welfare, — which I hope you will be so good as to gratify me in as often as you can.

[1] Edward Whitmore, who was at the siege of Louisburg and remained as governor after its capture in 1758. He was drowned in Boston harbor, December 11, 1761, aged seventy-one, and was buried under King's Chapel. Foote, *Annals of King's Chapel*, II. 213.

Copley to Jean Etienne Liotard [1]

BOSTON, Sep'r 30, 1762.

SIR,

This Letter will meet You accompanied by one from the Worthy Coll:l Spierring who has been so kind to give me his assistance for the obtaining a sett of the best Swis Crayons for drawing of Portraits. allow me Sir to Joyn my sollicitations with him that You would send as He directs one sett of Crayons of the very best kind such as You can recommend [for] liveliness of colour and Justness of tints. In a word let em be a sett of the very best that can be got.

You may perhaps be surprised that so remote a corner of the Globe as New England should have any d[e]mand for the necessary eutensils for practiceing the fine Arts, but I assure You Sir however feeble our efforts may be, it is not for want of inclination that they are not better, but the want of oppertunity to improve ourselves. however America which has been the seat of war and desolation, I would fain hope will one Day become the School of fine Arts and Monsieur Liotard['s] Drawing with Justice be set as patterns for our immitation. not that I have ever had the advantage of beholding any one of those rare peices from Your hand. but [have] formd a Judgment on the true tast of several of My friend[s] who has seen em.

permit me Sir to conclude with wishing You all Helth and happyness.

[1] Draft, in Copley's handwriting, unsigned and without address. Upon another sheet is written in a different handwriting: "A Monsieur Liotard fameux Peintre à Genève en Suisse." Liotard (1702–1790) was surnamed "the Turk" because of his adopting the Turkish costume. He is remembered chiefly for his delicate pastel drawings, of which the "Chocolate Girl" in the Dresden Gallery is one of the best known.

S. Fayerweather[1] to Copley

MR COPLEY,

After Waiting a Considerable time with much Uneasiness to know whether Judge Leigh's [2] Picture was sent to Carolina or no, at Length I'm Agreeably Surpriz'd to find it is Actually Gone, and I hope by this, it has Gott safe to its Destind Port, and that the proper Owner has joyfully took possession of it.

Upon Your Information in your last letter I immediately Wrote to Mr Leigh of your having sent from Boston his Honourd Fathers Effigy to Him, But Coud not tell By Whom, or What Vessel it Went; of this Be pleasd to Acquaint Me.

I have made the handsomest Apology to Mr Leigh in your Behalf, for the long Detention of the Picture; And not

[1] Rev. Samuel Fayerweather (1725–1781), graduated from Harvard College in 1743, settled in Newport, Rhode Island, in 1754, was ordained a presbyter in the Episcopal Church in England in 1756, and entered upon his mission at St. Paul's, Narragansett, in 1760.

[2] Probably Peter Leigh (1710–1759), Chief Justice of South Carolina. His only surviving son was Sir Egerton Leigh, whose controversy with Henry Laurens gave occasion to an interesting series of pamphlets before the War of Independence.

RECEIPT BY COPLEY, 1758

Boston May 20 1758.

Mr Thom.. Fayerweather to John Singleton Copley
to Painting a Picture in Miniature of Mr. Thomas Hubbert
one Guinnea in Geo. the Contents Recd J. S. Copley

only so, but wrote Him of your Assiduity and Diligence to Gett it on Board of a proper Vessel: And of your being obligd to Unshipp it once, by reason of the Ship's altering her Voyage for Another part of the World, after She putt up for Charlestown South Carolina. Upon the Whole, It will Much Rejoyce Me to hear from Mr Leigh which I Expect daily, and of Which you shall know. With Compliments To yr Good Mother I Subscribe y'r most humble Serv't

S. FAYERWEATHER.

NARRAGANSETT, Jan'y 7th, 1763.

[Addressed:] To Mr. John Copley, Limner, Near the Orange Tree In Boston. These Pr favr of Mr Mumford.

Captain Peter Traille [1] *to Copley*

SIR,

I received the favor of Yours, by the last Vessel from Boston and shou'd have sent for my Picture long ago but have not be[en] able to get a proper Oportunity. I shou'd be glad you would draw upon me for the Cash; and send the Picture when you can meet with a proper Conveyance.

It wou'd realy be worth Your while to make a Visit here. I am certain that y[ou would] get a Hundred or two £ ster'lg this summer. I shou'd be very glad to see You, and shou'd endeavor to make the Place as agreable to You as in my Power. I am Sir, Your Most Obedient and Humble Serv't

P. TRAILLE.

HALIFAX, 24th April, 1763.

[1] The name is not in the Army List for this year.

Copley to [Charles Pelham?]

BOSTON, Jan'y 24, 1764.

DEAR SIR,

I have receifd the Money (103.10.) Old Ten'r from Mr Box and sent the same by Miss Johana Dodge (as you desired).

I have entertain'd some hopes I should have the happyness of seeing You once more in Boston, before the small Pox had spread its contagion so far as to render it utterly unsafe for You to venture without the risque of Your health if not Your Life by catching that distemper; but I can now by no means advise You to see this distresst Town, till its surcumstances are less mallancolly than they are at present, which I hope will be in a few months, and which I pray God of his infinite goodness grant.

My dear Mamah sends her kind love and Blessing to You wishes You all imaginable helth and happyness in Your retreat, and her compliments with mine weit on the Coll'l [1] Mrs. Royall and the Young Ladys.

Our Brother Henry send his sincerest love to and best wishes for Your Happyness, and promisses strictly to observe Your good instructions to him, which were very sesonable, this being the first Day he has been able to draw sence You left us.

I have no time to add any perticulars about the small pox at present, only that it is very fatal, allmost every [one] being dead that has been taken with it, or remain dangerously ill. I hear there are several in the Country Towns that are broke out with it, perticularly two in Roxbury this Morn'g, which looks as if the callamity would be more general than we first expected.

---

[1] Isaac Royall, who married, March 27, 1738, Elizabeth McIntosh, and in 1775 went, with other loyalists, to England, where he died in 1781. Two daughters were living in 1763 — Mary and Elizabeth.

But that kind Providence may preserve You and the good family in which You are from any Personal share in this Callamity is the herty prayer of, Dear Sir, Your affectionate friend and Brother

J: S: COPLEY.

Thomas Ainslie to Copley

QUEBEC, 12 Nov'r, 1764.

SIR,

A few days ago I had Letters from Scotland by the Snow *Apthorp*, in which my Young Son of 15 Months Old went a Passenger to Glasgow, and as there is a Paragraph in one of them, which does great honour to You, I think it a Justice, due to Your Merite to accquaint you with it, and that too in my Father in Laws own Words:

We drank Tea with Grandmama Ainslie the afternoon of his Arrival, and being in the dineing Room, the Infant eyed your Picture, he sprung to it, roared, and schriched, and attempted gripping the hand, but when he could not catch hold of it, nor gett You to speak to him, he stamp'd and scolded, and when any of us askt him for Papa, he always turned, and pointed to the Picture. What think [you] of this proof of the Painters Skill in taking Your likeness?

Now, Sir, As I have ever had an Inclination to do You a Service if in my power, and the propagating of this Circumstance, which I have taken Care to do having not a little added to Your fame here, And as I am of Opinion that a Jaunt into this Country would rather add to Your Credite, and fortune, than deminish it; If You will come here for two or three Months in the Summer, so as to be here in June, I have a Room in my house at Your Service, so that Your Stay will be no Expence to You, and not only my family, but all those of Credite in the town would be glad to employ You. Be not overperswaded from coming, for certain I am Your Journey will be of Service to you and I shall have a pleasure in Entertaining You. I am, Sir, Your most hum'bl Servant

THOS. AINSLIE.

Let me hear from You by the post in the course of the Winter.

Copley to [an English Mezzotinter]

BOSTON, Jan'y 25, 1765.

SIR,

Out of pure regard to a good Old Decenting Cleargyman of this Town several Gentlemen have apply'd to me for the procuration of his portrait in Metzotinto. I therefore beg You will be pleasd to let me know on what terms You will undertake the same, and add to your demand for cuting the plate (which must be fourteen inches by ten [1] and containing only a head of the Rev'd Doc'r Sewell) [2] that of paper and Printing pr hundred. for as to number I shall want, that at present is alltogether uncertain, but I shall let You know in due time, leaving the plate in Your hands till I have a sufficient quantity Printed off, than desire the plate to be sent me with the last parcil of prints. I must beg You will not neglect writing to me the first oppertunity, for by the time Your answer comes to hand I shall have the Picture finishd and in proper Order to send. I shall likewise depend on Your perticular care in the preservation of the likeness that being a main part of the exellency of a portrait in the oppinion of our New England Conoseurs. be pleasd also to let me know the price of the different kinds of frames, as also that

[1] This was first written *twelve*.

[2] Dr. Joseph Sewall was minister in the Old South Church from 1713 until his death in 1769.

of Glass, and when You write direct to John Singleton Copley portrait Painter in Cambrige street Boston. I am Sir Your Most Obed't Humble Ser't

J: S: C.

PROPOSALS FOR PRINTING DR. SEWELL'S PORTRAIT

[Circa January 25, 1765]

Proposals for executeing a portrait of The Revd Doctr Sewell in Metzotinto by John S. Copley, which he promises to procure with all convenient speed to be done by the Ablest Master in London from a Painting done by himself, provided these his pro[po]sals are comply'd with, Viz: The Gentlemen who are desireous to forward the work must subscribe for prints to the amount of three hundred at three shillings and four pence per print, paying one half for any Number subscribed for at the time of subscribeing, the other half at the delivery of said prints: And upon Notice being given by Advertisement in the publick prints, or said Copley tendering the same to subscribers. Yet notwithstanding such Notice being given, They the subscribers do Neglect calling for said prints within three Months after such notice being given that, the said Copley shall not be accountable to them for any Moneys they have paid. And that in case the Picture should be lost in goin[g] to London, and if in the mean time The Father of mercys should take the Good Doctor to himself, by which means it will be impractable [for] said Copley to proceed in the Design, the Moneys paid by Subscribers shall be returnd, said Copley deducting for hi[s labor?] five pounds twelve shillings which is the price of said Picture.

Copley to [Thomas Ainslie]

Boston, Feb'y 25, 1765.

Sir,

Your kind favour came safe to hand, but not so soon as might have been expected, otherwise I should sooner have made my acknowledgements for Your proferd kindness, which I do now with all sincerity, and should receive a singular pleasure in excepting, if my Business was anyways slack, but it is so far otherwise that I have a large Room full of Pictures unfinishd, which would ingage me these twelve months, if I did not begin any others; this renders it impossable for me to leave the place I am in: but the obligation I am under I shall ever acknowledge as sincerely as if it was in my power to except of it. I assure You I have been as fully imployd these several Years past as I could expect or wish to be, as more would be a means to retard the design I have always had in vew, that of improveing in that charming Art which is my delight, and gaining a reputation rather than a fortune without that: Tho if I could obtain the one while in the persuit of the other, I confess I should be so far from being indiferent about either that I would willingly use great diligence for the acquireing of both, and indeed the mutual assistance they would render each other in their progress must naturally excite in me a desire for both, tho in diferent degrees.

I confess it gives me no small pleasure to receive the approbation of so uncorrupted a judgment as that of so Young a Child: it is free from all the fals notions and impertinant conceits that is the result of a superficial knowledge of the principals of art, which is so far from assisting the understanding that it serves only to corrupt and mislead it: unless temperd with a large share of good since: and might tend to excite some degree of Vanity did not my diligence for Years past in the study of nature, most ef[ec]tually convince me of this sad truth, that all human productions fall infinitely short of the bea[u]tys of nature.

The favourable opinion You have of my performance shows

a large share of goodness in You, as it is more than I can pretend to deserve unless indeavouring to do well shall be accounted a merrit. I am, Sir, with all Sincerity Your Obl[i]ged Humble Ser't

JOHN: S: COPLEY.

Captain Peter Traille to Copley

HALIFAX, 7th March, 1765.

DEAR SIR,

By a letter from my freind Captain Bruce I find my self under great Obligations to You, particularly in sending a couple of peices of your drawing in Crayons. I am sorry to have the Mortification to tell You that You are dissappointed in your good intentions by the unpardonable remissness of the Master of the Vessel. She was lost about 30 leagues to the westward of this port, and your drawings, together with several other things, have become the prey of the barbarous Inhabitants. I have taken every step to find out if any of them are recoverable, but can hear only of two of the prints which were purchas'd from Mr. Moffat. I beg leave, to assure You that not withstanding this Misfortune my Gratitude is not lessen'd, and I shall always esteem it as a real Pleasure to improve every Opportunity of acknowledging it. I cannot conceal the innexpressible pain this loss gives me, it robbing me of those patterns, by which I most sanguinely flatter'd me self to acquire some knowledge in the Art of colouring of which I have very disstant Ideas as yet. If it was not intruding on your Bussiness I shou'd beg a few Directions on this favorite Subject or some illustration by example as that easier followed than precept. I am with great regard Dr. Sir, Your Most Obed't and Humble Sev't

PETER TRAILLE.

Henry Pelham
"The Boy with the Squirrel"
From the original painting by Copley
in the possession of Mr. Frederick Amory.

A Bill for a Portrait [1]

Dr	Joseph Jackson Esqr. to J. S. Copley		Cr

1765 To one Portrait of his Daughter at eight Guineas } £11..4..0

By an order in favour of Wil- liam Miller } £9–6–8

By your Accot 1–17–4

Boston 25th March 1769 £11:4:0

Errors Excepted Per JOHN SINGLETON COPLEY.

Copley to [Captain R. G. Bruce] [2]

BOSTON, Sepr. 10, 1765.

DEAR SIR,

I have sent You the portrait of my Brother [3] by Mr. Haill, [4] who has been so kind to take the care of it and put it among his own baggage. Nothing would have been a sufficient induce- ment to have sent it so soon but the desire of confirming the good opinion You began to conceive of me before You left Boston which I would by no means forfeit, chusing rather to risque the Picture than the loss of Your esteem; indeed I be- leive it must be allowed I act with prudence in this respect if it is considered that should the Picture be unfit (through the changing of the colours) for the exhibition, I may not have the mortification of hearing of its being condemned. I confess I am under some apprehension of its not being so much esteem'd as I could wish; I dont say this to induce You to be backward in

---

[1] Boston Public Library, Chamberlain Collection, F. 4. 3. It is in Copley's handwriting.

[2] Captain of the *John and Sukey*, a merchant vessel.

[3] "The Boy with the Squirrel," Copley's first picture to be exhibited in London, 1766.

[4] Mr. Roger Hale, Collector or Surveyor of the port of London.

letting me know how far it is judged to deserve censure for I can truly say if I know my own heart I am less anxious to enjoy than deserve applause.

I doubt not You have seen Our good friend Capt. Traile[1] before this time. pray present my best regards to him and tell him I long to hear from him.

Capt. Jacobson is just arrived with the stamps which has made so much noise and confusion among us Americans. You will no doubt have heard before this reaches You of poor Mr. Howards[2] House being pulld almost down and all his furniture destroyd and himself with Docr Moffatt[3] (whose house and good shared the same fate) and Mr. Robinson being obliged to save their lives by flying on board the Kings Ship that Lay in the Harbour. the Docr and Mr. Howard are sence sail'd for Europe, But in Boston we demolishd the Lieut. Govournours House, the stamp Office,[4] Mr Storys[5] and Greatly damaged Capt Hollowells[6] and the Secretarys[7] Houses, sence which there is a strong Military watch kept every night which keeps the Town in quietness. I am Sir with all Sincerity Your Real Friend and Ser't.

JOHN: S: COPLEY.

[1] Captain Peter Traille.

[2] Martin Howard, a lawyer in Newport, whose house stood on Spring Street. His offense was publishing two pamphlets on the rights of the colonies. Hammett, *Bibliography of Newport., R.I.*, 66.

[3] Dr. Thomas Moffat, of Broad Street. With the stamp master for Rhode Island, Augustus Johnson, they were burned in effigy.

[4] A new building which some supposed to be intended for a stamp office. 2 *Mass. Hist. Soc. Proceedings*, x. 61; *Boston Gazette*, September 2, 1765.

[5] William Story, Deputy Registrar of the Court of Admiralty.

[6] Benjamin Hallowell, Comptroller of the Customs.

[7] Thomas Flucker (1719–1783).

J. Powell to Copley

LOND'N, 18 Octo'r, 1765.

SIR,

Herewith is Capt. Scotts Receipt for Two Cases of Frames Glasses etc. The Box of Craons I put Into Mr. Powells Trunk shipt by Capt Daveson. I hope will Turn out agreeable as I Took The pains To Go To The maker. The Cost as below, Capt Bruce and I both Expected by some of The Late ships To have seen your Bro[ther's] Picture as an Exhibision Peice, as would have been very agreeable To have Introduced You To The Knowledge of some of your Bror. Artists here. I am with Esteem yrs.

J. POWELL.

@ Box Cloths	2. 7
@ Box Craons	15
@ Case of Frames and Glasses.	6. 5
po[r]teridge & shipg	3. 6
	£ 9.10. 6

Peter [Pelham?] [1] *to Copley*

BARBADOS, April 28th. 1766.

MY DEAR FRIEND,

It is with a Sensible Pleasure that I set myself down to write to a Friend whom I ever lov'd & esteem'd and in whose Company I have enjoy'd so many pleasing hours. I hope you did not take it amiss that I left you so abruptly the morning I sail'd from Boston. But give me leave to say that when I whisper'd to you I imagined you would take the hint, and follow close

[1] Probably the son of Copley's stepbrother of the same name. Copley's reply to this letter is printed on p. 47, *infra*.

after me for I did not intend to return into my Father's and sisters presence again. I should read over and over again any even the shortest Letter I could receive from you, and should have wrote to you before this, but I have been engaged in Business and writing to my Father, and Sisters and those friends in Boston who favour'd me with letters, and must say I was not a little disappointed when I look'd over my Packet of Letters I receiv'd from Boston and heard nothing either of you or from you.

I will say it because my Heart bears me witness that, let me forget whomsoever of my Friends, I will that Mr. Copley shall not be obliterated from my Remembrance. Your honest, Droll and pleasant Brother Charles did me the pleasure of seeing the last of me in Boston, and amus'd me, and several of my hearty Friends in the ships Cabbin till we Cast off from the wharff. If he is with you please to make my Compliments and best regards acceptable to him as also my kindest respects, affection, and regard to your very worthy mama of whom I retain the most pleasing remembrance, and most devoutly wish she could enjoy only one twentieth part of the Health that I partake of. Please to remember me to your ingenious little Brother Harry whom I expect to see in a very respectable situation of Life by and by, owing to your great Care and Brotherly Love; also my Compliments and best regards to Mr. Pelham and Respects to the honble Family wherein he resides. more Compliments etc — Vizt. Compliments, best wishes and regards you'l please to present in my name to my worthy Friends Messrs. Winthrop, Prout and Lady, Miss Gerrish; Henderson and Lady, Shepherd and Lady, and all those by name whom you knew I lov'd and esteem'd. I am now on the Island of Barbados alias Garden of Eden, and while you my friend have been pinch'd with as severe

a Winter as ever was known, I have been enjoying the blessed-
est Weather and the most enchanting scenes human imagination can paint. If I was plagued at Boston it is all made up to
me in the enjoyment of my Health, and of every Pleasure that
my heart can wish. When I saild from Boston I had no more
intentions of tarrying between the Tropicks than I now have
of going to China, or to visit the Ruins of Rome, and Palmyra.
But in short I meet with everything so agreable here, and such
a Chance of making well for myself in life, that I think I cannot
in justice to myself return at least this year; if I should it will
be only to settle my affairs, and return here immediately.

It is well known of me that I did not launch out of my Country in order to get Business, because I not only had (very often)
more than my share, but was every day increasing it. But I
doubt not but you'l join with me in opinion that that is our
Country where we can live most happily. I can live infinitely
more happy here (absence of my dear Friends, and old Acquaintance excepted) than I can in my own Country, the Weather
being pleasant beyond Discription, and not so hot even in the
hottest season as with you; the People hospitable and generous
to a Fault, and the most polite, polish'd and gentile of any I
ever saw before.

It is with Difficulty my dear friend that a man can get away
from the Country where he receiv'd his birth and Education;
but when he has once broke the spell, and goes out into the
World he sees things that he never could see in his Father's
Chimney Corner, and has an oppertunity of making a Fortune
if he is commonly prudent. I could wish you was here most devoutly for the Climate would suit your Constitution, and Interest, I would not give Mr. Copley more than ten years to put
himself in his Chariot and four could he come here. There is

but one painter here and he has a prodigious run, and paints so admirably that I talk of leaving my abode in the Country, and taking a Room in one of the Publick Towns, and set up Portrait painting in Opposition to him, and doubt not I could excell him if my Charcoal was good.

I live in splendor here Vizt. at the Chief Justice's House who does me the Honour to profess himself my fast Friend and who will not stir from home even to take an Airing without me. This, with the Letters I carried from Boston, and those the polite Governour Scott [1] of Dominica has been pleas'd to send me, has been sufficient to introduce me into all the polite Company of this Island, so that I have neither friends to make or Connections to form if I incline to tarry.

It would give me pleasure to hear from you as often as you possibly can, and when you write please (under the Rose) to let me know how my father and sisters took my slipping away from 'em that morning, and how they bear my absence. I hope you visit 'em. Please to take care of my dear Sisters. I do not beleive I could love any man that did not regard and assist them, should they stand in need of it. I know not what is become of you all at Boston. I never hear from any of my friends there. I hope they han't forgot me. Farewell. God bless you, my dear Friend. you see I have only room to assure you that I am most unfeignedly and sincerely yours

PETER.

[Addressed:] To Mr. John Singleton Copley at his Seat near St. James Square, London Place, in Boston, New England.

·[1] George Scott, Lieutenant Governor, 1763-1768.

Captain R. G. Bruce to Copley

LONDON, 4th August, 1766.

D'R COPLEY,

Dont imagine I have forgot or neglected your Interest by my long Silence. I have delayed writing to You ever since the Exhibition, in order to forward the inclosed Letter from Mr. West,[1] which he has from time to time promised me, but which his extreme Application to his Art has hitherto prevented his finishing..

What he says will be much more conclusive to You than anything from me. I have only to add the general Opinions which were pronounced on your Picture when it was exhibited. It was universally allowed to be the best Picture of its kind that appeared on that occasion, but the sentiments of Mr. Reynolds, will, I suppose, weigh more with You than those of other Criticks. He says of it, "that in any Collection of Painting it will pass for an excellent Picture, but considering the Dissadvantages" I told him "you had laboured under, that *it was a very wonderfull Performance.*" "That it exceeded any Portrait that Mr. West ever drew." "That he did not know one Painter at home, who had all the Advantages that Europe could give them, that could equal it, and that if you are capable of producing such a Piece by the mere Efforts of your own Genius, with the advantages of the Example and Instruction which you could have in Europe, You would be a valuable Acquisition to the Art, and one of the first Painters in the World, provided you could receive these Aids before it was too late in Life, and before your Manner and Taste were corrupted or fixed by working in your little way at Boston. He condemns your work-

[1] Benjamin West.

ing either in Crayons or Water Colours." Dont imagine I flatter You. I only repeat Mr. Reynolds's words, which are confirmed by the publick Voice. He, indeed, is a mere Enthusiast when he speaks of You. At the same time he found Faults. He observed a little Hardness in the Drawing, Coldness in the Shades, An over minuteness, all which Example would correct. "But still," he added, "*it is a wonderful Picture* to be sent by a Young Man who was never out of New England, and had only some bad Copies to study." I have beg'd of Mr. West to be copious in his Criticisms and Advices to You. Mr. Reynolds would have also wrote to You himself but his time is too valuable. The Picture is at his House where I shall leave it till I have your Directions how to dispose of it. I could sell it to advantage, but it is thought more for your Interest to keep it as a Specimen. You are greatly obliged to Lord Cardross,[1] a Friend of mine, to whom I first sent it. He showed it to the most eminent Conniseurs, then gave it to Mr. Reynolds, who sent it with his own Pictures to the Exhibition. You are best Judge of your own Affairs, and whether you can with propriety accomplish a Trip for a few Years to Europe. Should you take that Resolution, I believe I may venture to assure You, that You will meet with much Encouragment and Patronage. Should it be in my little power to be of the least use to You, you may command me to the utmost. I am already very happy in having contributed to make your Merit so far known to the World, and hope it has laid the Foundation of your being the great Man Mr. Reynolds prognosticates.

I am obliged to write this in a very great hurry as I set out tomorrow on a Visit to Scotland. Pray remember me to my old Acquaintances at Boston. I have wrote to Mr. Scollay [2]

---

[1] Title of the Erskines.   [2] John Scollay.

and Mrs. Melville.[1] You have already my Direction, and I shall expect to hear from You. Perhaps I may see you in Boston next Year, but that at present is uncertain.

I had almost forgot to tell You, that in case you dont appear yourself, the Friends of your Art wish that you will paint another Picture to exhibit next Year, and Mr. West has promised to point out a Subject to You. Should you do so, send it to Mr. West who seems sincerely disposed to be your Friend. Mr. Reynolds is too busy and too great a Man to be active for You, tho he is also much disposed to serve You.

I have now a Favour to beg of You in turn, which is, that you will make me a Copy of my Picture I left with Mrs. Melville. I hope this will find You and your Familly well, — And either in Europe or America assure your self of my sincere Friendship while I am

R. G. BRUCE.[2]

Benjamin West to Copley

LONDON, August 4th, 1766.

SIR,

On Seeing a Picture painted by you and meeting with Captain Bruce, I take the liberty of writeing to you. The great Honour the Picture has gaind you hear in the art of Painting I dare say must have been made known to You Long before this Time. and as Your have made So great a Progr[e]ss in the art I am Persuaded You are the more desierous of hearing the remarks that might have been made by those of the Profession, and as I am hear in the Midst of the Painting world have the greater oppertunity of hearing them. Your Picture first fell into

---

[1] Probably wife of Thomas Melville.
[2] The letter was addressed to Mr. William Copley — Boston.

Mr. Reynolds' hands to have it Put into the Exhibition as the Proformanc of a Young American: he was Greatly Struck with the Piec, and it was first Concluded to have been Painted by one Mr. Wright,[1] a young man that has just made his appearance in the art in a sirprising Degree of Merritt. as Your Name was not given with the Picture it was Concluded a mistake, but before the Exhibition opened the Perticulers was recevd from Capt. Bruce. while it was Excibited to View the Criticizems was, that at first Sight the Picture struck the Eye as being to liney, which was judgd to have arose from there being so much neetness in the lines, which indeed as fare as I was Capable of judgeing was some what the Case. for I very well know from endevouring at great Correctness in ones out line it is apt to Produce a Poverty in the look of ones work. when ever great Desition [decision] is attended to they lines are apt to be to fine and edgey. This is a thing in works of great Painter[s] I have remark[ed] has been strictly a voyded, and have given Correctness in a breadth of out line, which is finishing out into the Canves by no determind line when Closely examined; tho when seen at a short distanc, as when one looks at a Picture, shall appear with the greatest Bewty and freedom. for in nature every thing is Round, or at least Partakes the most of that forme which makes it imposeble that Nature, when seen in a light and shade, can ever appear liney.

As we have every April an Exhibition where our works is exhibitied to the Publick, I advise you to Paint a Picture of a half figure or two in one Piec, of a Boy and Girle, or any other subject you may fancy. And be shure take your Subjects from Nature as you did in your last Piec, and dont trust any

---

[1] Joseph Wright (1734–1797), who first exhibited in London in 1765. Not to be confused with Joseph Wright (1756–1793), son of Patience Wright.

resemblanc of any thing to fancey, except the dispositions of they figures and they ajustments of Draperies, So as to make an agreable whole. for in this Consists the work of fencey and Test [taste].

If you should do anything of this kind, I begg you may send it to me, when you may be shure it shall have the greatest justice done it. lett it be Painted in oil, and make it a rule to Paint in that way as much as Posible, for Oil Painting has the superiority over all other Painting. As I am from America, and know the little Opertunities is to be had their in they way of Painting, made the inducement the more in writing to you in this manner, and as you have got to that lenght in the art that nothing is wanting to Perfect you now but a Sight of what has been done by the great Masters, and if you Could make a viset to Europe for this Porpase for three or four years, you would find yourself then in Possession of what will be highly valuable. if ever you should make a viset to Europe you may depend on my friendship in eny way thats in my Power to Sarve.

Your Friend and Humble Servent,

B. WEST.

my direction is Castle Street Leicester Fields.

[Addressed] To Mr William Copley Painter at Boston

[Endorsed] forwarded by Your Humbl Servt J. Loring.[1]

Francis M. Newton to Copley

SIR,

I am directed to acquaint you that on the 2d of Sepr. you was Elected a Fellow of the Society of Artists of Great Britain. Your attendance is therefore desired at the Turks Head

---

[1] Joshua Loring?

Tavern in Gerrard Street, Soho,[1] on Monday the 6th of Octr next at Six OClock in the Evening in order to be regularly admitted. I am Sir Your Very Humble Servt.

F. M. NEWTON Secy [2]

Sept. 3rd: 1766.

[Addressed.] To Mr. Wm. Copley of Boston in New England.[3]
[Endorsed] Octr. 13, 1767.

James Scott to Copley

DR. SIR,

This Informs you of my Arrivall in London. I have got the portrait safe home. it gives great satisfn.

I Expect I shall Sail the first week in Octr. I believe I Cannot posibly get your order Executed, before I sail Myself. My Brother is out of Town, 180 miles from London, and Engag'd all the winter; but however, I will not fail to Get some Able Hand to purchase for me all the Articles that requires inspection, beyond my Judgment.

I hope You are well and am with Respect Your Hble Servt

JAMES SCOTT.

5th Septr., 1766, LONDON.

[1] The Turk's Head was originally in Greek Street, and towards the middle of the eighteenth century removed to Gerrard Street. It was the headquarters for the Loyal Association during the rebellion of 1745, and after 1764 Johnson's Club held its meetings there. *Notes and Queries*, I. 114.

[2] Francis Milner Newton (1720–1794), a portrait painter. He was Secretary of the "Incorporated Society of Artists of Great Britain," and later of the "Royal Academy," a seceding body. See *Dictionary of National Biography*, XL. 367.

[3] Copley erased the word Wm., and wrote J: S: above it. Copley's reply is dated November 23, 1767.

Copley to Peter [Pelham]

Boston, Sepr. 12, 1766.

Dear Sir,

The receipt of Your kind favour of April the 28 [1] gave me the most sensable pleasure, as it confirm'd me in the opinion I always had that the tour You proposed would be attended with great advantage, both to Your helth as well as to Your purse. I most sincerely wish You a long continuance of every worldly Blessing. You have at present Your helth, are in a fine Climate, and are geting Money; those are Blessings that must smooth the ruget path of life and make it irksome to leave the World.

You are likly soon to be in a fair way of making Your fortune. You have many good frinds about You and as our friend Shakespear says, that which seasons all unfisickd helth. if this is the happy effect of leaving ones native Country, is it not strange any one should ever submit to the shackels which deprive him of such great Blessing[s]. especily when a little resolution would break em off. but this You will perhaps think strange doctrine to come from one Who is at this present, in spite of evry propose[d] advantage, tamely submiting to the Yowke he thinks so easyly shook off. but my friend You know my Bondage (if you seriously consider) is of a much more binding nature than the tie of Country. Your invitation to Barbados and incouragement come with much more force, as it should at the same time I made my fortune, give an oppertunity of injoy[ing] Your company. But beleive me, Dear Peter, when I can get disingage[d] from this frosen region, I shall take my flight to Europe, where tho I shall not find the warmth You

---

[1] Page 37, *supra.*

injoy in Barbados, I shall feel a much enlivening one. I shall
there be heated with the sight of the enchanting Works of a
Raphael, a Rubens, Corregio and a Veronese, etc., etc. here
give me leave to acquaint You, as You was privy to my sending
the portrait of my Brother to the exibition, that it was received
into the Collection, and as I am inform[ed] by severall who saw
it, and by letters to the Surveyer [1] and others, for I have not
yet [heard] from Capt. Bruce, it was much approved, and such
handsom things said of it that my Modesty would not permit
me repeat one of them but to You, who I have a better oppinion
off, than to think it would be made any use of to my disadvantage. a Gentleman writes to his friend in Rhode Island that
none but the Works of the first Masters were ranked with it.
and flatter myself you know me too well to suspect the rep[et]i-
tion arrises so much from Vanity, as a just senc of the Duty I
owe to Your friendship. what I owe to Your friendship, this is
an incouragement to me I confess, and adds new Vigeour to the
pencil. I have som foundation to build upon, some more sure
prospect of attaining what has cost me so many hours of severe
study, and given me resolution anough to live a batchelor to the
age of twenty eight.[2] however, I dont dispair, but I shall be
Married as I find Mericle[s] have not ceas'd, as You must
acknowledge when I assure You Mr P: [3] is Married to P[olly]
T[yler] has bot a farm at New Town and there set Down for life.

Your Hond. Father and Sister much long to see you and took
not amiss no more than my self You[r] sudden Departure. I am
Dear Peter Your Sincere friend and Sert.

J. S. C.

[1] Roger Hale.
[2] This would show that he was born in 1738, and not in 1737, as usually
stated. The Boston Records contain no entry of his birth or baptism.
[3] Charles Pelham.

Copley to Benjamin West

BOSTON, Octr. 13, 1766.

SIR,

I can by no means let this first oppertunity slip without making my acknowledgements to You for Your favourable Oppinion of the small portrait I sent to the exibition the last Year, and Your kind offer of obliging me in any thing in Your power, which I heard by way of My good friend Mr. Powell. This testamony of Your goodness, as I thot it unmerited so it was altogether unexpected, and has my most gratefull acknowledgements. I assure You when my Friend Mr. Powell told me of Your intention of wrighting, I could not forbear thinking hard he did not weit on You at the time of his coming away, as it would have given me the greatest pleasure immaginable to have had a letter from One of whom I entertain so high an oppinion, as an artist ingaged in the same studys with myself, and esteem as my Country man, from whom America receives the Same Luster that Italy does from her Titiano and Divine Raphael.

It seems almost needless to say how great my desire is to enter into a corraspondance with You, as it is very obvious that the pleasure and advantages would be very great on my side, and I doubt not the same benevolent disposition, that prompd You to express Your kindness for me, will incline You to add to my happyness by promoting that friendly intercourse.

As a compliance with Your desire will be ever pleasing to me, I shall not fail transmiting another small Picture for the exibition, which give me leave to trouble You with, as the stay of my friend Capt [Bruce] (to whose care I commited the last) in London is altogether uncertain, and I have no friend else that I am certain would give themselves the trouble of sending it to the exibition, unless You will be kind anough to take that trouble upon Your self, which will greatly Oblige him, who with great pleasure shall allways as at this time subscribe himself Your Obliged friend and Humble Ser't

J. S. C.

Copley to Benjamin West

Boston, Novr. 12, 1766.

Sir,

Your kind favour of Augst. 4, 1766, came to hand. It gave me great pleasure to receive without reserve Your Criticisms on the Picture I sent to the Exibition. Mr. Powell informd me of Your intention of wrighting, and the handsom things You was pleas'd say in praise of that little performance, which has increased my estamation of it, and demands my thanks which previous to the receipt of Your favour I acknowledged in a letter forwarded by Mr. Powell. It was remarkd the Picture was too lind. this I confess I was concious of my self and think with You that it is the natural result of two great presition in the out line, which in my next Picture I will indeavour to avoid, and perhaps should not have fallen into it in that, had I not felt two great timerity at presenting a Picture to the inspection of the first artists in the World, and where it was to come into competition with such masterly performancess as generally appear in that Collection. In my last I promis'd to send another peace. the subject You have sence pointed out, but I fear it will not be in my power to comply with Your design, the time being two short for the exicution of two figures, not having it in my power to spend all my time on it, and the Days short and weither cold, and I must ship it by the middle of Feby. at farthest, otherwise it will come too late for the exibition. but I shall do somthing near what you propose. Your c[a]utioning me against doing anything from fancy I take very kind, being sensable of the necessity of attending to Nature as the fountain head of all perfection, and the works of the great Masters as so many guides that lead to the more perfect imitation of her, pointing out to us in what she is to be coppied, and where we should deviate from her. In this Country as You rightly observe there is no examples of Art, except what is to [be] met with in a few prints indiferently exicuted, from which it is not possable to learn much, and must greatly inhanch the Value of free and unreserved Criticism made with judgment and Candor.

It would give me inexpressable pleasure to make a trip to Europe, where I should see those fair examples of art that have stood so long the admiration of all the world. the Paintings, Sculptors and Basso Releivos that adourn Italy, and which You have had the pleasure of making Your Studies from would, I am sure, annimate my pencil, and inable me to acquire that bold free and gracefull stile of Painting that will, if ever, come much slower from the mere dictates of Nature, which has hither too been my only instructor. I was allmost tempted the last year to take a tour to Philadelphia, and that chiefly to see some of Your Pictures, which I am informd are there. I think myself peculiarly unlucky in Liveing in a place into which there has not been one portrait brought that is worthy to be call'd a Picture within my memory, which leaves me at a great loss to gess the stile that You, Mr. Renolds, and the other Artists pracktice. I shall be glad when you write next you will be more explicit on the article of Crayons, and why You dis[ap]prove the use of them, for I think my best portraits done in that way. and be kind anough to inform me what Count Allgarotti[1]

[1] Francesco, Count Algarotti (1712–1764), author of *Letters upon Painting*.

means by the five points that he recommends for amusement and to assist the invention of postures, and weither any prints after Corregios or Titianos are to be purchased. I fear I shall tire Your patience and mak you repent your wrighting to one who makes so many requests in one letter.

But I shall be exceeding glad to know in general what the present state of Painting in Italy is, weither the Living Masters are excellent as the Dead have been. it is not possable my curiossity can be sattisfied in this by any Body but Yourself, not having any corraspondance with any whose judgment is sufficent to sattisfy me. I have been painting the head of a Decenting Cleargyman and his friends are desireous to subscribe for it to be scraped in mezzotinto in the common size of 14 inches by ten, but I cannot give them the terms till I know the price. I shall take it kind if when you see any artist that You approve You menshon it to him, and Let me know. I have seen a well exicuted print by Mr. Pether [1] of a Jew Rabbi. if You think him a good hand, be kind anough to desire him to let me know by a few lines (as soon as convenient) his terms, as the portrait weits only for that in my hands, and I shall send it immediately with the mony to defray the expence when I know what it is.

I am Sir with all Sinceri[t]y Your friend and Humble Sert.

J: S: COPLEY.

Captain R. G. Bruce to Copley

LONDON, 11th June, 1767.

DEAR COPLEY,

I have received your two Letters of the 16th and 18th of Febry. last, but the former Letter you refer me to I have never

---

[1] William Pether (1738?–1821). His "Jewish Rabbi" appeared in 1764.

received, so that I am quite at a loss how to dispose of the Picture which was exhibited last Year.

I am greatly obliged to You for the Portrait you have sent me. I have but just got it, as it was detained at the Custom House, and I had some difficulty, as well as Expence, to recover it; which made it unlucky that you did not send it, with the other, to Mr. Hale. I have not yet seen it, the Box not being opened, as Mr. West has desired it may be sent to him, that he may see your Performance in Crayons.

Your Picture arrived just in time for the Exhibition, and Mr. West did it all Justice, having the principal Direction of placing the Pictures there. I have been assiduous to collect the Connoiseur's Opinions of your last Exhibition. Mr West will tell You his in the Letter which I herewith send You; and the general opinion of the Society of Artists you may judge of by their Electing You a Member; their vote for which I also herewith send You. The general opinion was that the Drawing and Execution exceeded the last, and some went so far as to say it was the best Portrait in the Room in point of Execution; but you have been universally condemned in the choice of your Subject, which is so disagreable a Character, as to have made the Picture disliked by every one but the best Judges who could discern the Excellence of the Painting; so that it has not so universally pleased as last years Picture. I'm astonished that you should have suffered [Mr. Powel's vanity][1] to lead you into such an error. I waited on Mr. Rennolds on purpose to get his opinion, as of more Consequence than all the rest. He exclaimed against the Subject, but approved of the Painting, and perseveres in his Opinion that you only want Example to be one of the first Painters in the World. He dislikes your Shades; he says they

---

[1] The words in brackets have been erased and are almost illegible.

want Life and Transparency. He says "your Drawing is wonderfully correct, but that a something is wanting in your Colouring." I begd him to explain it, that I might communicate it to You, but he told me "that it was impossible to convey what he meant by Words, but that he was sure (by what you have already produced) he could make you instantly feel it by Example, if you was here."

You have his own words and may therefore judge what use to make of them. If you do not come over Yourself I hope you will still continue to exhibit, and establish a Reputation already so happily begun. At any rate I hope you are already enabled to raise the price of your pictures. If you have not I think you ought immediately. I hope You will be at some Pains to chuse a pleasing Subject for your next Exhibition, for it is not agreable to hear Dislikes exprest by even the most stupid and ignorant from such an accidental Circumstance.

I expected to have revisited America this Summer, but I beleive I shall now spend another Year in England, where I should rejoice to see You, and to render You every Service in my power. I hope your Mother and Brother are well. I doubt not but the latter is making great Progress in your Art, which he seemd to have so fine a Genius for. Your old Friend Capt. Traille is at Gibraltar, where he went about two Months ago. He continues to remember You with much regard, and is still assiduous in the Labours of the Pencil. He has parted with his Wife I believe totally. She lives with her Father in Somersetshire. A happy Riddance.

I beg you will continue to let me hear from You, and command any Services I can do You here. Mr. West seems much your Friend, and would be useful to You if you come to Europe.

He is making great Progress in History-Painting, and produced some capital Pieces this Year. He is at the same time a very agreeable amiable Young Man.[1]

Your last Year's Picture is still at Mr. Reynolds's, but I shall take it from thence in a few Days, and take great care of it till I have your Orders how to dispose of it.

I wrote to Mrs. Melvill and Mr. Scollay last Year, but I find my Letters never reached them. I write by this opport'y to Mr. Scollay and Mr. Kennedy and send the former a Sett of Mr Strange's last Performances.[2]

Remember me to your Mother and all Friends and believe me, D'r Copley, Your sincere Friend and humble Serv't.

R. G. BRUCE.

P : S : I must give you one Caution, which is, that if any of the Critical Reviews, Examinations etc., of the Exhibition (which have been published here) should fall into your Hands, to pay no manner of Regard to what they say, as they are most execrable Performances and universally condemned. The Artists depend on another Exhibition from You next Year. They already put you on a footing with all the Portrait Painters except Mr. Reynolds. If You have been able to attain this unassisted at Boston, What might you not atchieve in Europe? Your coming home as an Artist travelling for Improvement will cost you very little. I shall therefore hope to see You bring home your next Exhibition in Person.

This was first intended to go single but as I now enclose it and have not time to write it over again you'll excuse my scribling over the first Direction.

---

[1] West was born in 1738.
[2] Sir Robert Strange (1721–1792), an engraver, and long a friend of West.

Benjamin West to Copley

LONDON, June 20th, 1767.

SIR,

Dont impute the long Omition of my not writeing to you [to] any forgetfullness or want of that Friendship I first Shewd on seeing your works. My having been so much ingaged in the Study of my Bussiness, in perticuler that of history Painting, which demands the greates Cear and intelegance in History amaginable, has so intierly Prevented my takeing up the Penn to answer your Several Agreable favours, and the reception of your Picture of the little Gairl you Sent for the exhibition. It came safe to hand in good time. And as I am Persuaded you must be much interested in reguard to the reception it mett with from they artists and Publicks opinion in General, I as a Friend Take this oppertunity to Communicate it to you.

In regard to the Artists they Somewhat differ in Opinion from Each Other, Some Saying they thought your First Picture was the Best, others Say the last is Superior (which I think [it] is as a Picture in point of Exhecution, tho not So in Subject). But of those I shall give this of Mr. Reynolds when he saw it he was not so much Pleased with it as he was with the first Picture you Exhibited, that he thougt you had not mannaged the general Affect of it so Pleasing as the other. This is what the Artists in General has Criticised, and the Colouring of the Shadows of the flash wants transperency. Those are thing[s] in General that have Struck them. I Cant say but the Above remarks have some justness in them, for the Picture being at my house some time gave me an oppertunity of Examining it with more Exectness.

The General Affect as Mr. Reynolds justly Observes is not

quite so agreable in this as in the other; which arrises from Each Part of the Picture being Equell in Strenght of Coulering and finishing, Each Making to much a Picture of its silf, without that Due Subordanation to the Principle Parts, viz they head and hands. For one may Observe in the great works of Van dyke, who is the Prince of Portrait Painter[s], how he has mannaged by light and shedow and the Couler of Dreperys made the face and hands apear allmost a Disception. For in Portrait Painting those are they Parts of Most Consiquence, and of Corse ought to be the most distinguished. Thare is in Historical Painting this Same attention to be Paid. For if the Principl Carrictors are Suffred to Stand in the Croud, and not distinguished by light and shadow, or made Conspicuous by some Pece of art, So that the Eye is first Caut by the Head Carrictor of the History, and So on to the next as he bears Proportion to the head Carrictor, if this is not observed the whole is Confusion and looses that dignity we So much admier in Great works. Your Picture is in Possession of Drawing to a Correctness that is very Surpriseing, and of Coulering very Briliant, tho this Brilantcy is Somewhat missapplyed, as for instance, the Gown too bright for the flesh, which over Came it in Brilency. This made them Critisise they Shadows of the Flesh without knowing from whence this defect arose; and so in like manner the dog and Carpet to Conspichious for Excesry things, and a little want of Propriety in the Back Ground, which Should have been Some Modern orniment, as the Girle was in a Modern dress and modern Cherce [skirt?]. The Back Ground Should have had a look of this time. These are Critisisms I should not mak was not your Pictures very nigh upon a footing with the first artists who now Paints, and my being sensible that Observations of this nature in a friendly way to a man of Your Talents must not be Disagreable. I with the greater Freedom give them, As it is by this assistance the art is reasd to its hight. I hope I shall have the Pleasur of Seeing you in Europe, whare you will have an oppertunity of Contemplateing the great Productions of art, and feel from them what words Cannot Express. For this is a Scorce the want of which (I am senseble of) Cannot be had in Ameri[c]a; and if you should Ever Come to London my house is at Your Service, or if you should incline to go for Italy, if you think letters from me Can be of any Service, there are much at your Service. And be asshurd I am with greatest Friendship, Your Most obediant Humble Servent

BENJN WEST.

PS. I have Spoke to Several of our Mezzotinto Scrappers, and there Prices for a Plate after a Picture of that Sise is from fifteen Guines to Twenty Guines. Thare is Scrapers of a less Price thin that, but they are reather indefirent. I hope you will fevour us with a Picture the next Exhibition. In Closed I Send you a Copy of our Royal Charter and list of fellows, amongst whom you are Chosen one. The next which will be printed your name is to be inserted.

Captain R. G. Bruce to Copley

LONDON, 25th June, 1767.

DEAR COPLEY,

Since I wrote to You the 11th Curr't I was informed that a Letter had lain a great while for me at Mr. Myers's. Upon calling there yesterday I found your Letter of the 12th Novr. last, which, had they taken the trouble of putting in the Post Office, I should have received in course. I wish I had received it sooner, that I might have made your Acknowledgements to the Gentlemen therein mentioned. However I shall do it the first time I see them. Your Brother's Portrait I have removed from Mr. Reynolds's to Mr. West's, where I think it had better remain as a Specimen till you arrive yourself to dispose of it; especially as your last Exhibition is in the Hands of People where it will be of no use to You. With regard to the last Picture exhibited, you have the opinions of the learned in my Letter of the 11th, and the letter inclosed in it from Mr West. Upon the whole you have not pleased so universally as last Year, arising merely from the unlucky choice of your Subject. Among the Judges there are several who prefer the last, and of these are Mr. Hayman [1] and Mr. West, but Mr. Reynolds and the Majority prefer the first, because in that you have made the under parts of the Picture more subordinate to the principal than in the last, where they say the under parts such as the Dog, Parrot Carpet etc., are too brilliant and highly finished in proportion to the Head and Hands. The Nobility in gen'l have condemned the last for this excellent Reason, that "it is an ugly Thing." Let me therefore intreat You to ransack the whole Town and Country for a pleasing Subject for your next Exhibition. As the Society of Artists have chose You a Fellow of the Society (which you will find by a Letter, I have inclosed in my last, from the President) They will depend on your continuing to exhibit. I wish it was convenient for You to paint your next Exhibition Picture at the House of Mr. West, where you would be very welcome, and where you would receive some Assistance. I should think your Business at Boston could not, at any rate, suffer much by a Year or twos Absence, and the Expence would not amount to much. I am afraid you will delay coming to

[1] Francis Hayman (1708–1776).

Europe till the Force of your Genius is weakened, and it may be too late for much Improvement; and the Art be thereby deprived of a capital Hand. You are obliged to Mr. West and Mr. Hayman for being proposed as a Fellow of the Society. The former is so hurried that I have been obliged to teize him for the Letter I have sent You, much in the same manner as I did formerly to persuade You to finish the Picture, which is still surveyed here as an astonishing Performance. My Vanity is not a little flattered in having been the first to find out its Merit, since it has had such great and universal Applause in this Country.

Remember me to your Mother and Brother and my old Acquaintances in your Part of the World and believe me with much Truth, Dear Sir, Your sincere Friend and Serv't

R. G. BRUCE.

Continue to direct for me as usual.[1]

George Livius to Copley

PORTSMOUTH, NEW HAMPSHIRE, 3d. Sepr., 1767.

SIR,

I am desirous of having two family pictures copied in the best manner. If you will undertake it I will send them to you next week. I intend carrying the copies home which makes me wish to have them very perfect pictures, and was I not well satisfied of your ability I woud have ventured the originals to England. I shall send them to you if you think well of it, and can let me have them at the end of five weeks in Boston. The originals were painted by De Kelberg, and one of them has been allways held to be a good picture; the other I have been told by good judges has faults, and when I know your deter-

[1] This letter, sent by the *John Galley*, Captain Huline, was received October 13, 1767.

mination I shall be able easily in a few lines to you to point out any necessary alterations.

I shoud be glad of your answer by return of the post, also the price of a copy, as I do not at present well recolect it, they are half pictures. I remain, Sir, Your most obedt. & h'ble Servt.

GEORGE LIVIUS.

George Livius to Copley

PORTSMOUTH, N.E., 14th Seper., 1767.

SIR,

You shoud have heard from me in consequence of your letter had not the packett which was to have sail'd last week been delay'd 'till this time. I intend sending the Portraits by Captn. Fernald; he sails tomorrow. As to the price you wrote me it exceeds considerably what was customary with you when I was in Boston two years since, and at present is more than was expected by some Gentlemen here, especially for a copy; and I need not observe to you the very few opportunities you have of copying from so good a picture as one of them is. However all I shall add on this head is, that it shall be left entirely to your discretion. I have particularly to beg that nothing may be spared to have them as perfect pictures as you can make them for your own honor and the credit of New England, for as good pictures they may be observed in England and further convince many of your merit. I am sorry you have been disappointed by three or four days of receiving them, however I make no doubt but that five weeks from the date of your letter (the 8th. Instt.) will answer your purpose as to time, you shall hear from me if I shoud be delay'd longer, but I at present rely on having them at that time finish'd in Boston.

I remain, Sir, your most Obedt Servt

GEORGE LIVIUS.

P.S. They measure the Kitcat size. I find I can now spare you five weeks from this date, that is 'till monday the 19th of next month. The Alterations I woud chuse to have in one of the pictures are, 1st. the hand which holds the baskett of flowers. This I think is very badly foreshortned. The best way to remedy that in the copy may be by letting the mantle cover it, tho' I shoud prefer seeing the hand well foreshortned. The hair is also badly executed, as it is intended to exhibit hair that has been powder'd, careless in undress, but it looks more like grey hairs in its present dress, which woud be very inconsistant with the air of the picture, which has a youthfull appearance. The person's age was about 30 at the time of taking the picture, and a sure circumstance that they were not intended for grey is that at the time of her death the hair was light brown, which is the color I woud prefer having it drawn in. Another fault, thought so by those who remember the person, is the prodigious breadth of the picture across the shoulders (I dont mean the fall of the shoulders). This you will observe when you see the picture to be to a degree unnatural, tho I imagine it was intended to express the looseness of the bed gown; but it does not produce that effect. I woud chuse to alter the color of the bed gown from the flaring colour it is of to a more becoming and grave one, to a garnet purple for instance; but this I leave also to your fancy and taste. As to the other picture I woud chuse no alteration whatever in it; only an exact and good copy as possible. Care must be taken not to thrust the chisel too far in opening the case, there is a groove in the wood work in which part of the portrait is let in as it was a $\frac{1}{4}$ of an inch too small; you will observe the case is not to be opened on the broad part, but on the side on which the card is nail'd, which is to be gently wedged up with a chisel for fear of hurting the pictures, which are to be carefully drawn out of the grooves they are put into. And in packing up the pictures again you will take care to have them put facing each other, that they may not rub or be hurt. I shall be obliged to you if you will in time bespeak as good a case to pack up your portraits in, to be sent me here.

Copley to Francis M. Newton.

BOSTON, NOVR. 23, 1767.

SIR,

I received your very polite Letter of the 3d of Sepr., 1766, which gave me the first notice of my being Elected a Fellow of the Society of Artists of Great-Briton tho by some accident it did not come to hand till the 13th of Octr., 1767, otherwise I should sooner have acknowledged the seense I have of the compliment they have been pleased to Honour me with.

I beg Sir You will take the first oppertunity of making my acknowledgements to the President and Society for this testamony of their approbation, and the favourable reception they have given my works, and as I shall allways esteem it a real Honour to be of that Society, so I shall by constant application to my studys strive to deserve the Election; But as I am sensable the Honour of the Society depends on the promotion of the Arts, I cannot but reflect with concern on my present situation, which utterly deprives me of every oppertunity (but what Nature has furnish'd me with) of being aiding in this laudable work.

In a Country where their is neither precept, example, nor Models, to form the taste direct and confirm the practice I cannot take the sattisfaction or procure the advantages I might injoy in obeying Your sommons. But the tie of Filial Duty pleads my excuse for what might otherwise be thought to arrise from Inactivity I am, Sir, with all Due Respect, Your Most Obet. Humble Sert.

JOHN SINGLETON COPLEY.

Copley to [Captain R. G. Bruce?] [1]

[1767?]

But What shall I do at the end of that time (for prudence bids us to Consider the future as well as the present). Why I must eighther return to America, and Bury all my improvements among people intirely destitute of all just Ideas of the Arts, and without any addition of Reputation to what I have already gaind. For the favourable receptions my Pictures have met with at home has mad them think I could get a better Living at home than I can here, which has been of service to me, but should I be disappointed, it would be quite the reverse. It would rather lessen than increase their oppinion of my Works which I aught by all prudent methods strive to avoide. Or I should sett down in London in a way perhaps less advantagious than what I am in at present, and I cannot think of purchasing fame at so dear a rate. I shall find myself much better off than I am in my present situation. (I would be here understood to speak of the profits of the art only, for as I have not any fortune, and an easy income is a nesasary thing to promote the art. It aught to be considered, and Painters cannot Live on Art only, tho I could hardly Live without it). But As it is not possable for me, Who never was in Europe, to settle sufficiently in my mind those points, I must rely on Your Friendship and Mr.

[1] A fragment of the letter.

West to inform me. I have wrote You and Mr. West in the plainest and most unreserved maner what the dificultys are, and doubt not Your friendship and prudence will lead You to give all Due weit to the objections I have proposed; and if You think they are still sufficient to keep me in this Country, I shall strive to content myself where I am. I have been thee more perticular in this Letter Least the other should have miscarried, and doubt not You will write me answer as soon as possible, and prevail on Mr. West to Lay aside the pencil to remove my Doubts, for You cannot but know a state of uncertainty in affairs of consequence (as these are to me,) are very perplexing and disagreable. Beside if Your Answer [be] such as to favour my going, you know I have a Real Estate which I must dispose of, and a Great Deal of Business to settle, which must take up much time and will detain me another Year, unless I can hear soon from You.

Copley to [*West or Captain R. G. Bruce?*]

[1767?]

I observe the Critisisms made on my last picture were not the same as those made on the first. I hope I have not in this as in the last by striving to avoid one error fallen into another. I shall be sorry if I have. However it must take its fate. Perhaps You may blame me for not taking anoth[e]r subject that would have aforded me more time, but subjects are not so easily procured in this place. A taste of painting is too much Wanting to affoard any kind of helps; and was it not for preserving the resembla[n]ce of perticular persons, painting would not be known in the plac[e]. The people generally regard it no more than any other usefull trade, as they somtimes term it, like that

of a Carpenter tailor or shew maker, not as one of the most
noble Arts in the World. Which is not a little Mortifiing to
me. While the Arts are so disregarded I can hope for nothing,
eith[e]r to incourage or assist me in my studies but what I
receive from a thousand Leagues Distance, and be my improvements what they will, I shall not be benifitted by them in this
country, neighther in point of fortune or fame. This is what I
wrote at large in my last letter Datted [   ][1] as the only
reason that discourages me from going to Europe, least after
going I shall not find myself so good an artist, as to merit that
incouragement that would make it worth my while. It would
by no means be [   ] to go th[e]re to improve myself, and than
return to America; but if I could make it worth my [while] to
stay there, I would remove with Moth[e]r and Broth[e]r, who
I am bound by all the ties of Duty and Effe[c]tion not to Desert
as Long as I live. My income in this Country is about three
hund'd Guineas a Year, out of which I have been able to Lay
up as much as would carrie me thru and support me hand-
somly for a Couple of Years with a family.

Copley to Benjamin West [2]

BOSTON, Jany. 17th, 1768.

SIR,

By Capt [   ] I send You two portraits,[3] one in Oyl the
other in Crayons. with respect to the first I think common jus-

---

[1] Perhaps the letter preceding. Cunningham, in his *Lives of the British
Painters*, prints two extracts from letters of 1767 not found in this collection,
one to Captain Bruce, and the other to West.

[2] There are two drafts of this letter. The first one has many erasures, the
more important of which are given in the footnotes.

[3] Erased in first draft: "agreable to the promiss I made You in my Last, which
I am very desireous to hear of Your receiveing."

tice to myself requires some Apologys, that in case it should not answer Your expectations it may not be intirely at the expence of my Reputation. For altho it may be as good as my portraits generally are, yet for an Exibition somthing more may be expected, and that Artist is greatly to be pitied, who cannot occationally rise above the common level of his practice. Yet such has been my ill Luck, that this as well as the last Years I have not had the advantages I generally have for my other portraits. The reason of which is my not receiveing the Criticisms of the Artists and publick earlyer, and I prize them two highly to be willing to lose the advantage of them, which I should do at least one Year, should I paint my picture before they come to hand. Yet I find I had better submit to that inconveniance than to the evil of doing it in the depth of Winter,[1] the weither bein[g] too severe and time too far elapsed for such a work, considerin[g] at the same time that I am obliged to attend to a great [deal] of Business. Having no assistance I am obliged to do all parts of my Pictures with my own hand. However, I should not have had so many apologys to make for this portrait if Mr. Rogers could have spared time to have sat as I found occation for him, but the preparations for his Voyage to London took up so much of his time as to leave me to the disagreable necessaty of finishing a great part of it in his absence.

As to the other if I have not succeeded I must take all the blame to myself it. It is a plain head[2] and the only apology I have to offer is this, that as I never saw[3] any thing done in that

---

[1] Erased in first draft: "when the shortness of time the sever[it]y of the Climate at once conspire to appose the Art that can only thrive. But here I was doubly unlucky."

[2] First draft: "in Crayons." Erased in second draft: "in the most simple dress Imaginable."

[3] Erased in first draft: "more than three heads done in Crayons."

way that could possably be esteemd, I am more at a loss to know what will please the Coniseur. I prefered simplissity in the dress because, should I do any thing in a taste of Drapery forrain from or contrary to what is the prevailling fashon when the picture appears at the Exibition, it must displease. Nor indeed can I be suplyed with that variety of Dresses here as in Europe, unless I should put myself to a great expence to have them made. This picture bears the Likeness of a Young Lady who is known by some that may visit the Exibition and may be desireous to have a coppy of it, which I beg You will not suffer as I am under the strongest obligations both to her Parents and herself having given my word and honour that no Coppy shall be taken of it. What ever their reasons may be this is so binding upon me that I beg it as a thing of the last importance not to let any Body have it out of Your possession except while it is in the Exibition. After that is over I beg You will keep it till I shall direct how to dispose of it.

I am very ancious to hear of Your receiveing my last Letter, as it contained the reasons that have hithertoo deter'd me from a Voyage to London; and being uncertain weither they will be thought sufficent or not, and I can only be informd by You and My Friend Capt. Bruce, to whom I communicated the same. I should be glad to go to Europe, but cannot think of it without a very good prospect of doing as well there as I can here. You are sensable that three hundred Guineas a Year, which is my present income, is a pretty living in America, and I cannot think You will advise me to give it up without a good prospect of somthing at least equel to it, considering I must remove an infirm Mother, which must add to the dificulty and expenciveness of such [a] Voyage. And what ever my ambition may be to excell in our noble Art, I cannot think of doing it at the expence of not only my own happyness, but that of a tender Mother and Young Brother [1] whose dependance is intirely upon me.

I cannot conclude this long epistle without taking notice of the diference of the Exicution of the three portraits in Oyl I have painted for the Exibition. The first is Minutely finished and, as well as I can remember, I think pretty clean; the shades collected and thrown out of the principal part of the Picture. The second less minute not so clean, nor the shades so well dispos'd on the flesh. The last You will find differs from the other two, from the first in point of Minuteness, and the second in point of Cleanness and disposition of shades. Yet I am altogether uncertain weither it will please mor or less than the last, but I beg You will continue Your remarks in the same friendly [2] maner You have hither too done, which will very much Oblige Your sincere friend And Humble Sert.

John S: Copley.

P.S. To secure the pictures from the customs I have directed them to Roger Hale Esqr. Land surveyor at the custom house port of London, in the same maner as I did the last Year.

Copley to [Captain R. G. Bruce]

[*Circa* January 17, 1768.]

Dear Sir,

By this oppertun[i]ty I send the two portraits that I promist in my last, one in Crayons the other in Oyl, which I have Directed to Mr. Hale to secure them from the Customs, as I did the one I sent the last Year. I must beg you will be so kind as

---

[1] First draft: "who I am bring[ing] up to [the] same study with myself."
[2] First draft: "canded."

to see that Mr. West receives them for the Exibition. I intended to have sent them sooner but I found it more dificult to procure a subject than I thought I should. I really wish they may please but I assure you I have not had a Common chance sence the first I sent but have eigther been hurried by the shortness of time or the interuption of other Business or hindred by the badness of the weither. Perticularly in Mr. Rogers portrait I met with so much dificulty as not to be certain weither I should be able to finish the face before he saild or not till a few Days before he went for London, which was so dispiriting that if it is not liked you must blame him for all the Defects you find in it. He will acknowledge my observations to be true and I doubt not will do me justice in this perticular. He will remember I was Obliged sometimes to beg sometimes to scold in order to mak[e] the Dificulty of his compliance less than the neglect of his seting by which means I obtain[e]d as much time as I generally spend about a portrait of this size, which is by no means suffic[i]ent in my oppinion for an Exibition Picture. Indeed (I find however it may be with other painters) that mine are almost allways good in proportion to the time I give them provided I have a subject that is picturesk.[1]

Myles Cooper[2] *to Copley*

KING'S COLLEGE, NEW YORK, 5 Augt. 1768.
SIR,

By Capt Smith, who conveys this, You will receive 7 Guineas, the price, if I recollect, of the Picture. By the Same Gentleman

---

[1] The remainder of the letter is wanting.

[2] Myles Cooper was second president of King's College from 1763 to 1776. There are two portraits of him at Columbia University, one of which is doubtless the object of this correspondence. It has been reproduced in *Columbia*

I also send a Gown, Hood, and Band, by which to finish the Drapery. This, I doubt not, you will be able to execute, before Capt. Smith returns to New York; at which Time You will return the Gown etc. together with the Picture: and, if a Couple of Guineas will purchase the little Piece which I so much admired, the Nun with the Candle before her, You may send that also, which I will deposit in our College Library, as a Beginning to a public Collection. If the Picture does not please You, and I should visit Boston again, the next Year, I will take Care that it shall be there before me; that, when I come, it may receive your finishing Hand. I am, Sir yr. most obedt and very hble Sert.

MYLES COOPER.

Please to convey the Letter to Mr. Troutbeck.[1]

Copley to [Myles Cooper][2]

[1768.]

I received Your favour by C[apt.] Smith with the robe in good order. I am sorry it is not in my power to comply with Your reques[t] in sending it back as soon as You expected, but having been ingaged to sett out upon a tour of a week the next Morning, but will return it when Cap Smith makes his next trip. I likewise received seven Guineas the price of Your portrait. As to the Candle light In consideration of the use You propose to make of it I will part with it for two Guineas, as it is my desire to see some publick collection begun in America.

University Quarterly, I. 347. The other is either a replica by Copley or a copy by another artist. Mr. Edward R. Smith has discussed the history and relationship of the paintings in *ibid.*, XII. 299–301.

  [1] 'John Troutbeck was assistant rector of King's Chapel, 1755–1775.

  [2] An extremely rough draft of Copley's reply to the preceding letter, without address, signature or date.

I shall therefore send it with Your por[trait]. One box will contain the two but I [am] extreemly loath to send Yours till You sett again, for after it has been seen by everey body the finnish comes too late to answer the purposes desired.

Benjamin West to Copley

LONDON, Sepr. 20th, 1768.

DEAR SIR,

By your Friend Mr. Rogers I send you these few lines on the subject of your last letter to me. My long Silence on this head must have made you think by this that I had forgot you. But the more I reflected on your Situation, and those Points you have been Pleasd to Communicate to me, the More I found myself under the Necessity of a longer Deliberation and not to be too precipitate in writeing you my Opinion till I had Exactly assertaind that of Publick. I have with the greatest care Endavoured at their real Sentiments in regard to the Merrits of those Specimens you have been pleast to favour us with of your Painting at our Exhibition, And find by their Candid approbation you have nothing to Hazard in Comeing to this Place. The Plan I then offer for your Consideration is as follows: The length to which you have advanced in the Art of Painting shews the High light you hold that noble art in, and the venaration you must have for those great Productions with which Italy abounds, Tho perhaps amongs the liveing Masters of that Country you may not meet with a rival. But from the works of those dead to a Man of Powers they are a Source of Knowledge ever to be prized and Saught after. I would therefor, Mr. Copley, advise your makeing this viset while young and befor you determin to Settle. I dont apprehend it needs be more than one Year, as you wont go in pursut of that which you are not Advanced in, but as a Satisfaction to yourself hearafter in knowing to what a length the art has been Carried to. by this you will find yourself in Possesions of Powers you will then feel that Cannot be Communicated by words and is onely to be felt by those which Nature has Blessd with Powers.

As your Setling in England will be attended with a little famely, if your viset to Italy could be first accomplished I should think it would be better. But this yourself, Mr. Rogers, or your other Friends will be the best judges of. This seems to me the Plan that most affectually establishes you, and what is to be Accomplisdd without great Expance. this is what Occurs to me on this head, and candidly send it you as one that is your Friend. My Friendship I freely give, and if ever you should Come hear, I begg you'll make my house your home. I am, Dear Mr. Copley, Your Friend and Most obediant Humble Servent

B: WEST.

Myles Cooper to Copley

KING'S COLLEGE, NEW YORK, 24 Octr., 1768.

SIR,

I was so unfortunate as not to see Capt. Smith during his Stay here the last Voyage, otherwise, a Line should have waited on You at his Return. I am obliged to You for what you say concerning the Candle-Light, which You will please to send by Capt. Smith (who, I fancy, will be almost ready to sail, by the Time You receive this), and the Money [shall be re-]mitted to you by the first Opportunity. But, by the Same Conveyance, I must also beg of you to send my Portrait, finish'd in the best Manner You can; for, as to my Coming again to Boston, (considering what a Situation You are in, and I am afraid Things are not likely to change for the better) the Matter is quite uncertain: and, if ever I *do* see the Place again, it will hardly be before both You and I have seen Europe.

I have seen several People who have told me the Picture is exceeding *like* me; and if the Finishing is not so high, as You might have made it, on another Sitting; I will take all Care that the Circumstances shall be known to those who have either Discernment enough to taste its Excellencies, or Penetration sufficient to observe its Defects. I am, Sir with my best wishes for your Welfare, yr. most obedt. and very hble Servt.

MYLES COOPER.

Myles Cooper to Copley

KING'S COLLEGE, NEW YORK, 9th Jany, 1769.

SIR,

I was much surprized that you neither thought proper to send my Picture, as you were desir'd to do, by Capt. Smith; nor to give me any Reason for the Omission. Perhaps he might have slipt away as he has done from me, without your Knowledge of his sailing: but still you might have let me know that such was the Case. As for the portrait itself, the want of it cannot be attended with any great Inconvenience; but the Gown I think you are unpardonable for keeping in your Hands so long: And the *other* Picture, if I had been in possession of it, would, ere this, have been the Occasion of procuring some more, to my certain Knowledge, for our Library. I beg, Sir, you would send at least, my Gown by the first Opportunity, and remain, yr. most obedt. Servt.

MYLES COOPER.

Edward Holyoke[1] *to Copley*

CAMBRIDGE, Jany. 31, 1767.[2]

SIR,

This comes to desire you to delivr. Mr. Hollis's Picture to the Persons I shall send (as soon as may be) with an Order for it. It seems you say the Goven'r told you, you might take it to yor self, having 16 Guineas only for the new Picture, which I wonder at, for that his Excy. must needs know he had no more power to Dispose of it than the smallest man in the Governmt. But however, We shall not be sure part with the Picture, and if you must have more for the new Picture, let it be so, and as for yor letting us have it Cheaper, being for the College, I think you are in the Right rather to give what you shall see meet to allow in Gift to the College, in some other Way, I am Yor humble Servt.

E. HOLYOKE.

Myles Cooper to Copley

KING'S COLLEGE, NEW YORK, 21, Augt., 1769.

SIR,

I am extremely sorry, that, for a voyage or two before this, Capt. Smith should have made so much Haste, as to have prevented my Sending by Him the two Guineas which I am indebted to you for the portrait. The piece has been much admired; as well as the picture of myself. I should be very glad if You could persuade yourself to exercise your Art for a few

---

[1] Edward Holyoke was president of Harvard College, 1737–1769. He died June 1, 1769.

[2] The date was at first read 1769; but a closer examination, too late for transferring the letters to their proper places, proved 1767 to be correct.

Months in this place: I am satisfied you would find an unparalleled Degree of Encouragement, notwithstanding the common Complaint of the Scarcity of Money. Any assistance that I could lend you, you might depend on receiving. Capt Smith will give you the Balance of your Account; and you will oblige me by sending a Rect. for the whole by the Return of the same Conveyance. I am, Sr. Yr. most obedt. and very hble Servt.

MYLES COOPER.

Copley to [Myles Cooper]

BOSTON, Sepr. 24, 1769.

SIR,

I take this oppertunity to acknowledge the receipt of your kind favour by Capt. Smith. It gives me peculiar pleasure to find the pictures came safe to hand and were approved off. I am much obliged to you for the assistance you are so kind to offer me should I visit New-york. Although I cannot at present make that excursion for the exercise of my pencill, I may in some future time, when I shall be doubly happy in the friendship of one from whom an obligation will be no ways painfull. I am Sir with all Respect your Most Obet. Humle Sert.

JOHN SINGLETON COPLEY.

G. W. Schilling[?] to Copley [1]

SIR,

To fulfill my promisse per these few lines I do acquaint you that yr Pictur[e] is very wel received by all the world.

I am very glad and thank you kindly for your paines that you have taken in painting, and for all favours which you

---

[1] This letter is written in a somewhat trembling hand. It bears the stamp of the New York post office, April 3. The postage was four shillings.

have shewd to me. my Compliments to yr beloved lady Mother and whole famyly. I am with the utmost regard, Sir,

Your most humble servant

G: W: SCHILLING [?].

UTREGT the 18 8br. 1769
Pray excuse my scrable.

Captain John Small [1] *to Copley*

HEAD QUARTERS, NEW YORK, 8ber. 29th. 1769.

SIR,

The Miniature you took from my *Crayon* Picture has been very much admir'd and approv'd of here, by the best Judges.

Your picture of the General [2] is universally acknowledg'd to be a very masterly performance, elegantly finish'd, and a most striking Likeness; in short it has every property that Genius, Judgement and attention can bestow on it. The Gentleman who delivers you this Letter is Mr. Taylor of considerable Fortune in the West Indies, and of an accomplish'd Taste and education, improv'd by Travelling and observation; these circumstances induce me to make *so great a* Connoisseur accquainted with you, that he may have an opportunity of Observing that Genius is not confin'd to Europe, or the Eastern Countrys.

I Want *much* to have a Copy of my Crayon picture, Mr. Dumaresq [3] will Let you have the use of it for that purpose.

Mr. Taylor *soon* returns *hither*, and will do me the favor to

---

[1] (1726–1796). Long in America, as Captain of the 21st Regiment in 1765, Major Commandant in the 84th in 1775, and finally Lieutenant Colonel Commandant in the same regiment in 1780. He is prominently represented in Trumbull's picture of Bunker Hill.

[2] Gage?

[3] Probably Philip Dumaresque, a merchant of Boston.

take Charge of it; should it be any way inconvenient to him; (for I would by no means be troublesome) it can be sent by any other safe Opportunity, and you may draw on me for the price, or inform me to Whom I shall pay that Sum here or at Boston; Your Order shall be instantly accepted. If Consistent with your own oppinion and agreable to your Rules, I should be glad. The Face should be a Little higher in the frame, so that more of the body and drapery should appear; I think I mentioned this when I sat to you or about the time the first picture was finish'd; But I Leave it intirely to your own decision and shall be satisfy'd to receive it as you think propper to send it; should You approve of any Alteration of the above sort and that *a hand* may appear I would wish to have plac'd in that hand a paper, or part of a paper folded up and endors'd on the upper end with the Annex'd Superscription or Endorsement and as this may occasion a good deal more Labor and must be troublesome in some degree to you in the performance, I would by *no means*, propose this addition without also an Increase of the price. If you think proper to demand or charge it, be assur'd it will be chearfully paid. I beg an answer to this Letter As soon as convenient to you and am, Sir, Your Obedt Servt.

JOHN SMALL.

Direct To John Small Esqr Major of brigade at Head Quarters N York.

To appear on the before mention'd paper. General Return of the troops composing the Army in North America Boston 8ber 1769.

N. B. The words may be contracted if you choose it, the paper *by no means* to be broader than this annex'd pattern.

1766 Mr Isaac Smith to J. S. Copley Dr

 £
To painting his & his Lady's portraits
 on half Length at 15 Guineas —— 39 .. 4 . 0
To two carved Gold Frames for Ds —— 18 .. 0 . 0
          £ 57 . 4 . 0

Recd the contents in full
for John Singleton Copley

Mr. Eliot[1] to Copley

[1767?][2]

Mr Eliot's Compliments to Mr Copley. The President and the other Gentlemen of the Corporation think it would be quite improper to part with the Picture sent by Mr Hollis — are willing to pay Mr Copley for the other, but earnestly desire the small one may be put up to be ready when the President shall send for it.

Thurs: P: M:

Henry Pelham to Charles Pelham

BOSTON, Jany 17, 1770.

DEAR BROTHER,

This is to request of you to let Me know if you have yet found the Letter that you mentioned when last in town. Upon thinking of the Circumstances of that affair, we can form no probible conjecture but that it must be a person who has had some connection or Acquaintance with our hond. Father, either in England or here. I therefore submit it to you weither it would not be best to Incert an Advertizement in the News-paper for the Recovery of it. If it should be found and turns out to be of no Advantage ether to you or me, yet it will satisfy our Curiosity, and leave us assured that we have not lost any thing for the want of seeking it. If you think an Advertizement proper, be pleased to write one and send it and I will insert it in the paper. I would request you to make strict search, because it is impossable to know what advantages may be missed by the Family by its being lost. My Hond. Mama, who has been

---

[1] Andrew Eliot.

[2] See President Holyoke's note of January 31, 1767, p. 75, *supra.*

very unwell ever since you was in Town, joins me in tenderest love and Respects to yourself and Sister Pelham, hoping you are all well. I remain Dear Sir Your Affectionate Bror. and, Humble Sert.

H. PELHAM.

PS. There is a Report in Boston which gains Credit that Mr. Dickinson the pensilvania Farmer is dead, which gives the greatest concern to every Friend of the Libertys of America.[1]

Charles Pelham to Henry Pelham

NEWTON, Jany. 27, 1770.

MY DEAR BROR.,

I recd yours of 17th, and very much Commend the prudent concern you shew regarding the Letter I mention'd to you, and were it necessary shou'd have readily fallen into your proposal of Advertising it.

I had not the least apprehension that it related, or was interesting to me personally, but concluded you was the person meant, and by what I had heard, I judg'd it to be very Interesting; This imagination engag'd my utmost vigilence, by which after some search I receiv'd the Letter, and found it to be from Capt. Richard Lowry, half Bror. to Thos. Pelham.[2] The Letter is directed to Mr. Pelham. He says he had been absent and had heard nothing of the Family for 25 Years, but meant to address himself to Chas. or Wm., whichever might be Living. The purport of the Letter is a very tender enquiry after his Brethren, His Mothers, and our Fathers Familys; and a very earnest request that I will write to him concerning them.

---

[1] John Dickinson died February 14, 1808.
[2] Peter Pelham's second wife was Margaret Lowrey.

Sir   Boston May 1. 1789

On the 29th. Ult: Mrs Pelham departed
this Life, and on Monday next I purpose to en-
tomb her, when was it practicable I should
have been very glad of your Company, but fear
whether this will reach you before the Funeral
will over? You know the state in which she
has lain near two Years, no great percepta-
ble alteration took place till within these two
or three Months, ~~~ in which time she grew gradually weaker and weaker till within a ~~~
Week of her death when she sunk into a stupor
suffering great pain and distress, then gave up
Life without any struggle, thus has the good
old Lady left us, rather to congratulate than
bemoan her deliverance from a very long and
almost uninterrupted course of misery.

There is in the house some pictures
and Miss Scollay thinks some other things belonging to you, I shall be glad you would
send me an account of them, and your orders
concerning them, which shall be observ'd with
care and punctuality. My best regards
wait on you, being

                    Sir   Your most obedient
                            Hum: Serv:
                            Chas. Pelham

Henry Bromfield Esq.

I am sorry to hear your Mama was so unwell, but hope 'ere now she is better again. We are all (Thank God) in pretty good health; your Sister Pelham heartily Joins in Tender Respects to our Mama, in Love to you, and affecte. Regards to Mr. Copley and Lady. Your Godson[1] grows a clever Fellow, and will soon wonder that you do not come and Catechise him. Hilly[2] is Taught to express Duty and Gratitude to her Grandmama, and would be greatly pleas'd to pay her a visit. I pray God to Bless you and am Your Affecte. Brother

CHAS. PELHAM.

John Greenwood[3] to Copley

DR. SIR,

It has given me infinite pleasure from time to time, to see your masterly performances exhibitted here in London, and hope at the approaching Season to find no disappointment, as it will certainly be a very great one to me, if a Picture of yours is wanting. as it may hapen that subjects may frequently hinder your favoring us with them so often as one coud wish, I've tho't of one very proper for your next years Applause, and our amusement; I mean the Portrait of my Hond. Mother,[4] who resides at present nigh Marblehead, but is often in Boston. as I have of late enter'd into conections, that may probably keep me longer in London than I coud wish, I am very desirous of seeing the good Lady's Face as she now appears, with old age creeping upon her. I shoud chuse her painted on a small half length or a size a little broader than Kitt Katt, sitting

---

[1] Charles Pelham, Jr., born May 10, 1769.
[2] Helen, born April 2, 1867 or 1768.
[3] See *Dictionary of National Biography*, XXIII. 85.
[4] Mary (Charnock) Greenwood.

in as natural a posture as possible. I leave the pictoresque disposition intirely to your self and I shall only observe that gravity is my choice of Dress. I have desired her to write to you to be inform'd when 'twill suit you for her to come to Boston. if you could get it done by the time that Capn. Symms sails for London I shoud be sure of a safe conveyance.

In regard to myself, since I left the West indies I've been visiting most of the Courts of Europe, and admiring the thousand fine paintings that one finds distributed among them, tho' at present England bids fair to become the seat of the Arts and Artists. Almost every thing that is not immoveable is brot here, from every Country, as none pay so generously for real good pictures as the English — *tho' I must confess*, I think it begins somewhat to fall off. You'll be supprized when I tell you, that I have brot into London above 1500. pictures, and have had the pleasure of adorning some of the first Cabinets in England, so that I have had but little time to exercise my pencil, but now and then, have for amusement painted and scrap'd several pieces that have not been disregarded.

West goes on painting like a Raphael and realy out does every thing one could have expected. his Compositions are Noble, his design correct, and his Colouring harmonious and pleasing, and a certain Sweetness in his Charecters, that must please every one that beholds them. You certainly have seen prints after him, which will give you but a faint Idea of his Performances. we have several Exhibitions coming on, of old and new pictures, Prints, Drawings, etc., which form Mr Boydels Collection, so that for six weeks to come, you woud hear of nothing here but the Virtu — just as children in Boston for a fortnight before the 'Lection, prate of nothing else. it will please me to continue a correspondence with Mr Copley, and if I can be any ways Serviceable to him here in London he may freely comand me. I beg you'll accept my most sincere wishes for Your Welfare, and be assured shall Always be pleased with Your Success. I am with respects to all friends, Dear Sir, Yr most Obed. Humble Sert.

JNO. GREENWOOD.

MOUNT STREET the 23 March, 1770.

Henry Pelham to Paul Revere

THURSDAY MORNG. BOSTON, March 29, 1770.

SIR,

When I heard that you was cutting a plate of the late Murder. I thought it impossible, as I knew you was not capable of doing it unless you coppied it from mine and as I thought I had entrusted it in the hands of a person who had more regard to the dictates of Honour and Justice than to take the undue advantage you have done of the confidence and Trust I reposed in you. But I find I was mistaken, and after being at the great Trouble and Expence of making a design paying for paper, printing &c, find myself in the most ungenerous Manner deprived, not only of any proposed Advantage, but even of the expence I have been at, as truly as if you had plundered me on the highway. If you are insensible of the Dishonour you have brought on yourself by this Act, the World will not be so. However, I leave you to reflect upon and consider of one of the most dishonorable Actions you could well be guilty of.

H. PELHAM.

P S. I send by the Bearer the prints I borrowed of you. My Mother desired you would send the hinges and part of the press, that you had from her.

A Receipt for Money

Major Small.. Dr.

    To Mr Copeleys order for £7.10 / Sterlg. at par £13.6.8

    To freight a Box from Boston................... 4

                  New York Curry.   £13. 10. 8

         Recd. the above,

                        PASCHAL N. SMITH.

[Endorsed by Major Small] Receipt *in full* from Capt Smith for £13.10.8 New York Currency remitted by him to Mr Copely at Boston, in March 1770.

A Bill for Printing

Mr. Henry Pelham to Danl Rea Junr.·   Dr.

March To Cash Advanc'd for 12 Quire of Paper @ ¾   2

 1770   To Printing 575 of your Prints [1] @ 12/ Pr. Hund.   3:9:

                    L[awful] Money £5: 9:

         Contents Recd. Pr. Danl Rea Jun.

John Hurd to Copley

                    PORTSMO., 17th April, 1770.

DR SIR,

  By orders from Governor Wentworth I have putt on board this Sloop, Capt Miller, a Large Case with a Valuable Picture of one [2] of his favourite Friends which lately arriv'd from England, and by some bad Stowage in the Vessell has taken considerable Damage. The Governor desires you would receive

---

   [1] Probably Pelham's prints of the massacre. See previous letter.

   [2] Mr. Hurd has underscored "one" and written "Mr Jno. Nelson" in the margin.

it into your Care and do the Needful to recover and repair the Beauty of the Picture and the Frame, so as to reship it by return of Capt Miller. you may at the same time pack up the Frame of the Picture here, which you have the measure of and ought to have been sent before, together with the Governor's own Picture. I was much disappointed in not receiving it, when the Vessell arrivd here last, beg it may not be forgot this next Time.

You'll please to take all necessary pains to repair this Picture of Mr. Nelson, as the Governor setts great Store by it being a Present to him. he esteems it as an Elegant and choice piece of painting, the Taste of which he thinks you will be pleased with.

He desird me to renew his Invitation of your and Mrs. Copley's coming to Wolfboro' where he intends moving very soon, and tho' you may meet nothing very elegant there, he'll assure you of a hearty Welcome and some Employment for your Pencil. and you may depend on something of the same sort from us at Portsmo. as it lyes within our Sphere. I am with great Esteem, Your Most hum Servt.

JOHN HURD.

[Pr]ay my Complimts with Mrs. Hurds to Mrs Copley.

Henry Pelham to Charles Pelham

TUESDAY NOON, May 1, 1770.

DEAR BROTHER,

I have just Been to Mr. Barnards [1] Store, and am very sorry to inform you that he sat out this Morn'g for Kenebeck, where he tarrys 3 or 4 Weeks. I have therefore returned the Order and

---

[1] Probably John Bernard, of King Street, opposite Vernon's Head, who was one of the merchants being denounced at this time for "audaciously continuing to counteract the united sentiments of the body of merchants throughout North America, by importing British goods contrary to the agreement." *Boston Gazette* (Supplement), June 18, 1770.

should have been very glad to have done the Buisness more to your satisfaction.

As your man is waiting, I have only to subscribe myself your most Affectionate Brother

Hen'y Pelham.

P S. Accept of our best Love and Respects to yourself and Sister Pelham.

Henry Pelham to Charles Pelham

Boston, Tuesday Eveng, May 1, 1770.

Dear Brother,

I embrace the first Leasure Moment scince your Man Left Boston to appologize for the very engenteel scrawl I sent by him. I beg you would attribute it to the shortness of the Time, and not to any disrespect to a Brother whom I shall always take the greatest pleasure in Serving whenever it is in my Power. I enquired of the person who takes care of Mr. Barnard's Business if he had left any Orders respecting you Acct. But was i[n]formed he had not. My Mama sends her Love and Respects to you and Sister Pelham, and Blessing to Hilly and Charles; kindly thanks you for the present of parsnips; hopes the Gooseberry Wine she sent will prove agreable. Inclosed I send you two of my prints of the late Massacre, and a Newspaper containg. Messages between the L[ieutenant] Governor and the House, Extract from Lord Chatham's Speech, A sketch of the proceedings of our patriotick Merch's who have resolved to return to England 30000 £ st. worth of Goods imported contrary to agreement; the WISPERER. No. IV; the remonstrance of the City of London to his Majesty &c. &c.[1] By which you will conclude that they are in the utmost confusion in old

---

[1] The *Boston Gazette*, April 30, 1770.

as well as New England. What will be the final Result of these Altercations time only can discover. thus much seems to be certain that if there is not a change of Measures, and that very soon, the British Dominions will be plunged into one of the most dreadfull of all temporal Evills, into all the Horrors of a civil War. Yesterday Messrs. Hutchinsons who had a large quantity of Tea under the Custom house agreed to have it stored by the committee of Inspection 'till the Act is repealed.

A Vessell just arived who left London a week after Cap't Scott. Says the London Remonstrance was presented to the King by three Gentlemen at the head of the largest Number of People ever assembled together in London and was most graciously Received.

We greatly Rejoyce to hear that you are all well hope you will enjoy a continuance of that and every other Blessing. Brotr. and Sister Copley join me in tenderest Love and Respects to yourself, Sister Pelham, and Cousins Hilly and Charles. Hoping very soon personally to pay my respects, and catachize my son Charles at Newton. I remain, Dear Sir, Your Most Affectionate Brother, and Most Humble Servt.

H. Pelham.

P S. I must beg the favour of you Sir, to lock up the Newspaper in your desk till I come to Newton, as I find I cannot get another from the printer, and I should be Very sorry to be without one.

John Hurd to Copley

Portsmo', 4th May, 1770.

Sir,

I rec'd your favor of April with the Portrait Pictures per Capt Miller which are come to hand in good Order, but the

Frame designd for the Picture here is too small by half an Inch in the Wedth, that I fear it must go back again unless we find some other Use for it.

Mr. Nelson's Picture I think is well recoverd from the Ruin it seemd devoted to. The Governor is satisfy'd with it, tho' he hardly thinks it restor'd to its original Beauty.

He and his Lady return their Compliments to you and Mrs. Copley for yr. respectful Remembrance of them.

I am pleas'd with the Governor's Picture now sent, but I cant perswade Mrs. Hurd, nor my Children who were very fond of the first, that this Copy is equal to the Other. The Glass and frame is certainly not so good.

Inclosd you have the Governor's sett of Bills Exchange on Messrs. Trecothick and Apthorp of London for £30. 13.6 Sterlg, the Exact Ballance of your Acco't and which you'll please to credit him for Accordingly. Pray [give] my best Respects to your Father Clarke and all his good family in which Mrs. Hurd desires to join with our kind Complim'ts to Mrs Copley. I am with great Regard and Esteem, Dr. Sir, your most humle Servt.

JOHN HURD.

William Johnston [1] *to Copley*

BARBADOS, 4th May, 1770.

DEAR SIR,

Yours of the 6th. Jan'y I recd. and setting the motive asside from which it was wrote, be assured it gave me much pleasure; could I promise myself sucess, I would petition for a continuance of your favors. I will at a Venture. It is the humble

---

[1] Perhaps a son of Thomas Johnston, who was painter, engraver and japanner in Boston, and also a designer of heraldic work. John Greenwood, some of whose letters are in this volume, was apprenticed to him.

request of your friend Will: that as often as Opportunity presents, and your time cannot be better employ'd that you convey a few sentiments, which will ever be agreable and most gratefully received, as coming from my friend Copley.

I could wish to give you a more satisfactory account of the arms you are in search of, I well remember the talk of such a thing, but it never was carried into Execution, to my knowledge, for be assur'd I never had it possession in my life. It might possibly have been given to Mr. Parker who was at that time my partner. I was at Portsmouth a year and half after I left it as the place of my residence, and put up at Captn. Pearsons; no mention was ever made of it at that time. If I had had it I should have done it and return'd them both, for of what service could they be to me. You say that the Arms consisted of three Lions and a Stag for the Crest, if the arms are so well remember'd, the Loss is happily mitigated. I am sorry for the Loss of the other, if there was any particular Value put upon it, but cannot charge myself with having been instrumental to such a misfortune.

The next thing to be considered, I think is the boiling of oil, the purity of which article much inhances its Value. A few words would explain to you what you desire, but I choose to be methodical, for when method is strictly observ'd, we are not so apt to shake hands with Reason.

Now Sir the common practice of boiling oil among Common Painters; observe I say Common Painters, for what I am now about communicate is a knowledge you do not want to come at; but that knowledge which you would wish to be inform[ed] of, or made perfect in, is to me equally easie and shall be communicated in a future paragraph. You now undoubtedly will expect to be inform'd of the Common Painters method boiling

of oil, as I observ'd to you before altho it is not a knowledge
you are any ways curious about, yet I have promis'd and must
abide by it; from this Principle, that the complying with
Engagements is not only a Duty, but a Virtue, which every one
should cherish, and hold in the highest Veneration. Now Sir
this said information may not, and I dare [say] is not altogether
so neigh as you may imagine, for a thought has Just popt into
my head, the bear Idea of which, affords me such pleasure, that
I cannot indulge you with my promise till I have committed it
to writeing. It is this, the great satisfaction it would give me to
have a painting of my friend Copley's Head Either in Crayons
or oil, in miniature or what ever way will be most agreable to
him. I should wish to have it very like, but to be sure of that
I need only to desire it may be done by himself. I say the Common painters method is this, the Common painters method of
what? you are quite right indeed, to ask what, for I really like
to have blunder'd, but it must have occur'd to you from what
would have follow'd that the boilg. of oil was what I meant.
Well then (for we will be very Carefull this time) the Common
painters method of Boiling oil is this. Take any given quantity
of Oil put into an Iron pott, throw into it, a little red Lead put
it over the fire, and let it boil till such times as the froth sub-
sides, which is an Indication of its being boil'd Eno. Some
indeed try with a feather; when it is sufficiently Boil'd it will
scorch the Feather. Although this method does not alter the
Quality of Dryg. which is all they want, yet it has not the
property the other method gives it, for instead of its being
return'd to you Very black (which is ever the case from the
Common method of boilg.) it will be return'd to you as pure as
you put it in, and will hold its colour, and that in fact is what
you are in pursuit of.

Really, Sir, what I promised you in a future paragraph was design'd for this place, but upon sudden recollection find that the mark as well as word signifies the beginning of a new subject; a new subject let it be and confine the other to a new sentance. Mrs. Hobby is an only Sister of mine, not intirely unknown to you; and such is my affection for her, I should be very glad to have her picture in miniature, in water colours or oil, which you please tho: I must confess should like to have it in water Colours, for this reason, because there are several pictures in this Island lately arriv'd from England, that are thought much of, so far inferior to some I have seen of my friends, that they never can be nam'd with them, and to convince them it is not mere boast should be glad to have [it] as soon as you can conveniently do it. What ever your price is shall be remitted to you in specie, or any thing you may Fancy from this Island. Pray oblige me in this request. I think there was a picture done of Mr. Dipper: done in small life and given to Harry Liddle if you will give me a Copy of it in black and white Chalk, Just the head; or with a black lead pencil. I want it for a Lady, you shall receive a Compensation beyond your desires.

I have been in some parts of this letter, a little bordering upon the Shandean stile; that should it meet you on a Cloudy day, or when the weather had for a time been disagreable, brought on a languor and depression of spirits, to rouze you and make you forget the malady you then Labour'd under.

Now seriously to answer your request. Take a Glaz'd pipkin, made long in shape thus.[1] let it depend from the trammel into a Kettle of water, if you have a mind to force the drying property, you grind a little Vitriol or sugar of lead, and stir into it

[1] Here followed a crude sketch of a pipkin.

before it grows hot. this method will take 6 Hours at least, the water boiling all the time. I have put the Oil somtimes imediately into the water which method will render the oil as white as water it self, but in the boiling so divides the oil into numberless Globles that it is a considerable time before it will unite sufficently to get any great matter from the water.

The other will answer to your wishes.

N B never fill the Vessell with oil above two thirds full.

I see by the papers you have chang'd your condition,[1] and have taken to yourself a wife. I have [not] the pleasure of knowing your Lady by sight: but from the Charracter of that family in general, you must be the happy Man. I sincerely wish you both every hapiness you promis'd yourselves, or that your hearts can desire; it is customary upon wishing a new married Couple Joy to salute, but as this must be done by proxie, I cant with propriety employ a better hand than yourself; please to make a kiss acceptable to your Lady till such times as I can have the Honor of doing in *Propria Persona*. Well adieu, God bless you; write me as often as you can, and dont forget the News of the place you live in, and which I have so great a regard for. my kind regards to your Lady accept the same yourself and believe me to be with truth and sincerity Dear Sir Your affectionate friend, and Very Humble Servant

Wm. Johnston.

P.S Inclos'd is a pencil to assist you in the miniature. I forgot to tell you I have an Organists Birth worth £75 Sterl'g per Ann.

What ever you may have to send me: if there should not be

---

[1] Copley was married November 16, 1769, to Miss Susannah Farnum ("Sukey") Clarke, daughter of Richard Clarke, merchant.

any Vessell in Boston for this place forward them to Mr. Hobby at Middletown Connecticutt. If there should be a Vessell in Boston for Barbados, Direct for me to be left at the Attorney Generals Office. I. Veyow. I had like to have forgot one thing. I want a rough scetch of that little picture that is over the Door of Mr Chardon's Hall,[1] Time bringing truth to Light.

Captain John Small to Copley

Head Quarters, New York, May 15th, 1770.

Sir,

I was favor'd with yours *by Captain Pascal Smith,* who also Deliver'd to me, the Picture you were kind enough to Send me by him; it came Safe and undamag'd from the Voyage hither.

You'll see by the Inclos'd Accot. and Receipt that Captn. Smith has been paid, and Your Draught in his favor Duely honor'd.

Allow me now, Sir, to Congratulate you on your marriage, which I saw inserted in a Boston paper. I had the pleasure of hearing you Mention the Lady, *when I attended your Levee,* and with such warmth of Encomium as Convinc'd me of your serious and well plac'd attachment. Both from what you said *yourself* and the amiable Character I heard of her from others: I make no doubt of your having been happy in your choice and success.

I beg leave to assure you that I sincerly wish you Joy; A person of Your Merit and emminence in your proffession, deserves and ought to enjoy sweets of social and domestick

---

[1] Peter Chardon, who died in 1775(?). But see *Works of John Adams,* ii., 36.

happiness; as an additional and indeed the highest incentive of Endeavors to shine in so exellent an Art.

The Beau Monde here, have Mutter'd a good deal; on hearing of your happy wedlock; not from want of good wishes for you, but that as they consider that *agreable* Event *to you*, as a prevention of your Coming hither; which I assure you has been earnestly and eagerly wish'd by some of the finest women in the *World*. The fame of your performances had Long ago Reach'd them, and the Specimens which have recently made their appearance, have confirm'd them in the Idea of your Superior genius; and Excited the Wishes of numbers of Both Sexes; that your Leisure might admitt of *Even* a Short Visit from you: Indeed I dare say they might undertake to bespeak you for several Years Employmt at this place alone: but they now begin to Despair of the happiness of seeing You. The Generals[1] Picture was receiv'd *at home* with universal applause and Looked on by real good Judges as a Masterly performance. It is plac'd in one of the Capital Apartments of Lord Gage's house *in Arlington Street;* and as a Test of its merit it hangs between Two *of Lord and Lady Gages,* done by the Celebrated Reynolds, at present Reckon'd the *Painter Laureat* of England.

The Picture you sent by *Captn Smith;* is not only approv'd highly by the person it's drawn for, but greatly admir'd by Crowds of My Friends who come to Look at it. I shall only further observe that Nothing Indifferent can Come from the hands of the Ingenious Mr. Copely. I am Sir your oblig'd and very humble Servt.

JOHN SMALL.

[1] Gage.

John Wilkes to Nathaniel Barber[1]

PRINCES COURT, near STORIES GATE,
WESTMINSTER, Sept. 21, 1770.

SIR,

My Brother Hayley[2] has sent me from you a most Valuable present of a Picture which I receive with great Gratitude and pleasure from its being the recemblance of my dear namesake, and the merit of the Work it self. I was very happy to Observe to what a degree of excellence the most elegant art of Painting is Arrived in New England, and as you rival us in every essential good, so you now equal us in the refinements of Polished Life. I shall expect every thing good and intrinsically valuable from the Young Gentleman, whose Picture I admire, when I consider that he is educated under your care, and among the generous sons of Freedom in America, who remain undebauch'd by the wickedness of European Courts, and Parliamentary Prostitution. I pray heaven to give you great Comfort in him, and to permit him long to enjoy the Benefit of the virtuous example you set him! My most respectfull compliments ever attend the friend[s] of Liberty at Boston, and I beg you, Sir, to beli[e]ve me, with great truth and regard, Your Obliged, humble Servant,

JOHN WILKES.

[1] The letter to which this is in reply is printed in *Mass. Hist. Soc. Proceedings,* XLVII. 214. Barber had named a son Wilkes Barber, and sent to Wilkes a portrait of the child, then in his fourth year. Copley painted it. See *Copley to Benjamin West,* November 24, 1770.

[2] George Hayley, an alderman of London and brother-in-law of Wilkes. He was a member of the mercantile house of Hayley and Hopkins, with important American connections.

Henry Pelham to Charles Pelham

BOSTON, Nov. 12, 1770.

DEAR BROTHER,

Upon my Arivall in Town I began to execute your Commands, by delivering your Message to my Mamma. In Return she presents her kind Love to you and says that she expects to use her stove next Winter, but in the mean time you are intirely welcome to the Use of it, if you think it worth while to put it up 'till then.

I applyed Likewise to Mr Walley,[1] and Messrs. Green and Russell,[2] from whom I have procured a sett of the perpetual and Temporary Laws complete to the present time. The Temporary Laws were not to be had ready bound. The price of them you will see by the inclosed Notes.

By the papers I am Informed of the sudden Death of Mr Barnard,[3] and in Virginia of that of Lord Botetourt[4] both of which I most Lement. Thos Pelham is in a deep Consumption. He was first taken ill about three Weeks ago, has continued to grow weaker, and is now so dangerous that his Life is not expected from one hour to another. His Family is in the greatest Poverty and Misery.

I send you a new Specimen of the Abilitys of our Boston Poetess Phillis, which has undergone no Corrections what ever. Mr. Green, who examen'd her Poem on the death of Mr. Whitfield before it went to the Press alterd but one Word in the Whole, and that was the Word Stars instead of

---

[1] Abiel Walley?

[2] John Green and Joseph Russell, printers of the *Massachusetts Gazette* and the *Boston Post-Boy and Advertiser.*

[3] Francis Bernard, eldest son of Sir Francis Bernard.

[4] Norborne, Baron de Botetourt. See *Boston Gazette,* November 12, 1770.

star.[1] My Mamma, Bro'r and Sister Copley join me in kindest Love and Respects to your self, my Sister Pelham, Cousin Hilly and Charles. I am, Dear Sir: Your most affectionate Bro'r and most humble Sert.

HENRY PELHAM.

Copley to [Benjamin West][2]

BOSTON, NOVR. 24, 1770.

DEAR SIR,

I am afraid you think I have been negligent in suffering two years to pass without exhibiting somthing,[3] or writeing to you to let you know how the Art goes on this side the Atlantick. But be assured it is neighther because I have forgot my Friend, or have been less assiduous in the Labours of the Pencil than here to fore, But I find it extreemly dificult to procure Subjects fit and pleasing to entertain the Publick with. You are sensable in this country the hands of an Artist is tied up, not having it in his power to prosicute any work of fancy for want of meterials. Than my time is so intirely engrosed in painting portraits as to make it very dificult for me to exibit constantly; but the most meterial Reason of all others was the prospect I had of visiting Europe before this time. When I wrote you last I menshoned some obstruction in my way to making such a tour, and you have doubtless heard before this time I have increased the dificulty; yet be assured, notwithstanding I have entered into engagements that have retarded my travilling, they shall not prevent it finally. I will make all give way to

---

[1] Phyllis Wheatley.
[2] See *West to Copley*, June 16, 1770, referring to Dr. Jarves as bearer of a letter from Copley.
[3] Copley sent no picture to the exhibitions of 1769, 1770, 1773 or 1774.

the predominant passion of cultivating our Art. I am now painting a portrait of Mr. Greenwood's Mother for him, which he designs to place in the exhibition Room. But if I should have the good fortune to imitate nature with some degree of merit, yet it cannot please as an Eligent form equelly well imitated would do. I should therefore be glad to contrast that Picture of a subject in the Evening of Life with one in the Bloom of youth, but it will not be in my power, unless you shall think one lately sent to Mr Wilks[1] will answer that purpose. I had no thoughts of making such an use of it when I painted it. For this reason I beg you will do what you shall think best, but the party spirit is so high, that what ever compliments the Leaders of either party is lookd on as a tassit disapprobation of those of the other; and tho I ought to be considered in this work as an Artist imploy'd in the way of my profession, yet I am not sure I should be, and as I am desireous of avoideing every imputation of party spir[it], Political contests being neighther pleasing to an artist or advantageous to the Art itself, I would not have it at the Exibition on any account what ever if there is the Least room to supose it would give offence to any persons of eighther party, but at all events I should be happy in possesing your observations on it with cander and freedom. Before I conclude give me Leave to recommend to your notice the Bearer of this Letter, Docr. Jerves, a worthy friend of mine and fond of painting. Any favours shown to him will be acknowledged with the same Gratitude as if they were to, Sir, your Most Sin[c]ere Friend,

JOHN S. COPLEY.

[1] See *John Wilkes to Nathaniel Barber*, September 21, 1770. Copley's only exhibit in 1771 was "A Lady, half length." Society of Artists of Great Britain, Catalogue of Exhibitions, 1771.

Charles Pelham to Henry Pelham

NEWTON, Decr. 4, 1770.

DEAR BROR,

The bearer brings 1½ busl. Malt for our Mama, and 3 buss. for Bror. Copley, which being good, will afford you a great deal of wholsome Liquor.

We hear Mrs. Copley is safe in Bed, happily deliver'd of a fine Girl.[1] If so we heartily Rejoice with you all, especialy Mr. Copley and Lady, whom we Congratulate on this happy event. Hope her good geting up, and Pray for the Life and health of the little Lady. Pray acquaint them of our thus sincerely interesting ourselves in this pleasing occurrence.

I am not unmindful of the unhappy situation of poor Thomas's Family, and to relieve the Widow as much as is in my power am willing to take Tommy, and do my best for him till he is 15 years of age, Mrs. Pelham being heartily dispos'd to do her part for his well being; but as I have experienc'd the ill effects of taking a Child and not having them Bound, I am by no means willing to engage with Tommy unless his Mother is free and willing to Bind him till he is 15 Years old. I should be glad you would let her know this, and if she sees fit and promises to bind him, the Boy may come up with the bearer, and when I come to Town shall bring Indentures to execute, and shall engage to find him good Bed and Board, Cloathing and Instruction, in all which the honour of the Family will induce me to go beyond what is common in such Cases: I can say no more upon this Head.[2]

[1] Elizabeth Clarke Copley, 1770–1866, who married Gardiner Greene.

[2] "She desired me to present her kindest Love and respects to you and my Sister Pelham, and to let you know the scence she has of the kindness you will do her by taking Tommy: She expresses the greatest pleasure and satisfaction at

Its now very fine wholsome weather and a little Tour into the Country would promote any one's health, especially the Sedentary Persons; I therefore strenuously recommend your keeping the approaching Thanksgiving with us, but take me right; I do not invite you to a sumptuous feast, but to good wholsome Country Fare with undissembled friendship. If this suits you, my Doors were they animated with my Spirit would at your approach open of their own accord: Your Sister Pelham joins in saying we shall be glad to see you.

I hope our hond. Mama is well. Pray give our Duty and Love to her, and with Tender Respects to you, Mr. and Mrs. Copley,   I remain Yr. affecte Bror.

Chas. Pelham.

I should be glad of a Line by the bearer, as such kind of Folks rarely deliver a verbal message correct.

Copley to [*Charles Willson Peale*]

Boston, Decr. 17, 1770.

Dear Sir,

I received your favour of the 24 Novr: Your kind present which came to hand in good order. It gave me a twofold pleasure first because it is the portrait of that great man, in the most exalted carractor human Nature can be dignified with that of a true Patriot vindicatting the rights of mankind, and

having him under your Care and Government. She is perfectly willing to bind him, and has sent him with your Man." *Henry Pelham to Charles Pelham,* December 4, 1770. The mother of this Thomas was Hannah Cooper Gerrish Pelham, widow of Thomas Pelham. They were married in 1757 and had Elizabeth, born August 2, 1758; Penelope, born March 6, 1760; Thomas, born January 4, 1762; and Mary, born November 17, 1766 — all living in 1780. Thomas, Jr., was a baker, married Lydia Robinson, and died 1802. *N. E. Hist. Gen. Reg.* xxvi. 399.

secondly for the merit of the work itself and the fair prospect it affoards of America rivaling the continant of Europe in those refined Arts that have been justly esteemed the Greatest Glory of ancient Greece and Rome.[1] Go on Dear Sir to hasten forward that happy Era. how little so ever my natural abillitys or oppertunitys of improvement may be adiquate to the pro-moteing so great a work yet I should sincerely partisipate in the pleasure with those great Souls who are happily possessed of boath in a Soverain Degre.

The Aligory strikes me as unexceptionable in every part, and fully expressive of Ideas designed to convey. The Attitude which is simple is possed of great dignity with a becoming Energy, and from what the print expressd I am led to wish to see the Original, wher[e] the force of Colouring give Strength and perfection to the Clear Obscure.

Permit me to conclud with my sincere thanks for the kind notice you have taken of me and subscribing myself your sin-cere friend and Humble Sert.

J. S. C.

*A
Description
of the
Picture and Mezzotinto
of
Mr. Pitt,
done by
Charles Willson Peale,
of Maryland.*

The Principal Figure is that of Mr. Pitt, in a Consular Habit, speaking in Defence of the Claims of the American Colonies, on the Principles of the British Constitution.

[1] See next paper.

With Magna Charta in one Hand, he points with the other, to the Statue of British Liberty, trampling under Foot the Petition of the Congress at New-York. — Some have thought it not quite proper to represent Liberty as guilty of an Action so contrary to her genuine Spirit; for that, conducting herself in strict Propriety of Character, she ought not to violate, or treat with Contempt, the Rights of any one. To this it may be sufficient to say, the Painter principally intended to allude to the Observation which hath been made by Historians, and Writers on Government, that the States which enjoy the highest Degree of Liberty are apt to be oppressive cf those who are subordinate, and in Subjection to them. Montesquieu, speaking of the Constitution of Rome, and the Government of the Roman Provinces, says, "*La Liberté croit, dans le Centre et la Tyrannic aux Extrimetés:*" And again, "*La Ville ne sentoit point la Tyrannie, qui ne s'exercoit que sur les Nations Assujettis.*" And supposing Mr. Pitt, in his Oration, to point, as he does, at the Statue, it makes a Figure of Rhetoric strongly and justly sarcastic on the present faint Genius of British Liberty, in which Light, Gentlemen of Reading and Taste have been pleased to commend it. The Fact is, that the Petition of the Congress at New-York, against Acts of meer Power, adverse to American Rights, was rejected by the House of Commons, the Guardians, the Genius, of that Liberty, languishing as it is.

An Indian is placed on the Pedestal, in an erect Posture, with an attentive Countenance, watching, as America has done for Five Years past, the extraordinary Motions of the British Senate — He listens to the Orator, and has a Bow in his Hand, and a Dog by his Side, to shew the natural Faithfulness and Firmness of America.

It was advised by some, to have had the Indian drawn in a dejected and melancholy Posture: And, considering the apparent Weakness of the Colonies, and the Power of the Parent Country, it might not perhaps, have been improper to have executed it in that Manner; but in Truth the Americans, being well founded in their Principles, and animated with a sacred Love for their Country, have never disponded.

A
DESCRIPTION
OF THE
PICTURE AND MEZZOTINTO
OF
Mr. PITT,
DONE BY
CHARLES WILLSON PEALE,
OF MARYLAND.

THE Principal FIGURE is that of Mr. PITT, in a Confular Habit, fpeaking in Defence of the Claims of the AMERICAN Colonies, on the Principles of the BRITISH Conftitution.

WITH MAGNA CHARTA in one Hand, he points with the other, to the Statue of BRITISH *Liberty*, trampling under Foot the Petition of the CONGRESS at NEW-YORK.——Some have thought it not quite proper to reprefent LIBERTY as guilty of an Action fo contrary to her genuine Spirit; for that, conducting herfelf in ftrict Propriety of Character, fhe ought not to violate, or treat with Contempt, the Rights of any one. To this it may be fufficient to fay, the Painter principally intended to allude to the Obfervation which h tn been made by Hiftorians, and Writers on Government, that the *States which enjoy the higheft Degree of Liberty are apt to be oppreffive of thofe who are fubordinate, and in Sufpicion to them.* MONTESQUIEU, fpeaking of the

the present faint Genius of BRITISH Liberty, in which Light, Gentlemen of Reading and Taste have been pleased to commend it. The Fact is, that the Petition of the Congress at NEW-YORK, against Acts of meer Power, adverse to AMERICAN Rights, was rejected by the House of Commons, the Guardians, the Genius, of *that* Liberty, languishing as it *is*.

AN INDIAN is placed on the Pedestal, in an *erect* Posture, with an attentive Countenance, watching, as AMERICA has done for Five Years past, the extraordinary Motions of the BRITISH Senate——He listens to the Orator, and has a Bow in his Hand, and a Dog by his side, to shew the natural *Faithfulness and Firmness of* AMERICA.

IT was advised by some, to have had the INDIAN drawn in a dejected and melancholy Posture: And, considering the apparent Weakness of the Colonies, and the Power of the Parent Country, it might not perhaps, have been improper to have executed it in that Manner; but in Truth the AMERICANS, being well founded in their Principles, and animated with a sacred Love for their Country, have never desponded.

AN ALTAR, with a Flame is placed in the Foreground, to shew that the Cause of Liberty is sacred, and, that therefore, they who maintain it, not only discharge their Duty to their King and themselves, but to GOD. It is decorated with the Heads of SIDNEY and HAMPDEN, who, with undaunted Courage, spoke, wrote, and died in Defence of the true Principles of Liberty, and of those Rights and Blessings which GREAT-BRITAIN now enjoys: For, as the Banner placed between them expresses it,

SANCTUS AMOR PATRIÆ DAT ANIMUM.

A CIVIC CROWN is laid on the Altar, as consecrated to *that* MAN who preferred his Fellow-Citizens and Subjects from Destruction!

THE View of W——H—— is introduced in the Back Ground, not meerly as an elegant Piece of Architecture, but as it was the Place where —————— suffered, for attempting to invade the Rights of the BRITISH Kingdoms: And it is observable, that the Statue and Altar of BRITISH Liberty are erected near the Spot where that great *Sacrifice* was made, through the Necessity, to the Honour, Happiness, Virtue, and in one Word, to the Liberty of the BRITISH People.

THE Petition of the Congress at NEW-YORK, and the Representation of W——H—— point out the Time, and almost the Place, where the Speech was delivered.

THE chief Object of this Design will be answered, if it manifests, in the least, the Gratitude of AMERICA to his Lordship. It will, with Tradition, unprejudiced by the Writings of *Hirelings*, who are made to glide in with the courtly Streams of FALSHOOD, be the faithful Conveyance to Posterity of the Knowledge of those GREAT THINGS which we, who are not to be imposed on by " the busy Doings and Undoings" of the envious Great, have seen

An Altar, with a Flame is placed in the Foreground, to shew that the Cause of Liberty is sacred, and, that therefore, they who maintain it, not only discharge their Duty to their King and themselves, but to God. It is decorated with the Heads of Sidney and Hampden, who, with undaunted Courage, spoke, wrote, and died in Defence of the true Principles of Liberty, and of those Rights and Blessings which Great-Britain now enjoys: For, as the Banner placed between them expresses it, *Sanctus Amor Patriæ dat Animum.* A Civic Crown is laid on the Altar, as consecrated to that Man who preserved his Fellow-Citizens and Subjects from Destruction!

The View of W——H——[1] is introduced in the Back Ground, not meerly as an elegant Piece of Architecture, but as it was the Place where ——[2] suffered, for attempting to invade the Rights of the British Kingdoms: And it is observable, that the Statue and Altar of British Liberty are erected near the Spot where that great Sacrifice was made, through sad Necessity, to the Honour, Happiness, Virtue, and in one Word, to the Liberty of the British People.

The Petition of the Congress at New-York, and the Representation of W——H—— point out the Time, and almost the Place, where the Speech was delivered.

The chief Object of this Design will be answered, if it manifests, in the least, the Gratitude of America to his Lordship. It will, with Tradition, unprejudiced by the Writings of Hirelings, who are made to glide in with the courtly Streams of Falshood, be the faithful Conveyance to Posterity of the Knowledge of those Great Things which we, who are not to be imposed on by "the busy Doings and Undoings" of the envious Great, have seen.

Extract of a Letter[3]

I am pleased with your Remarks on Mr. Peale's Performance, but wish you had been less sparing of them — A Incident of

---

[1] Whitehall. [2] Charles I.
[3] A broadside measuring $7\frac{1}{2}$ in. $\times$ $12\frac{1}{4}$ in.

Yesterday affords me Occasion to add to your Remarks: — One of the Mezzotinto's was brought into Company, when all agreed it was Very clever; but some thought it "not like Mr. Pitt."

You, my Friend took the fair Side, and remarked only on the Beauties of the Piece — Pray preserve your good Humour from being ruffled by the Objections made by my Companions, and receive what occurs to me on the Subject.

Perhaps it was hazardous to offer to the Public a Portrait so unlike the old Pictures, which have been long known among us — Very few have Seen any other Representation of the Great Man, and we know how Strongly First Impressions work on the Imagination: And, what is yet more disadvantageous to the Painter, not only First Impressions, but many Years intimate Acquaintance with the old Piece, has probably So fixed that Likeness in the Mind, that, were Mr. Pitt himself to be of a Sudden present, and appear a Contrast to those Pieces, there would not be a total Want of weak Minds, who might even struggle to conceive he was like himself — preferring the Likeness with which they were so intimate. But between the old Copies and the present, I do not see that great Disparity that is pretended: Pray attend to them, and make all due Allowances — Twenty Years between the Drawing the one and the other — such Difference in his Age! — In the one he is in modern Dress, with Neckcloth, a Wig, and full Suit: In the other, with his natural Hair, a loose Roman Habit, and Neck bare. I am assured that Gentlemen, who had seen the Proof Copy, and among them, Dr. Franklin, thought Mr. Peale's a very good Likeness of the Great Patriot, as he is at this Time worn down with Sickness and Years, — and with Fatigue in the Service of his Country.

The Pillar at the Back of Mr. Pitt signifies Stability in the Patriot and his Principles. — You see the dark lowering Clouds, and disturbed Air, representing the alarming Times; and yet at a Distance, you observe a calmer Sky, tho' not altogether clear — Hope of better Times.

Copley to John Greenwood

BOSTON, Jany. 25, 1771.

DEAR SIR,

Your very kind favour of March 23 came to hand and afforded me much pleasure, as by it I learned you were in a situation of all others the most desireable to the Lovers, boath of the fair Sex as well as the arts. I trus[t] you will excuse my not writing to you sooner, but really my ingagement were so many as to make it some what dificult. No engagement should have hindred me from answering your favour, had I not fully intended to have finished Mrs. Devereux portrait for Capt. Simms to have carried, but was prevented from my design by several surcumstances, the most meterial that of the weither being so very hot as to make it inconvenient for the Old Lady to come to Town, and so the Letter I posponed writeing till Capt. Simms sailed, who promisd to call but I suppose forgot it. But beleave me your nex[t] favour, if I should omit answering so long, I will make a better apology for than this. But trusting in your goodness I will suppose myself acquited this time, and proceed to other matters. First then permit me to congratulate you on your Marriage in which state I sincerely wish you Long Life and all Imaginable happyness. It gives me great pleasure to find the Arts travill[i]ng Westward so fast it gives me hopes they will one Day reach this Country however destitute at present it appears of every affection for them. Your tour through Europe must have affoarded you great pleasure and the more so as you have had so many Capitol Picture[s] in you[r] possession. I should think myself happy in such an oppertunity of contemplating the works of those Renowned Masters. I sincerely rejoice in Mr

West's successfull progress towards the summit of that Mighty Mountain where the Everlasting Lauriels grow to adoarn the brows of those Elustrious Artists that are so favour of Heaven as to be able to unravel the intricate mazes of its rough and perilous Asent. It gives me pleasure to receive your Approbation of the Work I have Exibitted heretofor, and am sorry the Distance make it impossable for me to be constant. I should be glad never to miss an exibition, for by it the Arts are kept in health as the Body is by Exercise. I shall be happy if the portrait that accompanys this (of your Mother)is approved. I shall be impatien[t] to hear the Criticisms on it. Do be perticular either in your praises or condemnation of [it]. Dont be afraid that finding fault with it will have any other effect than to make me more assiduous to do better, nor praising than to encouraging me to be diligent. If you can remember the others I should be glad of a comparison, by which I shall be better able to judge what path to pursue for the future in the [*unfinished*]

Petition relative to the Powder House

[January 29, 1771.]

To the Freeholders and Inhabitan[t]s of the Town of Boston in Town-meeting Assembled.

The Petition of the Subscribers, Freeholders and Inhabitants in the town of Boston humbly sheweth. That (considering the many and fatal Accidents that happen by the explosion of Magazines of Powder in Large popolouse Citys) your pe[ti]tioners apprehend their Lives and properties in common with the rest of their fellow-Citizens to be very insecure from the powder house being situate where it now is. They therefore pray the town to take the matter into their serious Consideration and make such application as they shall think effectual for its removal. And your petitioners as in duty bound shall ever pray.

Boston, Jany. 29, 1771.

Jno Barrett.	Benja. Greene.	Nathl. Gloover.
Edm: Quincey.	Ja. Richardson.	Oliver Greenleaf.
Danl. Hubbard.	William Henshaw.	Sa Salisbury.
Richard Clarke.	Sam Partridge.	Stephen Cleverly.
John Winslow.	Samuel Doggett.	John Amory.
Martin Brimmer.	Saml. Dashwood.	Herman Brimmer.
Thos. Leonard.	Jno Soley.	John Gore.
Saml. Prince.	John Deming.	John Moffatt.
Adino Paddock.	Jos Green.	Nathl. Balston.
Saml Abbot.	Nicho. Boylston.	John Scott.
John Timmins.	Thos. Flucker.	John S. Copl[e]y.
David Greene.	James Perkins.	Wm Davis.
Nicholas Bowes.	Sol. Davis.	James Bowdoin.
Wm: Bowes.	James Perkins.	John Erving.
Thomas Brattle.	Silv. Gardiner.	Thos. Hubbard.
Benjn. Edes.	W. Molineaux.	William Vassell.
John Gill.	Joseph Sherburne.	Wm. Phillips.
Paul Revere.	Saml. Eliot.	Stepn. Greenleafe.
Nath. Waterman.	Henry Stanbridge.	Thomas Cushing.
Edward Holliday.	Ez Price.	John Hancock.
John Avery.	Benj. Church.	Saml. Adams.
Frans. Johonnot.	John Sweetser Junr.	Ph. Dumaresq.
Rufus Greene.	Jonathan Simpson.	Robt. Pierpont.
John Box.		

[Endorsed:] Copy of the Petition relative to the Powder House.[1]

Charles Pelham to Henry Pelham

Newton, March 28, 1771.

Dear Bror.,

Ever since I enter'd upon House keepg we have had almost constantly one or other in our Family who prov'd a trouble and a pest to us, But of all Creatures that ever came under my Roof

---

[1] See *Boston Record Commissioners*, xviii. 44; xxiii. 78, 79.

Betty Pelham[1] I seriously think seems to be the worst, and has prov'd an affliction to us almost to render us distracted. On Friday last she came; we receiv'd her kindly, bid her welcome, and did all in our power to convince her of our Sincerity; On Saturday she threw out hints of a great dislike to the Country, and a want to go home, go home; We hearing it, soothed her, told her the strangeness of it might at first make it irksome, but a little use would render it more agreeable, especially as her Aunt and I shou'd do our utmost to bring her up in Credit and render he[r] capable of making a Reputable living; On Sunday she fell into strange kind of Fitts of what sort I cant say, for by her Pulse, her feeling etc. we cou'd not discover that any thing ailed her, and cou'd get nothing out of her but that she wou'd return to Boston if she went on Foot, for she should die; every thing was administer'd that could be thought of, but she refus'd taking any thing and would spurt out what was put into her Mouth; On Monday she harpt all day about going home. I told her she should not go home, that she was come for her own good, and that she must behave better, or I should find means to make her; On Tuesday she fell into her fitts again; which she suddenly threw off upon the approach of a good Loin of Veal which we had for Dinner; however I thought meat might hurt her and prescrib'd a Porrenger of Water Gruel; The Docr. coming in, We desir'd him to consider her case, and after examining her, he only hinted that she was somewhat in the case of Mary Magdalene. The remainder of the day she continued her old strain of dislike to the Country that she could not bear to see the Trees, and must go home, or shou'd die; On Wednesday her fit, (Damoniac I could almost find in my heart

---

[1] Elizabeth, daughter of Thomas and Hannah Pelham. She married William Higgins.

to say) came on again, Mrs. Pelham told her to go up stairs and lay down, but she made as if it was no way in her power so to do, upon which Mrs. Pelham greatly alarm'd call[ed] me. Upon hearing me call'd Madam got up and walk'd upstairs. I went up to her, but could get nothing out of her, only that she must go home or should die. I desir'd Mrs. Pelham to cause a Bowl of Tea to be made, which was carried to her, but she said she would not touch it, nor would she take any thing at all; but we found in a Drawer a hoard of Milk Bisket which she had privately conveyed there, I suppose to eat when she chose to be in her fits; she says her Mother told her at parting that if she did not like, I must send her back again; but I cant think her Mother wou'd so affront me; I have now sent her home, and would give any thing that I had not sent for her, not only that we sent off a Girl which we had, to make room for Betty, which is an injury to us, as we have a sick Child, but that I would not upon any Accot. have had Mrs. Pelham so frighted and per- plext. Thus have I given the heads of Bettys History at New- ton. Paper would fail me to give all the particulars, but as I expect to be in Town in a few days shall then let our Mama know this matter more fully. If you have opportunity shall be glad you may let Bettys Mother know the Contents hereof, but dont give her this Letter, as I have no Copy of it, and shou'd chuse it might be with you as a Register of what I aver to be fact: I own I blame my Self for taking her after what your Mama said of her, who I now further find is a good judge of Mankind. I talk'd with Docr. Spring [1] concerning the size of the Cloth which was to contain his Portrait, he said he knew nothing about it, and wou'd leave it to you. I recommended the half length, to which he readily agreed, and is ready to Set.

[1] Rev. Samuel Spring.

I have not had good oppertunity to speak to Mr. Meriam about his Daughters, but shall do it soon, in the mean time hope to see you here, and think the sooner you can begin with Docr. Spring the better, however my desire to serve you may lead me astray, and will therefore leave it to your own and Mama's consideration.

Hilly has got pretty well, Chas. is still very poorly but we hope mending. I hope our Mama is at least as well as usual, pray present her our joint Duty and Love. Mr. Copley and Lady with their little Dear I hope are well, pray give our Love to them. I think I need not say that whenever it suits you to come to Newton we shall be very glad to see you, I hope you are convinc'd of that; Accept our hearty Love and good wishes, and Recognise me as Dear Harry, Yr. Very affecte.

CHAS. PELHAM.

If Mr. Copley has got the Oyl he spoke of should be glad the bearer might bring 6 Flasks. I inclose a Line to Bettys Mother pray Seal it and let her have it.

Henry Pelham to Charles Pelham

BOSTON, March 29, 1771.

MY DEAR BROTHER,

Your Letter of yesterday, gave me a Narrative of Behavour, the most surprising I think I ever met with. To see a girl of Betty's Age, who can receive no advantages from her Station or Rank in Life, or from her Parents Character, taken from poverty and Misery, placed in a Family where she might have had all the Benefitts of Example, Education and Instruction, have been brought up in a way, in which she might have enjoyed Happiness, have been a Comfort to her Friends and a

Credit to herself, to see a Girl with such Advantages, forfeit all favour [of] her Friends, deliberately, and with such Agrevated Circumstances spurn and reject their profered Kindness, and return to her native Obscurity, shews such a depravity of Heart, such a totall want of every generouse and humane Sentiment, a proneness to Vice and Folly, as truly astonishing, as Malencholly. When that ruin is compleated, to which she seems to [be] hastily advancing, your and my Sisters Trouble (in which we sincerely pertake) I doubt not will be fully recompenced, by the heartfelt Satisfaction, of having Offered that Assistance, and protection, which she has so disgracefully refused. I communicated the contents of your Letter to her Mother she expressed the greatest Affliction, and uneasiness, said she was very sorry, you had so much trouble and Vexsation, and would be glad to see you when you come to town. We are much pleased to hear of Coun. Hilly's recovery, hope Charles will soon enjoy his former health. I return my sincere thanks for your kindness in procuring me Buisness at Newton.

The kind expressions of your Attachment likewise calls for my warmest acknowledgements. The Affability and kindness I have experienced from you and my Sister assure me of your sincere Affection. Be assured of a hearty Welcome, whenever your Bu[s]iness calls, or permits you to come to Boston, where we long to see you. My Mamma, who is as well as can be expected, with Brother and Sister Copley, join me in Love and Respects to yourself, my Sister Pelham, and Cousins. I am, Dear Sir, with great truth and regard, Your Affectionate Brother, and most Obliged Humble Sert.

HENRY PELHAM.

Captain Stephen Kemble [1] *to Copley*

[Before April 17th 1771.]

Mr. Copely will inform Captain Kemble if he inclines to come to New York in the Spring, or Summer. If he does, he will specify the time he proposes to stay, and the number of Picktures he would undertake to draw, and mention his Price for Busts, half Lengths, and whole lengths, of Men, Women, and Children. Capt. Kemble will then send Mr. Copely, the Names of those, who will employ him, that Mr. Copely may be at a Certainty.

Copley to Captain Stephen Kemble

[No date.]

SIR,

Major Goldthwait communicated to me your memorandom desireing to know the price of the Different sizes of portrait and what number I would undertake to do at New York.

As to the number it will be determined by the time it may be in my power to stay. should I go in May toward the end of the Month and sooner it will not be in my power to go and come away in Sepr. I may be able to engage 12 or 15 half Lengths, or in proportion to that, reck[on]ing whole Length as two half Length[s], and half Length Doub[le] the busts. More I could not engage without a Longer stay. and I can not say at present it would be in my power to stay beyond that time, tho this is not quite certain. The pric[e] of Whole Lengths 40 Guineas, half Length 20, ¼ peices or Busts 10. Weither Men or Weomen makes no differenc[e] in the pric[e] nor does the Dress; but Chil-

---

[1] See *New York Hist. Soc. Collections*, 1883, 1884. He held a commission of captain in the British army from January 24, 1765, in the 60th Regiment, commanded by Jeffrey Amherst.

dren in the ¼ peaces will be more, because of the addition of hands, which there must be when a Child is put in that size; [1] but should the hands be omitted, the picture may be smaller and than the price will be the same as for a Mans or Womans without hands. But if hands they will be something more tho the pric[e] will be not exceeding 15. According to maner size of the Picture you will see by this my pric[e] is greater I have set than what I have here. But the Reasons are so obvious why it should be that I think it needless to menshon them [*fragment*]

Captain Stephen Kemble to Copley

New York, 17th April, 1771.

Sir,

I am sorry a short absence of mine, and a little negligence on the part of some who were desired to procure subscribers to your Terms, has been the means of delaying an Answer to your Letter of the 20th of March. But I have now the pleasure to acquaint you that twelve ½ lengths are subscribed for (two Busts to a half Length,) and I make no doubt as many more will be had as your time will permit you to take. I hope this delay in answering your Letter will not prevent you from undertaking your Journey to this place I am Sir Your most Obedient Servant,

STEPH. KEMBLE.

List of Subscribers

[April 17, 1771.]

We the undermention'd Persons do promise to have our Pictures drawn by Mr. Copley, agreable to the Sizes set opposite to our Names. —

[1] Erased: "which is not the case with grown people."

Lengths........half Lengths.......Busts

	Lengths	half Lengths	Busts
Mrs. Gage................................		2..............	I [1]
Mr. Ogilvie[2]..			I
Miss Johnston[3].............................		I...............	
Captain Maturin[4]			I
J. Mallet [5]..			I
Mrs Morris[6]..			I

[The rest of the page has been lost]

Lengths..........½ Lengths..........Busts

	Lengths	½ Lengths	Busts
Captain and Mrs. Montresor[7]			2
Mr Barrow................		I...............	
Mr. Sherbrook[8]		I........	
Mrs Mc. Evers[9]........................			I
Mrs. Mortier[10]			
M Hust and Lady........................			2
Mr Kemp[11]................................			

[1] It is uncertain whether this figure was intended to be erased.

[2] Probably Rev. John Ogilvie (1722–1774), assistant at Trinity Church, New York.

[3] Thus far, and possibly the next name, in Kemble's handwriting.

[4] Gabriel Maturin was a captain in the 31st Regiment, from June 17, 1767.

[5] There was a Jonathan Mallet, a surgeon of the 46th Regiment, from August 31, 1757.

[6] Probably Mrs. Roger Morris, a sister of Frederick Phillips, proprietor of Phillipsborough and a loyalist.

[7] John Montresor, whose "Journals" are in the *New York Hist. Soc. Collections*, 1881.

[8] Miles Sherbrook. See *Journals and Correspondence of Samuel Blachley Webb*.

[9] See Copley to Pelham, August 17, 1771. James McEvers, and his son Charles, were the leading representatives of this family.

[10] Abraham Mortier, a deputy paymaster-general.

[11] John Taber Kemp was attorney-general of the province of New York.

Henry Pelham to Henry and Thomas Bromfield [1]

BOSTON, June 6, 1771.

GENTLEMEN,

Mr Copley, before he sat out for New York, desired me to transmitt a memorandum of some Articles, which as he is in great want of he requests you would ship by the very first Opertunity.[2] You will oblige him by being perticular as to the Size and Quality of the Glass there being a great Difference in the Thickness and Clearness of the New Castle Crown, some of it being not inferior to the London Crown. You will please to procure the Cloths of the very best kind, the last you sent not being equal in goodness to the price. The inclosed Bill you will pass to his Credit. As my Brother resides all Summer at New York, you will direct the things to me at this place. I am Gentlemen your most Obedient, Humble Sert.

HENRY PELHAM.

Memorandum

185 Squares of very best New Castle Crown Glass each square measuring 10½ Inchs. by 14½ Inchs.
200 lb. Wt. of ground White Lead.
50 lb of putty.
2 ozs. of finest Vermillion.
1 pint poppy Oil.
3 pound Brushes.
3 half pound Do.
12 half Length Cloths.
6 kitkat Do.
12 ¾ Do.

[1] Merchants, London. Henry Bromfield married Hannah Clarke, a sister of Mrs. Copley.
[2] Erased: "and which in case of a War, he begs you to insure."

12 Hog hair tools of the smallest Size for portrai[ts].
3 Oz. Italian White Cha[l]k.
2 Oz Italian Black Do.

Benjamin West to Copley

London, June 16th, 1771.

Sir,

It was with great pleasure I received your letter by Dr Jarves as it informed me of your health and your intentions of Coming to Europe. I am still of the Same opinion, that it will every way answer your Expectations, and I hope to see you in London in the corse of this year, Where I shall be happy in rendering you all the Service lays in my Power.

Your Picture of Mrs. Greenwood was exhibited and did great honour.[1] The other Picture you mentioned I have not seen but I hear them much spoke of. The arts Continue to receive great in Corragement. To London at preassent seems to be the onely place in Europe where a man is rewarded for his productions in the Art of painting. You will excuse the shortness of this letter and be assur'd I am with great respect, Your Obediend Huml. Servt.

B. West.

Copley to Henry Pelham

New York, 16 of June, 1771.

Dear Harry,

We are now fixed in a very comodious House in this City. We arrived here on Thursday night and our Journey perfectly agreable, and has contributed a great deal to my looks. I can-

---

[1] In the catalogue of 1771, it appears as "A lady, half length." Anderson, who saw the picture at Lord Lyndhurst's sale in 1864, describes it as the portrait of an old lady leaning on a Pembroke table.

John Singleton Copley
From the original miniature by Copley
in the possession of Mr. Henry Copley Greene

not say Sukey has improved so much in looks as myself, tho she is very well. Our Journey was not attended by the least unpleasing surcumstance, but was delightfull beyond all expectation. Our Horses held out wonderfully well and brought us with great spirit forty Miles the last Day of our Journey. I come now to say somthing of this place, but really I have not been yet able to attend to anything but that of getting myself a little settled, that I may go to Business, and I beleave you will think I have done pretty well to be ready to begin Mrs. Gages portrait tomorrow, which I propose to do, considering I have had but friday and Saturday to Deliver several Letters and get suitable Lodging. The City has more Grand Buildings than Boston, the streets much Cleaner and some much broader, but it is not Boston in my opinion yet. I have seen the Statues of the King and Mr Pitt, and I think them boath good Statues. I find it so expencive keeping horses here that I think to send the Mare back. Mr. Joy will take her, if he is not provided. This you will let me know by the next post. You may assure him she is as good to the full as he thought her. I beleive he cannot easily get so good a Creature. He offered me fifty-five Dollars, so do you agre with him according to your own discression, and I will send her by the next post, and take the chance of Buying in the fall. I want my Crayons much and Layman and Drawings. Do see Mr. Loyd, and find when Smith will sail, for I shall not be able to do long without them. Cloath there is anough here. Give our affectionate Duty to our Mamma. We long to hear from you. Hope you have wrote by this post, but I cant know till to morrow. We are ancious to know how Betsey is. let Mr. Clarke know we are well and send our Duty. I am your Affectionate Brother,

J. S. COPLEY.

You will find in one of the Draws of the Desk some Gold
Buttonholes. Do send me 3 or 4 of the Best of them when you
send the other things, or shall write by a private hand.

Benjamin West to Shrimpton Hutchinson [1]

SIR,

Mr. Temple having made Application to me in behalf of
your Son's studying the Art of Painting under me, and finding
my Objection to having Young Gentlemen in my House as
Students for a certain Number of Years, the Particulars of
which Mr. Temple will inform you. Tho' this may deprive
your Son of coming to England for some Years longer, yet in
my Opinion it will by no Means prevent his being a Painter.
If it so happens that he should not come to England, my
Advice is that he may be indulged in the Pursuit of the Art
by his own Observations after Nature, and that he may the
more speedily accomplish it, I beg he may be permitted the
Use of Colours, tho' this is not the modern Receipt to make
a Painter. Yet if I can judge from the Works of the great
Masters, who are dead, they thought an early Knowledge of
Colours, and the Use of the Brush highly necessary. For Example, Raphael and several other great Painters of those Times
painted many fine Pictures (which are now to be seen) before
they had obtained the Age of fifteen; so it appears evident to
me, the great Object they had in View was to surmount, early
in Life, the mechanical Difficultys of Painting, that is the
Handling of the Pencil and the Management of Colours, that
their Hand might keep pace with their Ideas, so as to receive

[1] There are two copies of this letter, with trifling variations. They were
inclosed in Shrimpton Hutchinson's letter to Copley dated August 24, 1771. It
is possible that the one here printed is the original sent to Mr. Hutchinson,
though it is not in West's handwriting. See postscript. Shrimpton Hutchinson,
born September 10, 1713, was son of William and Elizabeth Hutchinson.

Pleasure from their Performances. This convinces me that young Artists should receive great Pleasure from what they do, as it is that alone can compensate for the great Fatigue which must arise from the prodigeous Length of Time necessary to make a painter, let him have ever so great a Share of Genius. I mention this that he may early in Life be acquainted with the Making of Pictures, and qualify himself for a Painter, and not a Drawing Master. You have a strong Instance on your Side of the Water (in Mr. Copley) to what a Length a Man may carry the Art by his own Assiduity. He is better qualified for coming to Europe now than he was seven Years ago. If it is not convenient for your Son to come to England, let him advance himself as Mr. Copley has done, and he will find himself equal to the first in Europe. I should think from what I have heard of Mr. Copley he would have a pleasure in communicating to him the Knowledge of Colours. I write my Opinion on this Matter with greater Warmth than I should have done, had I not been once in your Son's Situation, which I have found since my Arrival in Europe was the most fortunate Circumstance that could have happen'd to me: My having no other Assistance but what I drew from Nature (the Early Part of my Life being quite obscured from Art) this grounded me in the Knowledge of Nature, while had I come to Europe sooner in Life, I should have known nothing but the Receipts of Masters.

If at any Time I can be of Use to your Son, by communicatg. my Thoughts to him, either in America or England, I shall with the greatest Pleasure do it. I am, Sir, your most obedient humble Servant,
                                                    BENJA. WEST.
LONDON, 18th June, 1771.

PS. You will excuse Incorrectness as Illness prevented me writing the above Letter.

Copley to Henry Pelham

NEW YORK, June 20, 1771.

DEAR HARRY,

I must not omit so good an oppertunity as the present to let you know we are well, and that painting much engages the attention of people in this City and takes up all my time. I have begun three portraits already, and shall as soon as time permits fill my Room which is a very large one. We have experienced great sivility from several people, as well from those to whom we were recommend[ed] as others into whose knowledge we have fallen here. The Gentleman[1] who is the bearer of this is desireous of seeing my Room in Boston. You'l therefore weit on him, and be kind anough to go to Mr. Clarkes and let the family know we are well, and shall write to them by Mr. Loring who goes from this place on Monday next. We desire our most Affectionate Duty to our Mamma, to Mr. Clarke, Love to your self and all our Brothers and Sisters. We are very impatient to hear from you and Mr. Clarke's family. Do write us by the first oppertunity. As it grows late, I must conclude with subscribeing my self your Affectionate Brother,

JOHN SINGLETON COPLEY.

PS our compts. to Miss Peggy McElvain and all friends.

Henry Pelham to Copley

BOSTON, June 23, 1771.

MY DEAR BROTHER,

By your favour of the 16, we had the pleasure, the inexpressable Pleasure, of hearing of your and my dear Sisters being

---

[1] Mr. Harmonside.

commodiously fixed at New York, after the agreable and safe
Journey, which you say, has contributed so much to your looks.
We are greatly Rejoyced to find that you are so well. hope the
change of Air and Exercise will confirm your and my Sisters
health. It is with pleasure that I can inform you that our
Hond. Mamma (whose kind Love and best Wishes she desires
may be presented to your self and Lady) has been in very tolerable Health for her, since you left us.

I saw a few days ago, my Cousin Betzey, at Roxbury, she is
as hearty and well, as when you saw her. she is I think the
finest Child of her Age of any in New England. Now I am
speaking of Children, I must not omitt informing you, of an
Occurrance, which has afforded us a great deal of Entertainment as well as Satisfaction. on Saterday afternoon the 15
(as if inspired) took a Horse and Chaise, called and saw my
little Friend, as above, and thence proceeded to Newton, to
spend the Sunday. I had a pleasant and agreable time 'till
Sunday Eveng. 10 o'Clock, when my Sister Pelham was taken
very ill, and after sending 15 Miles for a Doctr. was safely
delivered the next Morning, of a fine Son, whom they call
Peter. Since which my Brother informs me by Letter, that
"*she is as Cleaver as can be expected for one in her case.*" He
farther says, "*When you write to Mr Copley please present our
kind Love and Regards to him and Lady, and you will naturally
inform him of the late interesting event in my Family, of which
we may say, you was almost an Eye Witness.*" Mr Clarke and
Family are all very well. I communicated your Letter to them,
they were exceedingly pleased to hear of your safe arrival,
desire their kind Love to you and my Sister. I spoke to Mr.
Joy relative to the Mare, he says it is not reasonable that he
should give the five dollers he offered for the Bargain, 'tho he

still stands ready to take her at the price you gave, provided she returns safe and sound, of this you will inform me more particularly the next post. About a Week ago Mr Otis[1] called upon me. told me that you had left some Money with me, for him, and would be glad if I could let him have it. I told him you had left sundry Debts to collect, that I had not yet got them in, but that I hoped it would soon be in my Power to wait upon him. I shall wait your express Orders with regard to this Affair. I have not been able to find, but that he is as well, as he used to be. And I hope, will be capable of defending your case. You will consider weither (as his purse from his long Confinement may be low) he may not if he dont soon receive his Fee, get affronted and soured, and neglect if not abandon your case. He told me, that it was determined, that there should be no adjournment of the Court. So that the tryal must be in the begining of September, if it is to come on this Fall. you will do well likewise to consider, weither if you have Mr. Otis and Coll. Putnam[2] it would not be best to have the Case tryed at the next term. Mr. Otis told me that the bill for the removal of the Powder House, has had three readings, and past the House, so that it seems now to be in a very fair Way; in my next, I hope to be able to inform you that it is enacted. The Repairs go on very briskly, the upper House will be in motion to Morrow.[3] It is I think the unanimouse Opinion of all your Friends, that the Expence is not at all adequate to the looks, of a hiped Roof upon the upper House. The plan they

---

[1] James Otis (1725–1783), then suffering from the effects of an assault made upon him by Robinson, a Commissioner of the Customs.

[2] James Putnam, of Worcester, in whose office John Adams studied law. He left Massachusetts a loyalist, and settled in Fredericton, New Brunswick.

[3] Copley's house on Mount Vernon, the land owned by Copley extending from Joy Street to low water mark.

think is in every other respect perfectly compleat, but the want of that, they look upon, as a very great Omission. Aided by their Advice, I have ventured to give orders for its being done in that manner; as the time would not admitt of consulting you. Mr Lechmere[1] was a few days ago, at your place, he told the workmen, that he thought it one of the finest Situations in the Province, and that had he have known of it, he would have bought it at all events; will this please you? Smith sails perhaps in a fortnight, perhaps a Month, is quite uncertain which. I have twenty things to ask, twenty to say, but have only Room to subscribe myself with my most Affectionate Regards to my Sister, Your Loving Brother,

HENRY PELHAM.

PS. Write often and send no blank Paper.

Henry Pelham to Copley

BOSTON, July 7, 1771.

MY DEAR BROTHER,

I have to acknowledge the Receipt of your's (per Mr Harmonside) of the 20 of June, which gave us the pleasure of knowing that you and my Sister were well at that time. Mr Loring ar[r]ived here last Fryday Eveng. but as we have not yet received your Letter we can only know that you was well when he left york, that you had began severall pictures, and had received an Invitation from Philadelphia but had refused to go. he further informd us that you had not received your trunk from Providence which surprised me as your not mention[in]g it in your Letters made me suppose you had duly

---

[1] Richard Lechmere, of Boston, who died in England in 1818, having left Massachusetts with other loyalists.

received it. I was extreemly dissapointed in not having a Letter by the post the last Eveng as it might have been wrote a Week after Mr. Loring Left New york. My Mamma is as well as can be expected for her. she desires her kindest Love to yourself and My Sister. begs you would write by every Opertunity. I saw little Betsey the last Thursday, she is exceeding hearty and well.[1] Mr. Clarke and Family are all very well. It is with pleasure That I communicate two peices of Intelligence which I doubt not will give you some Satisfaction. The Powder-house bill is passed into a Law in which it is ordered that there should be two Magazines erected, one in the town of Watertown, the other at the Back of the Hills near the Pest House.[2] The Generall Court have appointed a Committee (amongst whom is Mr. Hancock) to build the Magazines with all Convenient Speed.[3] Thus has this affair so long wish'd for and heretofore unsuccessfully attempted been brought about by a little Assiduity and Aplication. I saw Mr Pepperrell last thursday he told me that he and Mrs. pepperrell had determined to keep Lucy as they like her exceedingly and think she is the best Servant they have met with.[4] He invited me to dine with him the next day when he paid me 40£ sterg for her. Luce herself is very much pleased with her place. Ag[r]eable to contract with Mr. Joy I have made the first payment of a 100£ L.M. He has got the upper house to its place. You cannot Imagine how much it has improved that side of the

---

[1] First draft: "has got a most noble pair of trumpeters cheeks."

[2] Passed July 5, 1771. *Mass. Acts and Resolves*, v. 167.

[3] On July 4 the House of Representatives named Hancock, Ebenezer Thayer, Jr., and John Remington to be a committee, together with such as the Council should nominate. *House Journals*, 1771, 106.

[4] Probably William Pepperell Sparhawk, who took the name of William Pepperell, and married Elizabeth Royall.

Common it draws the attention of most people who all agree in its being one of the pleasantest situated places in the Province.

I have applyed to Mrs. Dawson for rent, but I have really no expectation of getting any. she makes a most lamentable preachment about the unreasonableness of paying Rent for a place so much out of Repair. says she will apply to the Fence Viewers to have the Fences made upp. as to that I informed her that they could nor would not do any thing between a landlord and tenant; if they did they must pay for it themselves. She further said that she prefers reserving the Rent and paying it to yourself when you come home and that she don't like so many Landlords. Have you received the ½ Guinea from Mr. Balch for the dutch picture. I can not conclude without again reque[s]ting that you would write often and largely. Present my most tender Regards to My dear Sister, accept the same yourself and beleive me to be yours most Affectionately,

H. PELHAM.

P.S. Bror. and Sister Pelham desires their kindest Love to yourself and Lady. Complime[nts] from Mr Pepperell and Lady. Miss Peggy McElvane. Mr Edward Green and Lady say thet the only [way] to make atonement for not calling there will be to write to them. When you write to me send the lines Mr. Joseph Green made up on Mr Checkleys Picture.[1] The Governor has informed the house that he is instructed not to sign any tax bill unless the salerys of all crown Officers are freed from paying Rates.

P.S. 2d. My mamma has just received your letter. Mr. Clarke and Family desire their kindest love. No more Room.

[1] They are printed in Slafter, *John Checkley*, i. 5.

Henry Pelham to Copley

BOSTON, July 11, 1771.

DEAR BROTHER,

By Capn. P. Smith you will I hope receive in good order your Layman, Crayons and Drawings and Major Bayard's Picture. The Crayons and gold Button holes are packed in the same Box with the Layman, the Drawings and Paper underneath Major Bayards Picture. My Mamma received with the greatest Pleasure your Letter of 23d of June tho' of an old date, as by it she had the Satisfaction of knowing that you and my Sister enjoyed so good a Degree of Health. She desires her kindest Love and Blessing to you and my Sister, begs that you would take Care of yourselves and not Lett the Gayeties and Pleasures of New York (by exposing you to Colds) have any tendency to impair the pleasing prospect of a confirmed state of Health. We are all pretty well. Mr. Clarke's Family are all well. Betzey I have not heard from since this day week, she was well then. The Account you give of the City, of your Buisness, etc. are very agreeable; continue those Remarks. You say you have seen two of Mr. West's Portraits. Let me have some Account of them. Your Directions with respect to the Repairs at the Common, the sale of the House, Papers to Coll Putnam etc. I shall punctually observe. It is time that I had my full directions with Regard to your Lawsuit, as the Court will sit in about a Month, and it may require some preveious time to write to and hear from Coll. Putnam. As I have received no Answer to my Letter sent per Post of June 23d I am entirely at a Loss what to do respecting Mr Otis's Fees. Sha'n't you be able to Procure at New York some Lime Trees for continueing the walk from Mr Hancock's?

We beg that at a proper Season you would send us a Barrell of Newton Pippins and a Barrell of the fine New York Water-Mellons.

I must before I conclude remonstrate against your not writeing. your last Letter was dated June 23d 18 Days ago, and how long it may yet be before we hear I cannot at present say. We must beg you would let us hear oftener. Present my kindest Love and Respects to my Sister. Miss Peggy's Compliments. Inclosed is a Letter from Mr. Edward Green. I must subscribe myself in Haste Your most Aff[e]ctionate Brother and Humble Sert.

HENRY PELHAM.

Copley to Henry Pelham

NEW YORK, July 14, 1771.

DEAR BROTHER,

This Eveng I devote with pleasure to you as I know it must give you pleasure to be inform'd of every surcumstance attending our situation here I will give you a minute detail and of the maner in which Sukey and myself spend our time. But to begin with the most important. Sukey and myself are very well; she is imployed in working on muslin, and myself in the Labours of the pencil. We commonly rise by six oClock in the morng, breakfast at 8, go to our respective Labours till 3, when we dine; at six ride out, and since we have be[en] here I have by no accident Lost more than one Day, as there is so many that are impatient to sit I am never at a loss to fill up all my time. My large Chamber is about 9 feet high and 20 feet long and near as broad, with a good room ajoining it, the ligh[t] near north. I have begun 4-½ lengths 6-¼ peaces 1 Kitcat. When

we came here Capt. Richards's [1] portrait (at Mr. Sherbrooks[2])
[was] so much admired that vast numbers went to see it. Mr.
McEvers[3] (from whom by the way we have received great
civility) spoke to Mr Sherbrook to send it to my Chamber
where it is [as] much esteemed [as] I Could wish. As I am vis-
ited by vas[t] numbers of People of the first Rank, who have
seen Europe and are admirers of the Art, I was glad to have
a Picture so well finish'd. Most of them say it is the best
Picture they ever saw and all agree in its being an admirable
Picture. I saw a miniature the other Day of Governor Martin [4]
by Miers which cost 30 Guineas and I think it worth the
Money. the Gover'r says he sat at least 50 times for it. We
have not found the wether uncomfortably hot; a great deal of
rain has injured the hay. We have been at Long Island. It is
pleasant tho the soil [is] not very good naturaly. the ferry is
about a mile over. Most of the provisions come that way, but
is by no means so well tended as Charles Town ferry, tho it is
six times as dear. We have been at Bloomingdale twice at the
widow McEvers's (about six miles out of this City), and this
week are to go to Mr Apthorp's that is about a mile farther.[5] I
beleive you will think we take a good share of pleasure, but I
find I can do full as much Business as in Boston, having no
interruptions and very Long forenoons, and punctually attended. I received your Letters of 24 of June and 7 of July.
Mr. Joy thinks he aught not to give the five Dollars he Offer'd
when I was in Boston, but he did not consider I beleive that it

---

[1] Charles Lloyd Richards was a captain in the 95th Regiment.

[2] Miles Sherbrook.   [3] James McEvers.

[4] Josiah Martin (1737–1786), governor of North Carolina from 1770 to the out-
break of the War of Independence.

[5] Probably Charles Ward Apthorp, whose house stood on what is now Ninth
Avenue near Ninety-first Street.

would cost 8 Dollars to carry her to Boston; besides she is as good as she was than and well worth the money. But I have met with a good pasture since and shall keep her here till I return, and than I shall be as willing to part with the Horse at 14£ sterling as with the Mare at 55 Dollars. They boath exceed my expectation. With regard to Mr Oatis I think it odd he should be in such hast to call for his fees considering the uncertainty of his helth permiting him to do the Business. I saw Coll. Putnam and he dont expect any fees till the time of tryal. I think you had better ask Mr Clarkes oppin[i]on about it. It is mine that you had better assure Mr. Otis he shall have his fees before the time of Tryal. If you cannot get the money you will write to me and I will send it without any doubt, for I told you I would do so. I think the Cause had better be tryed this term if there is no adjournment. You may let Mr Otis know I thought there would be an adjournt. and expected to be in Boston before that time. This must be managed with some address but let him know he shall certainly have his fees before tryall. I would have you attend the tryall and be vigilent; if you can do no otherwise you and Sigorney must give him part, but not if you can possably avoid it. When I was in Boston he told me the Coart would be adjourned, Putnam and Addams the same, and there has been no meeting of the Coart since. I therefore wonder Mr Otis should say it has been determined otherwise. It must be a fetch to get the money and nothing more. Have you got the Money from Sigorney for sundrys? I should be glad, if I am not too late, you would put in the Box a frame and Glass and paisted paper with Major Bayard's portrait, as I have one to do here.

I am happy to find you are all well by yours of the 7th instant. You were misinformed relative to the Trunk. It came in good season. I am happy in hearing of the Powder house Bill pasing. Take care to save the fence and get Mr. Hancock to put some Locust Trees their. If he will not, the Selectmen may, as it will be of publick utility. I am glad you have sold Lucy; I wish you could sell the House. You say you were advised to put a hipt Roof on the uper House, but you did not say who advised to it that could be depended on. I am glad people like the situation and that the Repairs go on briskly. If it is not two late I should like to Direct how to make the Sashes somthing different from what is usual with you. This you may let me know next Letter. A pattern of Chinese for the Top of the house I will send you, as I think they excell in that way here. I hope Mr. Joy will be more carefull to do every thing in the best maner than if I was present, that I may find every thing to my sattisfaction. See that he puts studs where the Doors are to be, if wings should be built, and for two Windows in my great Room. Let there be three Windows in the Side of the Kitchen, beside that in the little Entry. Otherwise it will be Dark. As to Mrs. Dawson I think she imposes on me. You may let her know the Lease is not of my giving, and if she does not like to stay and pay her Rent, she may move out of it directly, for I am accountable for the Rent and must lose it if she dont pay it, and I will not lay out one farthing more farther, nor any one else, and she must pay the money to you. I think there aught to be two Windows in the west side of the Chamber I shall paint in. It will tend much to keep it cool and pleasant when it will be convenient to open them, and I am inclined to think it would be best to put the Windows in the Room below now. It is so much more extended. We might contrive to have 2 Windows north of the Wing and a door into the Wing, if the Wing should be ever added. This I think must be attended to.

You know the Wing might extend lengthwise from the house. This would certain give two Windows north of the Wing in the Chamber and Lower Room. We send our Affectionate Duty to our hond Mamma Love and congratulation to Mr [and] Mrs Pelham Compts. to Miss Peggy Mr. and Mrs. Green to Mr. Boylston Family and let me know how he is. I would have the Windows put in the north side of my Rooms as above, for should I not add Wings I shall add a peazer when I return, which is much practiced here, and is very beautiful and convenient, and I think it as well to shut up a Window as to cut out one. Therefore put in 2, but for the Door put the studs only. You must think weither it will be best to put the Door next the Chimney or in the Middle. Your Affectionate Brother,

J. S. COPLEY.

Sukey thinks the Kitchen without Windows on the north will be very hot; I think so too. Wish the Clossets could be contrived better. If it will not be too late next Letter I write I will send you my thoughts on it.

Henry Pelham to James Putnam

BOSTON, July 16, 1771.

SIR,

I transmitt to you, by Mr. Copleys Directions, the inclosed Papers, viz. Copy of Mr. Pratts Minutes in the case of Banister *vs* Cunningham;[1] and Copies of the Depositions of Mr. Lovell and Mrs. Church.

[1] Thomas Banister purchased about 1709 the eight and a half acres which Copley owned, known as Mt. Pleasant. In 1733 his son, Samuel, mortgaged this property to Nathaniel Cunningham, whose son of the same name inherited it. There is no record of its sale to Copley, but two of the Deed Books (Nos. 112 and 114) are missing. When Copley transferred the property to Otis and Mason

My Brother has desired me to furnish you with any Papers, etc. that you may want from this Place, as Occasion requires. You will therefore please to inform me (by a line per Post) of what is requisite, and it shall be immediately forwarded to you. I am with the greatest Respect, Sir, Your most obedient and Humble Servt.

HENRY PELHAM.

Copley to Henry Pelham

NEW YORK, July 24, 1771.

DEAR BROTHER,

Sukey and myself have just finished a rich repast of which I wish you and our Mama had been partakers; it was on a fine pine, of which there is great plenty from one shilling Lawfull Money to 7 pence a peace, which you will no doubt think cheap anough. When you wrote me some time ago you desired I would send no blank paper; you may depend on it I shall not send my Letter in a Cover, because the postage will be double if I should. But you must not expect I should sett up so late to night as to fill up this whole paper, for We propose rising so early tomorrow Morng. as to take a ride before Breakfast. I have received your Letter by Smith, the Layman, etc., in good order. He arrived last Sunday. And Your Letter by the Last post by which I have the happyness to know our Mama and all our other friends were well. I pray Heaven they may continue so, and that we May have an happy meeting in the fall.

in 1796 the title was subject to a claim of the heirs of Nathaniel Cunningham, and this claim may have been the basis of the lawsuit mentioned in these letters. The tract was thus described in 1733: "A tract of land with a dwelling house thereon on the N. W. side of the Training Field, containing 8½ acres with the flatts, bounded S. or S. E. on the Common or Training Field, W'ly on Charles river or a cove, and in part on John Leverett and Mr. James Allen, on whom it also abutts N. E. ly. E. on Sam'l. Sewall."

I have by that memorable Epistle the happyness to know Likewise that you have a good talent at scolding which you have well improved, and wraught up in that Letter. you say you have not had a line for 3 Weeks; but you may remember Sukey wrote to her Brother in that time, by which you might have been informed we were well. You was at a loss likewise what to do with Mr. Otis. now that was a sad affair, and Mr. Otis could not be so unreasonable as not to think your not hearing from me a sufficient apology. Could any thing have turned out better or furnish'd you with more powerfull means of suspending the giving him his fees? If I had done it on purpose I should have thought myself wise therein.

When I saw Mr. Putnam he informed me should be glad to know assuredly of Mr. Goffs purchaseing Land and taking a quit claim from Banister, and I think nothing so forceable on all such occations as full proof of the fact. This do then. Get Mr. Green, or who else you shall think proper if you cannot do it yourself, in a way as private as may be best to examin[e] the Records at Cambridge. There you will find who he has purchased of or taken quit Claims from. Mr. Shurbourn who writes for Mr. Goldthwaite would do it for Mr Sigorney and me. I think him the best person because he understands the nature of those things so as to do it with more ease and certainty. You must mind weither the name was Goff or Trowbridge, or you may be puz'led. I cannot send you the lines on Checkley this time. I have [not] received the ½ Guinea, nor have I been able to contrive the Clossetts yet. The Pencill goes on very briskley and I have no time. Mr Green's letter shall have an answer. Sukey and myself are well. we desire our Love to all our friends Duty to Mama and Mr. Clarke. Your Effect'te Brother,

J. S. COPLEY.

Henry Pelham to Copley

BOSTON, July 28, 1771.

MY DEAR BROTHER,

Could you conceive the Pleasure I take in receiving a Letter from you, you would (I doubt not) write much oftener. Your very acceptable favour of the 14th. Inst. is now before me. by it we receive with infinite Pleasure, the agreable Account of your and my dear Sisters being very well. We reflect with great Satisfaction upon our hopes being happily accomplished, bee assured you are ever attended by our best Wishes for your Health and Happiness. The Account you give of your Buisness as well as Recreations are very satisfactory. You say you saw a Miniature Picture of Governor Martin by Meirs. I wish you had given me a more perticular Discription of it as well as of Mr West's Pictures that you mentioned in a former Letter. let me know something about them. Mr Otis I have not yet seen but I shall in a day or two. The Box with Major Bayard's Picture I hope before this is safe in your Possession, so that it is difficult for me to put a Frame and Glass into it. Your Friends that advised to a hiped [roof] were our Hon'd Mamma Mr Clarke, your two Brothers, Messrs. Jack and Isaac Clarke, etc., etc. Some of the Sashes are made. I have stoped those that are not 'till I can receive Directions which must be as soon as convenient. I dont comprehend what you mean by a Peazer.[1] explain that in your next. Don't forgett to send the Pattern of the Chinese. I spent Commencement Day at Cambridge, while I was there I mett Coll Putnam at Mr. Murray's[2] Chamber. I hapned

[1] On the transformation in meaning of this word see Albert Matthews in the *Nation*, LXVIII. 416.

[2] Samuel Murray, of the Class of 1772.

luckely to have the Coppies of the Papers with me, which I delivered him, he gave me the same Account he gave you, about the adjou[r]nment. I want your full and Perticular Directions for the law suit as to the largeness of the Fees, the Persons to whom and the time when they are to be given. What is to be done with Messrs. Payne[1] and the two Quinceys?[2] but of this you must let me know soon. Thus much for Buisness. My Mamma is tolerable well for her, she sends her kindest Love and best Wishes to yourself, and my Sister with her intreaty's that you would take the utmost Care of yourselves. I heard yesterday from my Cousin Betzey. (by the way I am very much affronted that you made no Inquiries after my dear little Neice. I suppose you have forgot her, therefore I don't address the Paragraph to you but to my Sister, to whom I beg my kindest Love and Respects may be acceptable). she is very hearty and well, has got two teeth and cuts them very easy. she is a very good Girl and is excellently tended. I see her frequently. We have had a most Remarkably fine Summer. hay is very plenty and Cheap. — Mr Otis's Action against Commis'r Robinson[3] for an Assault come on at the Inferior Court last Thursday Morn'g. The Tryal lasted 'till Saterday Morn'g, when the Jury bro't in a verdict in Mr Otis's favour with 2000£ St. Damages. Pray write often. I am with Regard yor Loving Bror.

HENRY PELHAM.

1st. P S Mr Clarke and Family are all well. Compliments I am desired to present from Mr. Green and Lady Miss P. McElvane etc., etc., etc., etc. I have neither time, Room nor Inclination to write about 500 Names.

---

[1] Robert Treat Paine (1731–1814).   [2] Samuel and Josiah.
[3] John Robinson. See 2 *Proceedings*, x. 72.

2d. P. S. Mr Boylston[1] is very ill his Friends have little or no hopes of his Recovery. Mr. Pelham I have not seen this ten days. They were well then except Peter who has been like to die. he is now better.

Copley to Henry Pelham

NEW YORK, Augst. 3d, 1771.

DEAR BROTHER HARRY,

I received your favour by the Post and am happy in hearing you and our Hon'd Mamma are well. The same information I now give you of Sukey and myself. we desire our Most Efectionate Love and Duty to her and Love to all our other friends, in perticular to yourself. my time is so much engrossd by Business that all I can spare is little anough for recreation so that you must excuse all the enaccurys in my Letters. I have began Painting to the amount of 3 hundred pounds Sterg. shall take four more and than Stop. We experiance such a Dispostion in a great many People to render us happy as we did not expect, but I must go to Business as it grows late. You say you dont know what I mean by a Peaza. I will tell you than. it is exactly such a thing as the cover over the pump in your Yard, suppose no enclosure for Poultry their, and 3 or 4 Posts aded to support the front of the Roof, a good floor at bottum, and from post to post a Chinese enclosure of about three feet high. these posts are Scantlings of 6 by 4 inches Diameter, the Broad side to the front, with only a little moulding round the top in a plain neat maner. some have Collums but very few, and the top is generally Plasterd; but I think if the top was sealed with neat plained Boards I should like it as well.

---

[1] Nicholas Boylston (1716–1771). See Quincy, *History of Harvard University*, II. 214.

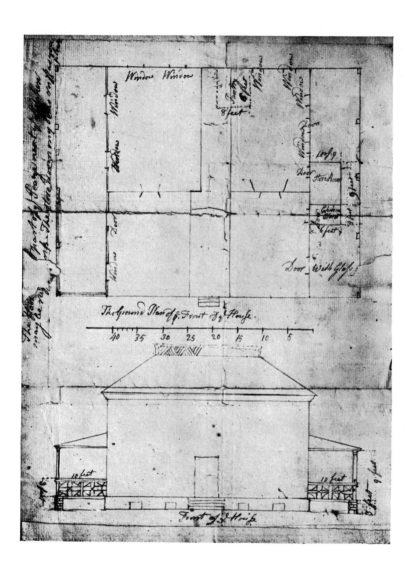

The Ground Plan of ye Front of ye House.

40 35 30 25 20 15 10 5

Front of ye House

these Peazas are so cool in Sumer and in Winter break off the storms so much that I think I should not be able to like an house without. I hope you will find it not much addition to the Expence to add them as I have drawn them in the Plan. you will see I have not drawn accurately. the Distanceing of the Post, Windows, etc., I have left to you. you can make them tourn out right. You see I have Drawn the Chinea Clossit Store Room in the east piaza, which containing things the Cold cannot injure, will be better there than in the Kichen, and I suppose not more expencive; and the Pantry I have left in the Kichen a[s] proposed when I was in Boston, Because I can find no other place for it, unless it was put where the Store Room is now, and the store room put out side of that, and the China Clossit as I have dotted in the Plan. the shape will be long but convenient anough and this will make the Pantry warm anough; But you must consult Joy in this. If the Piazas are added I should lik to have one window in the best Parlour, and a Door the top of which shall answer to the Window; but when you shove it up so high as to Clear the head (which it may be by opening a way through the plate above it) the part emidately under it shall open like the Lower half of a Shop Door. if you can contrive better, do. the East Peaza need not be sealled at all, but left rough. the foundations is not continued but only Coins at proper distances. I should have the Roof to pitch from under the Arkitraves of the Chamber Windows hipt every way and as flat as possable. I cannot send you the Chinese pattern yet. see what Mr. Joy will expect for this addition of Peazas, and let [him] know I think it cannot be much, becau[se] I would have them done at once, if they wont be Expencive. you need not tell him so; but if £200 Old Tenr[1] would do it you

---

[1] A trifle over £26 sterling. See p. 147 for Mr. Joy's estimate.

migh[t] conclude upon it without my orders. The floor of the
Peazas except that next the Kitchen should be Pitch Pine. As
to [the] Lawsuit, I must give Putnam 10 Guineas and Otis the
same; But if there will be an adjournment dont Guive to Otis.
tell him I shall be at home before that time. dont be too Liberal
with the Lawyers; they will not do the work one bit the better.
as to Pain Consult Mr. Goldthwait. if they are not sattisfied
Let them know You are sure your Brother will do what is
handsom by them when he returns. I know you are apt to be
Liberal, but remember money once gone never returns. Remember Sigorney is to be half. Send by the first oppertunity
from Boston 2 half Length Gold frames and 2-¼ Cloath frames
likewise Gould. I am with Great Effection Your Brother,

J. S. COPLEY.

Henry Pelham to Copley

BOSTON, August 15, 1771.

DEAR BROTHER,

The near approach of the Courts sitting, makes me solici-
touse about your Law suit. The last Evening, I receiv'd two
Letters from Coll. Putnam, in one of which he says:

The superior Court sets at Boston the last Tuesday of this
Month; I can't attend on Mr. Copley's Cause that Week, if I
could, it is very uncertain whether the Court will sit, to do Buisness at that time: you had better therefore get the Cause put off
till the Adjourment in the Fall: When I hope to be better able to
attend the Cause than at present. In the meantime I shall take
all due Care as far as my health will permitt. PS. If the Cause
must come on the first Week of the Courts setting, and can't be
delayed let me know, and I will endeavour to attend.

Now what I want, is your most perticular and express Orders, Whether your Cause shall be tryed at the first setting of the Court, or whether it shall be put off till the adjournment [in which Case it] can't be sooner than the middle of November. On the one hand, you will consider the state of your Lawyer's Health; Collo. Putnam you know, is an invalid, and his health is so very precarious, as to render his travelling, in such a season, very difficult; often impossable. Mr Otis, you are likewise sensable, has no certainty of his Health; he is now very well, but how long that may continue, is very uncertain; these Considerations, Operate in favour of its coming on, as soon as possable. On the other hand, if it is put off 'till the adjournment, you will be able to attend the Tryall yourself. You will likewise consider, that if the tryal is put off till November, and anything should prevent its being then tryed, it must go to the spring term, when it is very bad travelling. It has been put off, upon your motion, sundry times already, which should make you cautious of putting it off, when you can bring your Lawyers together with such favourable Circumstances; and the oftener you put it off, the more difficult you may find it, when you have greater Occasion for it. I have just seen Mr. Otis. he says, he is entirely ready for speeking. I shall endeavour to have the action, so ranged as either to have it tryed now, or in November. I imagin you wont need soliciting for an immediate answer to this Letter, when you consider, that if you write by the return of the same post that Carries this, it will be two or three days after the Court opens, before I can receive your Letter. I must therefore intreat, that you will not neglect letting me have an immediate answer. I am just going to write to Coll. Putnam, so have only time to subscribe myself, your loving Brother,

HENRY PELHAM.

P. S. We are all well, accept of Love, from our Mamma, Mr. Clarke and Family, Mr. Startin[1] and Lady, myself, etc. The same, to my Sister.

Invoice of Merchandise

Invoice of Merchze shipped by Henry and Thos. Bromfield in the Thames Capt. Jno. Derby; on Acco. of Mr. Jno. Singleton Copley; consigned to Mr. Henry Pelham at Boston.

No. 1 a Case qt.

No.
       ⎧ 6   fine half length Cloths.... 4/ ......1.. 4.
1..   ⎨ 6. d? Kit-Cats............. 2/ ....12.
       ⎩ 6..d? Three Quarters...... 1/6...... .. 9
2..   ⎰ 6..d? fine ticking half Lengths 4/ ......1.. 4
       ⎱ 6..d? three Quarters........ 1/6...... .. 9
              The Case 2: 6   4   6

2 a Box qt.

12 fine Tools........................ .. 3. 8
5 Brushes........................ .. 3. 8
3 oz. Italian Black Chalk.... 2/ 6
3 oz.   do   White........ 1/ 3
2 oz. fine Vermillion......... 2/ 4
lb   oz
1..   2 fine white Poppy Oil 5
50 lb Putty................. 4d...... ..16 8
       Bladders, Bottle & Box 1   6   2   3   6

3 Case

                    feet   Ins
185 Squares best Newcastle ⎱ 195.. 3. 9d   7   6   6
    Crown Glass 14½ by 10½ ⎰
            Box etc...............   5   6   7 12

4 A Keg
   Wt.   Ct. 2..0..19
      Tare 12
      Nett 2..0.. 7 Grod. white Lead. 35/ 3 12   2
               Kegg.............   2   6   3 14   8

[1] Charles Startin, who married Sarah, a sister of Mrs. Copley.

Charges

Entry & Shipping...........................	5 6		
Primage & Bills Lading.....................	3 3	8 9	
Commission on £17 19 5 @ 2½ p Ct..........		9	
Errors Excepted.		£18 8 5	

London 17th August 1771.

HENY & THOS BROMFIELD.

Copley to Henry Pelham

NEW YORK, August 17, 1771.

DEAR BROTHER,

Mrs. Copley and myself have this Even'g returned from Mrs. McEvers's at Blooming Dale where we have been two Days. I have been taking her portrait there, and finding Smith sails tomorrow morning I sit up late to write a line to you to let you and our Hond. Mamma know we are well, and have been so ever since we left Boston, which is a great blessing. I have wrote to Brother Jona'n [1] at large and it is now late, so must be very short for we keep good hours. I have not been able to send you the Chineese yet, for I hardly get time to eat my Victuals; but I will send it soon. I forget weither or not there was to be a Clossit in the Keeping Room. if the Clossits are made in the Peaza as proposed in my last Letter so as to be contiguous to the Keeping Room, I would by no means have any by the Chimney. I am likewise determined to have no door into the Kitchen from the Keeping Room. I dined at Mr. Yates's 3 Days ago, where I noticed two such spaces with side boards in them which were very convenient. the Arches were somthing in this maner. I should like to have them left open the same Depth they are now, or if there should be the Clossit in the Peaza, and

[1] Jonathan Clarke.

those Spaces will receive a side board in one and a Table in the other, which will be very convenient.

If Mr. Joy would as leaves wainscott the Lower part of the Painting Room as plaister, which I should think would be as Cheep, I should prefer it. I dont remember weither I did not put an odd number of Posts to the Sketch of the Peaza I sent you; if I did, it was rong and I suppose that you would correct it. the Number should be even, so as to have steps from the Middle which would lead into Fennows Pasture, steps of about seven or eight foot Long somthing in this manner [1] I must have Windows from my great Painting Room into it. those Windows having new fassioned Blinds such as you see in Mr. Clarke's Keeping Room Will keep the Ligh[t] out from that side, and allways occation a Draught of Air. Mind I dont mean to tie you up in any thing; you must contrive the place for Windows, Doors, etc. yourself. I dont know but it would be better to have the Steps at the End of the Peaza than at the side, as the Door from the best Room cannot be opposite to those Steps: in which Case their might be the odd number of Posts in this manner. indeed I think this would be best. however only let me know the expence. if it is not much, as I think it cannot be, I would have the Door and Windows orderd Accordingly, and the Peaza might be built after I return to Boston.

I am with Effectionate Duty to our Hon'd Mamma Love to yourself in which Sukey Joins me Your Effectionate Brother,

JOHN S. COPLEY.

You have never said anything of Snap. I hope he is well and a good Boy. if he continues to do well he will merit my Care

[1] A small rough sketch, not reproduced.

and tenderness for him and I shall reward him According on my return. I am obliged to write in a very Slovenly Manner for want of time, which I hope will [be] deem'd a sufficient excuse.

Shrimpton Hutchinson to Copley

BOSTON, 24th August, 1771.

SIR,

I take the first Opportunity of sending you a Letter from the ingenious Mr. West,[1] which came inclosed in one to me from that Gentleman for my Instruction in bringing forward my Son in the Art of Painting, and on the other side I give you a Copy of it for your Perusal, in hopes that you will likewise favour me with your Sentiments on the Subject, and let me know if any Compensation can be made to you by me or by his Services to entitle him to your Instruction in the Knowledge of Colours, which will determine in my Mind the Time of sending him home to England, as I find by Mr. Temple's Letter Mr. West will be very friendly to him on all Occasions. It gives me pleasure to hear by Capt. Smith and many Gentlemen from the Southward that you are in Health, and command as much Employment as you think proper to undertake, and wishing you and your Lady a safe Return to your native Town, I conclude with due Regard for you and Esteem for your Merit. Your humble Servant

SHRIMPTON HUTCHINSON.

P S I am sensible Genius, Industry, and long Practice must be united in the Painter to make him eminent and am therefore anxious my Son should improve his Hours usefully, and Time

[1] See page 118, *supra.*

will determine whether he has Genius. Taste may be acquired
by his future Travels, which I hope he will have the Advantage
of, and am encouraged in it by the Offers of my Friends.

Copley to Henry Pelham

NEW YORK, 25 Augst., 1771.

DEAR BROTHER HARRY

When you wrote me last so pressingly for an Answer you
should have consider'd I might have been out of Town; therefore you should not have delay'd writeing so long that an accident of that sort should possably take place. now this was the
very accident that prevented my writeing an Imediate answer.
I slept out of Town the night before and it is the custom to
send the letters to their respectiv[e] proprieters, and it was not
brought me till after the Post had been gone an hour. I was
very much mortified and shall be doubly so if you have not been
active in bringing on the Action; for it is my judgment to have
it come on by all means, and in order to make amends as much
as possable for this delay I have wrote to Coll. Putnam by this
Post informing him that I send you my peremtory orders to
have the Cause try'd if possable, so that he will hold himself in
readyness or go down to Boston at the time to which the Cause
stands assigned, according to what has past between you. however write him, if their is time for him to receive your Letter,
and go down to Boston before the time to which you ranged
the Cause for. I would not for any consideration whatever
you should not procure a Tryal this time, and cannot but be
surprised you should be so timid as to weit one moment for my
orders. Act for me as if for your self, and you will do wright.
the letter to Coll Putnam has taken me up so much of the

Dear Brother   Boston August 2nd 1771.

— — — I hope you have too great an Opinion of
our affection and Regard to think it necessary that I sho
should describe the pleasure we enjoyed upon the Receipt
of your favours of the 24 of July. August 3 & 17. Your own feelings upon
some similar Occasion better than my pen can give you
an Idea of our Satisfaction ... a Satisfaction heightened into Hap
piness by hearing that you & my dear Sister were well.

As this Goes by Mr Stanton — I shall be as her truly
in answering your letters and in setting you know the
situation of things here as his unexpected departure give me an
We thank you for your kind Wishes. With regard to the fine Apples
I am much pleased that you have such plenty of fine
fine Apples and are very glad you have had such plenty of
so delicate a Fruit but if we may judge from the price we
have had greater plenty than you you have hed here than at New
York. with you they were from a shilling to seven
pence here they from a shilling to 2 pence and excel
ent Fruit too. — You tell as rain from what I say
about Blank Paper by by to tell me to not
Letters in a Cover — you tell me now I must not expect. I should
sett up so late to nights as to fill up this whole paper —
that is very clever indeed! not write for better than three Week!
will expect several things. that you wont set up so late
that you will write often
& that you will send no Blank Paper (I repeat it for all
your sneer about a Letters being covered) but above all I ex
pect that you would take the utmost Care of your Health a
Man and his Wife being one I think less to you that
that in this last and most important Expectation My Dear

Even'g that I can only send you this scrip, for I must rise earley. Sukey and myself are very well desire our Duty to our Dear Mama, Love to you and all our Brothers and sisters, comp'ts to all Friends. I am, Dear Harry, your Effectionate Brother,

J. S. COPLEY.

Henry Pelham to Copley [1]

BOSTON, Augst. 25, 1771.

DEAR BROTHER,

I hope you have too great an Opinion of our Affection and Regard, to think it necessary, that I should describe the Pleasure we enjoyed upon the Receipt of your severall Favours of the 24th of July, 3d. and 17. of August. Your own feelings upon some simular Occasion, can give you a better Idea of our Satisfaction, than my Pen — a Satisfaction, heightened into Happyness, by hearing that you and my dear Sister, were well. In return for such agreable News, I can inform you, that our hond. Mamma enjoys, as she has done for some time, a pretty tolerable degree of health, for her. I have been very well scince you left Boston.

As this goes by Mr. Startin, I shall be as perticular, in Answering your three last Letters and in letting you know the situation of things here a[s] his sudden departure will permitt.

We thank you for your kind Wishes, with regard to the Pine Apples, are very Glad you have had such plenty, of so delicat[e] a Fruit, but if we may judge from the Price, we have had greater plenty here than you have had at New York. with you, they were from a shilling to sevenpence, here from a Shilling to two pence, and excellent Fruit too.

---

[1] There are two drafts of this letter. The first bears the date July 4, 1771, which has been changed to August, 1771.

You tell me, *You must not expect I should sett up so late to night as to fill up this Paper*. That is very clever indeed! not write for better than three Weeks, and than tell me I *must not expect etc., etc*. Yes, dear Sir, I will expect severall Things: that you won't sett up late, that you will write often, that you will send no blank Paper (I repeat it for all your sneer about a Letter's being couvered), but above all, I expect that you will take the utmost Care of your Health. a Man and his Wife being one, I think it needless, to Say that in this last and most important Expectation, my Dear Sister is included. You have receved your Layman etc. I am glad of it. I think my self very happy in possessing a talent, which, is so very neacessary and usefull, and which produced your fav'r of July 24. I hope you will render it unneacessary for me to excersise that talant again.

Agreable to your directions, I have got Mr. Sherbourn to examine the Records at Cambridge, for a Quitclaim to Mr. Goff, But he can find no such Instrument upon Record. there is a quitclaim from Mr Jno. Banister, to Mr. Inman of a peeice of Land, for the sum of five shillings.

The Window Sashes are made much as you would have them, narrow but very deep. I have observed the Windows of several Houses, lately painted, in a manner that I greatly like, and which makes the Glass look much Larger, and the Bars appear very slender. it is by painting the putty, with a dark Colour, nearly approaching to Black. The Glass you propose over the Door, would be very convenient, but I think the venetian Door would be much Handsomer and Pleasanter. Paper Mashe Gilt, Mr Gore[1] makes for thirty shillings O. T. per Yd.; if it is white, half that price; but the Goodness ought to be regarded. I wish you could send a small peice from New

---

[1] John Gore, of Boston, painter and merchant.

York to Compare. I thank you for the lines on Checkley's Picture. The Peaza's which you describe, appear to me, to be very convenient, as well as pleasant. Capt. Joy has given me an Estimate of the expence. it turns out more than you expected, £63 L. M. he says is the lowest he could afford to undertake to do it for. The stuff comes to near 40£. The gold frames shall be forwarded as soon as possable. The Arches at the sides of the Chimnie in the Sitting Room, I like, but there is no determining about the Closetts, without knowing weither the Peazas are to be built or not. I will speak to Capt. Joy about the wainscot in the Painting Room. You putt an odd number of posts, in the Peaza, which was right, as there is four Windows, which makes five Peers. I think upon the whole it would be best to have the steps at the front End.

In answer to your inquiries after Snap, I take a pleasure in informing you; that he has been well, except one fit, which he had since you was away, but it was so much less violent, than any of his former ones, that we are in great hopes that they will entirely leave him. Each fit has been essentially less Violent than the preceeding one, he has behaved himself very well and is a cleaver Fellow. Since I began to write this Letter, he came up, asked me if I was writeing to New York, and beged that I would give his Duty to his Master and Mistress, and tell them that he was very glad to hear that they were well. Antony is well.[1] Having thus exibited Snap and Antony to View, I begin to think it is time to produce myself. I have but Just returned from Newton, where I have been exerciseing the Pencill. In my way I called up at Jamaica, and saw my Cousin Betzey, she is in charming Health, looks as fatt and hearty as you could Wish, she cutts her teeth very easy. My Brother Pelham and

[1] A dog.

Family are well, desire their kindest Love and Regards may be presented to you, and my Sister. Little Peter has been exceedingly ill, but has recovered again, and is now in a fine promiseing way. I have now upwards of 500£ worth of Buisness in Hand. I have been trying to etch a little thing, an Impression I Inclose.

Agreable to your desire, I inclose a Plan of the House. The Entrance into the great Room, and the Room over it, were objects of great Moment, and what has cost Capt. Joy and my self much Study and attention. The principle Object, we had in View, was to mak[e] the passages not only convenient, but answ[e]rable in Looks, to the noble Rooms, to which they lead. a secondary Pursuit, was to prevent the other parts of the house, being encroached upon and being a thoro'fare to these Rooms. These Objects, I believe, we have accomplished, in the best Manner, the Place was capable off.

I entended to have given you an exact section of the entry and staircase, but Mr Startin, going sooner than I or even himself expected, I can only send you a rough sketch, drawn by the eye only. You will *be able* to understand the Plans, with a little attention. take notice, that the Rest of the front Stairs, the rest of the back Stairs, and the passage between the two marked AAA are all upon a leavel. To make the thing as plain as possable, let us take a Walk up stairs. We have now mounted 13 Steps, and are upon the Rest. This you see is Circular, it is so made to avoid having Closetts in the Great Room, the small peice that Comes into the Room Capt Joy says, can easily be hid, by throwing an Arch from the Chimnie to the Partition, which will be Very hansome. This rest being circular, affords as much passage Room as, if it was square, and will more naturally lead us up to the small Rest B, and into the painting Room. I beleive, it will look as well, if not better than square; if you have any Objections to this plan, you must let me know them as soon as possable. The upper Room will be about 8 feet 9 Inches under the Beam. Your great Room will be a very fine one, 24 feet long, 17.6 feet Wide, and 10 feet high. We discovered the other day, that the Chimney in this Room has no Funnell, one of the foolishest peices of Buisness that could be, to build a Chimnie without a passage for Smoke. We have had most excessive hot Weather, this Month. It has been the death of several People here, and had like to have been Fatal to Capt. Joy. he was at the Common one morn'g about 3 Weeks ago, about 7 o'Clock, he was [so] over come, as to endeavour, with the Assistance, of one of his Men to get home, which with difficulty he affected. within a few Minutes after, he was to appearance almost dead. Docr. Bulfinch [1] was called, and pronounced him a gone Man, but by the application of Medicine he after a time brought him to his Sences again; but it has left him soo Weak, that last Monday the Doctr. permitted him to Walk, for the first time, as far only as Mr. Laughton['s] Shop, bottom of the Lane. Mr Boylston, you will doubtless have heard, is dead, he has left 5000 Dollars, to Harvard Colledge. *But to conclude*, is a reviving Sentence after a long and dull Sermon. I doubt not you will think it as reviving after a long and dull Letter. My Mamma desires, her kindest love and Blessing to yourself and My Sister. Present my most affectionate Regards to my Sister, Accept the same yourself, and beleive me to be with truth and Regard, Dear Sir, Your most Affection[at]e Brother and most Humble Sert.

HENRY PELHAM.

---

[1] Dr. Thomas Bulfinch (1728–1802), father of the architect. See Bulfinch, *Life and Letters of Charles Bulfinch*.

BOSTON, Septm. 2d, 1771.

MY DEAR BROTHER,

I receiv'd your's of the 25 Inst by which I am sorry to find, you are very anxious to have your Cause bro't to an Issue, this sitting of the Court; sorry, only as it has not been in my Power, to answer your Expectations. Beleive me, when I say, I was much Chagrin'd, when I was obliged to apply to Mr. Quincey, to have your Cause put off to the November Adjournment. My Reasons for doing it, were the difficulty of Coll. Putnam's Attendance, and the bad state of Mr. Otis's Health. Coll. Putman in a letter to me says —

You tell me in your's of 15 Inst that Mr. Copleys Cause stands for the second Saturday of the Courts sitting. You must remember that is a time when I can't possably attend; because it is the same Week the inferior Court sitts at Worcester and I am not now certain it will be over in one Week. if it should I may attend the second Week in Septmr. if the Cause can't be putt off with more Convenience 'till the fall Adjournment, which I should choose. If our Court finishes the first Week in Septmr. as I hope it will and Mr. Copleys Cause must come on the second; Give me timely notice and I will be there.

Thus you will find, that had there been no other Obstacle, your Cause could not have been tryed, till the second Week in Sepmr. in which Week, the Court will sit only two Days, viz. Tuesday and Wednesday. on Tuesday, there was a Cause assigned by the Court, so that the time was reduced to one day. The third Week in Septmr. the superior Court sitts at Worcester. Mr. O—s's health is such, as renders it (in the opinion of most People, perticularly of the Court) quite improper, to trust a Cause of that importance and difficulty to his Care. At some times he is raving, at all times he is so bewildered as to have no dependance placed upon him. He tóld me, that the Court had peremtorally ordered the Cause to be tryed on the ensueing Thursday. upon enquiry, of Mr Quincey and Mr. Winthrop, I found it was a great Mistake. In short He is too well to be dismissed from the Cause, too unwell to manage it. Had it been possable, I should have engaged Mr. Payne to have spoke, but Mr O—s thinking himself capable, precluded that. I shall write to Coll. Putnam, next post, to inform him that the Cause has gone off to November. I should be glad, that you would instruct me, about the finishing the body of the upper house, as also about painting and papering the same, about Wood for Winter. Inform me, where I shall gett some more Money for Mr. Joy. As it will be impossable to have both houses finished, so as to go into them with safety this Fall, it is proposed to have the upper house finished so as for either us or you, to move into it when you come back. My Mamma is tolerable well. I have got a Violent Cold increased by going out to a Fire, at New Boston, the other Night. Betzey is well, she paid us a Visit the last Week. Present our love etc. to my Sister, accept the same yourself, I am, Yours, most Affectionately,

Henry Pelham.

Copley to Henry Pelham

New York, Sepmr. 9th, 1771.

Dear Brother,

Your Letter of the 2d. Instant came to hand. it gives me peculiar pleasure to hear our Dear Mamma is so well, and our other friends, yourself excepted, in health. this makes every other disappointment quite tolerable, nothing in this Life being of importance in comparison with that. Sukey and myself are in full possession of this inestimable Blessing at this time, and indeed have been so ever since we left you. we grow impatient to see you all, but must not expect that Blessing till late in the fall. I find it a great work to finish so many pictures, as I must do every part of them myself. however patience will accomplish it all in due time, and I shall have more sattisfaction when I return from my present assiduety. send me by Smith the frame and Glass formerly menshoned and Receipt for Varnish in your next Letter.

I am sorry my Cause has been posponed till Novemr., but I hope it is for the best, and would have you apply to Coll. Putnam prior to the Coart's sitting to send you word what time will be convenient for him to attend, and you can then have the Cause ranged for that Day: and with regard to Otis you must run no risque; if their is the least doubt about his state of health, Paine must be the man. I hope you have not advanced him any Money.

I am sorry the House will not be fit to live in this Winter. you had better get the upper one done at all events. I think their is only some Window Shutters and Doors to make, in which you must be as frugal as possable. as to the Cornishing the Rooms (except those in Joy's estimate) I think it needless to be at the expence of it; only get the neet low prised papers, carry them to the Sealing and with the Border the Rooms will look well. the House we lodge in is so and looks very neet and fit for the firs[t] Gentleman in this City to live in. this you will understand is in respect to the two front Rooms and Chambers. Mr. Joy is by his agreement to Cornis those he makes new. as to the painting you know how your Mamma would have it done. it is for her and I would have you please her in that and every thing else. I hope you will soon receive Colours from

London and Glass, etc. as to the Chimneys I think if your
Mamma is determined to put up the stove, I should think it
needless to have Jambstones. plaster painted will look as well
and your Mamma will never make fire in the Best room; so
plaster will do as well their too, but Connecticut Stone hearths
I think will be best. I only menshon these things. you must
please our Mamma, but you know my plan is frugallity and
this way of finishing the Chimneys accurs as being as good as
any and much Cheeper; but if the Stove is not put up, than I
think the Keeping Room should have Jambstones. But judge
in this matter with prudence yourself. as your Mamma shall
not move this Winter you may lay in your own wood, and when
we return wee will look out for ourselves and doubt not we shall
do well. you must mind what Mr. Joy was to do in his agreement that you don't pay for anything included in that. I should
think the Doors that go from the front Rooms and front
Chamber must be included in finishing the Entry. this you
must take Care of. you want Money, but how can I answer
your question, Viz, where you shall get some, when you have
not informed me from whom you have received any, how much
you have got, and Who owes? let me know when you write
next. their is an Acct. of Mr. Hancock of about 20 Guineas,
which I suppose if you are in want you may have. as to my
receiveing Money here I have received none yet, nor do I expect
to till I am coming away, when I shall receive it in Bulk. Coll.
Lee owes, but I am very loath to take that. it is on interest,
and nothing less than absolute necessity would induce me to.
I Wonder the Peazas come to so much considering the Plainness
of them. I should not conclude did not you want to know on
Acct. of the Clossits. you must talk with Joy about the Price
of the Posts plain, and so is every thing else indeed. however

see. if you can get no abatement I will have them done, and as I sketch'd in my Letter 2 or 3 Weeks ago, would have the Chinea Clossit and store Room in the East Peaza leaving a passage from the front to that part that is contiguous to the Kitchen; and what you have Drawn for the Store Room in the Kitchen shall be the Pantry. the Size is good, but only the one Door into the Entrey. than where you have markd a Clossit and Entrey I would have all open to the Kitchen and a very large Window or two of those old one to the north for Air in hot Weither, and I think the Plan compleat. make no Door from the Keeping Room Directly into the Kichen.

J. S. COPLEY.

Our Effectionate Duty [to] our Dear Mamma. [L]ove to all other friends. I have received a letter from Mr. West he say[s] Mrs. Deveroux's Picture was Exibitted and did me great Honour. Shrimton Hutchinson has a letter that compliments me much from West. no blank paper.

Henry Pelham to Copley

BOSTON, Septemr. 10, 1771.
MY DEAR BROTHER,

I think it needless, to intrude upon your time, by telling you, what I hope you know allready, the Pleasure we take in hearing from you. I was a little, a little did I say? I was greatly disapointed, in not receiving a Line from you, by the last Post, but that was agreably compensated, by hearing afterwards, from Mrs. Startin, that you and my dear sister were well. Your not writing, I attribute to your Buisness, which you say takes up all your time, an ill effect proceeding from a good Cause.

We are, thank God, in very good Health. My Mamma is

tolerably well, my Cold has left me. Miss Betzey I have not seen or heard from Scince my Last.

Inclosed, is Captn. Paschall Smith's Receipt for a Box of Frames, which I hope will arrive safe to hand. The Frames are (I think) as good as any that have been done, and are such, as I hope will please the Taste of the Gentry at New York. If you should have Occasion for more, you would do well to lett me know as soon as possable, that they may be ready to goe by Capt'n Smith, when he makes his next Trip.

Your Lawsuit — in my last, per Post, I informed you perticularly of that. As the Superior Court setts by adjournment in November, and as I suppose, you won't be at home till the middle of October, I submitt it to you, weither it would not be best, that Mr. Payne should prepare himself for speaking in the Cause. Mr. Otis you can not have the least dependance upon, he has been raving distracted, several times the last Week. If you should determin that Mr. Payne is to speak, it would be best that he should know of it, as soon as possable, that there might be no Excuse, for his not being prepared, for want of time. Mrs. Sigourney wants very much, to have Mr. Josiah Quincey for a speeker; he tells her, that he will have nothing to do in the affair, unless he can speak. Mrs. Sigourney will be entirely satisfied with your determination.

Your Works, at Mount Pleasant, go on very Briskly. The upper house is in it's place. It has the Cellars finish'd, the Chimnies built, the Back part erected. The Roof finished entirely. It makes a very noble appearance, and its situation is pleasant beyond Discription, beyond Idea.[1] I could wish the lower house stood three feet higher upon its foundation, This House is also in a fine forward way. The Back is framed

---

[1] Erased in first draft: "the conception of the most lively Imagination."

erected and Boarded, Chimnies altered, Roof entirely finished, rough pertitions and rough Ceilings up throughout the House. Captn Joy says, he shall be ready for the Plastering, in about a Fortnight, and that you may come into the House this fall with all safety. I wish the matter of the Peaza's was determined, as some things depend upon them. for instance, if it was determined to have them, the Windows might be placed so far out, at the ends of the House, as to allow Room for the Box casing for the shutters, without lessening the Rooms. It ought to be determined upon, before the House is Clapboarded. The front and one end of the upper house must be new Clapboarded, will you give me directions about it? the Clapboards on the other end are very good. Who is your Glazier? Mr Gooch [1] has spoke to me, to know if you will give him the jobb, he would be very glad to have it. Mr Moses Pitcher has likewise applyed to me, he would be much obliged to you for your employ, in the Glazuring, Papering and Plumbing Buisness's. Mr. Miller would be glad to serve you, in the Papering Way. he desired me to mention it. he says he will work as Cheap and do his Work as well, as you can gett it done in Boston. He is at Work at the upper house. Mr Winter hopes, you will be so kind, as to lett him do what Iron Work you may want. Mr., —— I forget his name, no matter, would recommend slate as vastly preaferable to shingles, and would be proud to serve Mr Coplin. I dont recollect any Body else, that I have to recommend. Would it not be best to give one good coat of paint, to the Roofs of the Houses? it appears to me as well as to others, that it would be a great benefit, much more than the expence. The Chinese Rail — Did I inform you that you are like to have a fine Crop of Potatos?

[1] First draft: Mr. Gough.

You would do me a great Kindness, if you would procure me, if it is to be had at New York, The Church Prayer Book in Latin. I am not able to get it here. If you can get one, please to send it by Smith. In my last Letter, that per Mr Startin, I gave you a discription of the stair case, since that we have made Considerable Alterations in the Plan, much for the better. The Passages to the two great Rooms will be much more Roomly,[1] and much easier of access. it would be very difficult to describe it in a Plan. I have contrived to have your painting Chamber, very commodious for painting a whole length Picture. This I will discribe by a Plan.[2] The Part of the Room marked A is made considerably higher than the rest of the Room B. This part of the Room A will be made 9 or 9½ feet high, and will be extended 9½ feet from the Great Window. This I think will be ample Room.

Capt. Joy has made the front of the lower House 11 Inches higher, which makes it look much better. I had like to have forgot to put you in Mind of the Lime trees, for the continuance of the Walk, from Mr. Handcock's. it will be a fine time to send them, by Capt. Smith when he returns, it will take 36 Trees to go to the Water. The Apples that I mentioned in a former letter, a Barrell of Newton Pippins, a Barrell of Golden Pippins, and some fine Large New York Water Melons. I have promissed one of these last, so that I shall depend upon them. News, by a Vessell in 5 Weeks from London, we are informed, that Mr. Wilks is Chosen Sherriff of London. That the Lord Mayor, Aldermen, and Livery, have presented another Remonstrance, in which after enumerating many greviances, they request his

[1] Erased in first draft: "Roomy."
[2] There is a similar plan in the first draft, but less carefully drawn, and giving fewer details. The first draft also has this drawing.

Majesty to Restore them their Rights, And Peace to this unhappy, and distracted Nation, by a speedy Dissolution of Parliament, and a Removal of his Majesty's present Wicked and despotic Ministers forever from his Councils and Presence. They were answered, by a peremptory refusal, and a severe reprehe[n]sion, for using such indecent Language. My Mamma present[s] her kindest Love and Blessing to Yourself and My Sister. Accep[t] my own Love and Compliments, present the Same to my Sister. My Compliments attend Mr. Startin. I am Dear Sir, Your most Affectionate Brother, most obed[i]ent, and Humble Sert.

HENRY PELHAM.

P S. Rememr. it is the 10 of Septr. also Rememr. October is approaching, and also that Boston stands in its old Place.

Post Script.   BOSTON Sepr. 10 PM

DEAR BROTHER

I did not intend after so long a letter as that of this date to have wrote so soon but this is to let you know that you can procure Lime Trees from Spriggs Mr. Handcock's Gardner. He will furnish Trees Plant and Warrant them for 18 Shillings O. T. a peice. this I imagine will be Cheaper than they can be procured from N. Y. for, considering Risque, Frieght etc. Spriggs's Trees are four Years old and 12 feet High. If you think proper to have them planted this fall (which I think by all meens would be best) let me know as soon as conveni[ent], that there may be a first Choice. Mr Sprigg says he can supply you with every Fruit Tree, flowering Tree except the Tu[lip] shrub or Bush that you can want. that he will plant them and not receive his pay till it is known weither the Tree etc. lives or not, and that he will supply you as Cheap and as well as any

Gardner in America. For Compl. I refer to my long Letter. I am as there your most Affectionate,

HEN PELHAM.

P. S The Tulip Trees are plenty with you and it would be no damage if you was to send some of them by Capt S. Good night.

Copley to Henry Pelham

NEW YORK, the 20 of Sepr. 1771.

DEAR BROTHER,

Your favour by Capt Smith I received yesterday and shall answer paragraph by paragraph. The frames came safe to hand and I hope will do, but shall know better when they have been seen by those who will want frames, and soon as possable if they will answer you shall have my orders.

As to my Lawsuit I think you had better write to Mr. Payne let him know when the Cause must come on and desire him to be ready. let him know Mr Putnam and Mr Quincey is engaged with him and they must pursue the common practice with respect to speaking, for I am determined to do nothing to give offence to Mr. Payne. let Mr Payne know I depend on his being ready. But dont you tell this to Mr. Quincey; he need know nothing of your Charges to him and my absence is a sufficent covouring. for if Quincey Leaves me, I had rather it should be at the time of Tryal than sooner, and indeed I dont think I shall be at home so soon as the Cause will come on, and if you manage well my Absence may be turned to good Acct. for you know you cannot with any reason affront Mr. Payne, and I left no perticular Direction for Mr. Quincey to speak, Suposeing the Attourneys would take proper care and do what was proper by me and one another. but be sure direct

Payne to be prepaired. furnish him with any papers he may want etc. The Works at pleasant Mount go briskley — I am glad of it. The Peazas you have my Mind upon, but I dont propose they shall be built until I return; only the House finishd, so that they may be done when I return; for I think they will be better done under my inspection. The front and one end of the upper House you say must be new Clapboarded. I am willing to have it done, but agree with Joy for every thing. if you don't like the Price, don't get it done. Who is my Glaizer? I shall like Gooch as well as any one, if he does the Work as Cheep. see others first and see how low you can get the Work done: and as to plumbing, that is within Joy's estimate, if by plumbing you mean leads for Windows. I had as leaves Miller should paper as any one, provided he does it as Cheep; but I cannot take notice of all those who desire to be recommended, so I shall leave them and you do Your best. I have no objection to painting the roofs. The Chineese I will send within a fort-night. I am Glad you have improved the plan. I have been all a long Ancious about the roomlyness of the Passages and am so now about the hight of that which leads to my great Room. I hope you will take care of it, as you may ruin the House by a mistake in that. I like your alteration in my Chamber. Mrs. Copley thinks Locust Trees much better than Lime. I am of the same oppinion. the Way to Judge is to go at a distance and see if the Locust will not be so high that you may see the house under the bows. I think they will and that the Lime will intercept the sight. The Locust is much quicker Growth and much Cheeper etc. Mellions we have none this year better than in your Market. Pippins I will take Care of. it is now very late and I must to bed, for we rise earley to set out for Philadelphia and shall be back in about a Week. When I must work like a Beaver. Mr Startin Mrs. Copley and myself are in perfect Health. Our Most Effectionate Duty to our Mamma and Except our Love yourself, and remember us to all friends, perticularly to Mr. and Mrs Green. I shall write to him by Smith. Your Effectionate Brother,

JOHN S. COPLEY.

Mrs. Syme to Copley

Mrs. Syme presents her Compliments to Mr. Copely — She has been in Expectation all this Summar of receiving her Father's picture that she understands he has sat for frequently. Will be obliged to Mr. Copely if he will forward it as soon as possible.

LONDON, 21st. Septem'r, 1771.

Henry Pelham to Copley

BOSTON, Septmr. 24, 1771.

DEAR BROTHER

I have only time to acknowledge the Receipt of your's of the 9th Instant and to assure you that it is with greatest Satisfaction that we hear that you and my dear Sister still enjoy that health you have before given me so pleasing an Account of. My Mamma is as well as can be expected. She desires her kindest Love and Blessing to you and my Sister. she takes very kindly the Respectful and tender Sentiments you express for her. We are Glad that you are impatient to see Boston, but are very sorry to find that your buisness will detain you till late in the fall. We must begg that you would not delay coming till the Weather is cold and disagrable. Your directions with regard to the Lawsuit [and] the Repairs at Mount Pleasant shall be observed. I have talked with Capt Joy about the Peazas. he says that he could not possably do them a farthing under 63£ and at that is affraid he shall not be able to make days Wages. I am drawing an Elivation of the House with the Peazzas. it will (if Possable) have the advantage of the first most Beautifull Plan. The Peazzas extend the Front and by their being open makes it appear higher. Comformable to agreement, Capt. Joy put up a small plain square look out, but it has given such generall Disgust that I was obliged to have it taken down. it is the generall Opinion that there ought to be something taisty atop of the House, or nothing at all. For the present I have directed the Roof to be finished with a scuttle. Severall People have applyed to me to know what you propose to do with the upper House, because they would be glad to hire it. Capt. Joy is again Sick. he has been very ill abed these two days. his head is very much swelled and he is not able to speak, occasioned by his catching Cold, after a great Quantity of Physick he had taken.

The Frame and Glass, I should have sent had I not forgot it till after Smith Sailed. At Bottom is the Receipt for Varnish. I have rece[i]ved Money from Messers. Sargent, Fenno, Barrell, Goldthwait, Pepperell, Hancock and Mrs. Watts. I have about 90£ O. T. by me. Mr Jno. Green owes, as also Mr. Flucker, Mr. Loring and Mrs. Martin. These I wait your directions before I apply for the Money. Mr Jno. Clarke told me he should write by this Opertunity. I have not seen Betzey lately. She was well a Few days ago. I intend to see her soon. Painting I am full off. Mr. Barrell going for Philedelphia afords me this Opertunity of writeing. By the way, I hope you and my sister have had a Pleasant Ride. you have become great

Travellers. I wish I could see the Original or a Copy of Mr. West's Letter to you. I have seen his to Mr. Hutchinson. I saw Mr. William to day. he told me that the two great American Artists Mr. Copley and Mr. West almost entirely engaged the attention of the Coniseurs in Britain. I am Obliged to conclude in great Hast with my most affectionate Love and Regards to my dear Sister and your Self. Your most Loving Brother and Humble Sert.

HENRY PELHAM.

P. S. every body desire their Compliments to Mr. and Mrs. Copley.

Copley to Henry Pelham

NEW YORK, the 29 of Sepr., 1771.

DEAR BROTHER,

We have just arrived at this place after a very pleasant Journey. Philadelphia, We thought a place of too much importance not to Visit when we were so near it, and perhaps might never be able to see it so conveniently if we missed this oppertunity. we sett out last Thursday week, the Weather very fine, and reach'd the City on Saturday Eveng. I have seen several fine Pictures with which you would have been Charmed had you been with us. at Mr. Allen's [1] (to Whom General Gage was so obligeing as to give me a letter) We saw a fine Coppy of the Titiano Venus, and Holy Family at whole Length as large as life from Coregio, and four other small half Lengths of Single figures as large as life, one a St Cecelia, an Herodias with John Baptists head, Venus lamenting over the Body of Adonus and I think a Niobe,[2] I cannot be certain. The Venus and Holy

---

[1] William Allen (1710?–1780), chief justice of Pennsylvania.
[2] This was first written Nioby.

Family I will give some account of, the others I will leave till I can give it you by word of mouth. The Venus is fine in Colouring, I think beyand any Picture I have seen. and the Joints of the Knees, Elbows, etc. very Read. and no Gray tints anywhere to be found. the hair remarkably Yellow and I think the face much inferior to any other part of the figure in releiff and Colouring. there is no minuteness in the finishing; everything is bold and easey; but I must observe had I Performed that Picture I should have been happrehensive the figures in the Background were too Strong. The Holy Family is not Equil to the Venus in Colouring; it suffers much by the Comparison, tho I do not think it indiferent in that part neither, but might be pronounced fine in Colouring was not the Venus compaired with it. But what delights us in this picture is that universal finishing and harmoniseing of all parts of it. I have made a slight sketch of it which will give you a better Idea of the Disposition when you see it than any thing I can say. in the Back and fore Ground every leaf and shrub is finish'd with the utmost exactness. The flesh is very Plump, soft and animated, and is possesed of a pleasing richness beyand what I have seen. in short there is such a flowery luxsuriance in that Picture as I have seen in no other. On our return we saw several Pictures at Brunswick. I have no doubt they are by Vandyck. the Date is 1628 on one of them. they were painted in Holland. it is without doubt, I think, Vandyck did them before he came to England. I should be glad you would see when he came to England, and let me know in your Answer to this. in those Portraits there is a freshness equeil to any thing you can conceive. they are ½ lengths and on Board, with all the minuteness of finishing of the orniments belonging to the Dress which is the fashon of the Times. the painting has not suffered any thing from the time they have been painted. they are now as perfect and fresh as ever as if painted but yesterday. I have just been informed Smith sails at 8 o Clock tomorrow and it is now ten o Clock, so this letter designed to go by the Post shall take passage by him; but I promised to write to Mr. Green by Smith. but what can I do? I came to Town at 2 o Clock this Day, and Now hear he sails tomorrow Morn'g. do apologise to Mr. Green in the most Effectual Manner by telling him the truth. give Mrs. Copley's and my Love to Mrs. and Mr. Green.

Sukey and myself are in good health and desire our Effectionate Duty to our Dear Mother, to yourself; our Love and desire to be remembered to all our friends.

please to inform Mr. Clark we are well, and give our Duty to him, etc., etc., etc. let Mrs. Startin know we left her better part safe and well in Philadelphia on Thursday Morng. Sukey has not time to write. Adieu and beleive me Your Affectionate Brother,

JOHN SINGLETON COPLEY.

Copley to Henry Pelham

NEW YORK, 12 of Octr., 1771.

DEAR BROTHER,

Capt Montresor[1] going this Day for Boston give me an oppertunity of informing you we are in good health, and desire our most Effectionate Duty to our Mamma and Love to your self. I received your favour by Mr. Barrell, by which I see who you have received money from, and think the amount to be about 14 hundred pounds, which I should have thought sufficient for Capt. Joy till I return, as the work I suppose will not be quite

[1] John Montresor (1736–1799).

compleat. but be that as it may, I would have you get the money from Green if possable. I wrote you so some time ago and wonder you should weit my orders for that. I would have you be as urgent as possable for it, for I don't think it so safe as I could wish. you know there is an note of hand in the middle Draw of my Desk for it. Get Mrs. Martin's, [and] Mr. Loring's. I should not chuse you should ask Mr. Fluker. I hope you have got Mrs. Dawson's. Likewise some from Hudson, tho you have not menshoned it. I hope you will be able to make out till I return. I should have been Glad you had informed me how much you have paid Mr. Joy. the Bearer Capt. Montresor is a Gentlemen we have received great Civility from. his Lady is Daughter to Docr. Auckmuty[1] to whom I had a letter from Mr. Walter,[2] to whom make my Respectfull Compts. when you have oppertunity, and to all our other friends, perticularly Mr. and Mrs. Green, and beleive me your Effectionate Brother

J. S. COPLEY.

I have parted with the two small frames, but cannot yet give orders for more. because I would have none come but what are engaged. you must let me know the price of the small ones; I know that of the Large ones. let me know what you paid Welch for Carving and Whiting for Gilding and Give my compts. to Capt Joy. tell him I am very sorry for his repeated indisposition. I am in extreem hurry adiew.

[1] Rev. Samuel Auchmuty (1725–1777), assistant minister of Trinity Church, New York.

[2] Rev. William Walter (1739–1800), rector of Trinity and Christ Churches in Boston.

Henry Pelham to James Putnam

SIR,

BOSTON, October 2, 1771.

The Superior Court stands adjourned to the 3d Tuesday of November at which time Mr. Copley hopes his Cause may be bro't to a Tryall. He desired me to enquire from you the time that will be most agreable for you to come to Boston. as I am directed to get that time affixed that will be most convenie[nt] for you. My Brother desired me also to inform you that Mr. Otis's Health is such that he can have no hopes of his Assistance he has entirely given up all thoughts and expectations of obtaining it, and that Mr. Payne is the Gentleman that is to speak with you in the Cause. You will be pleased to give me as early notice as possable of the time you propose to come to Boston.

If there is any Papers, etc. that you may want from this place, I beg you would inform me by a line per Post and they shall be immediatly forwarded.

I am with Respect Sir your most obedient and Humble Servt.

HENRY PELHAM.

Henry Pelham to Miss Barrett

[1771.]

Mr. Pelham presents his respectfull Compliments to Miss Barrett, acknowledges the receipt of 3 Guineas for her portrait. begs leave to return his thanks for the very polite Manner in which she sent them and for the fine present with which they were accompanyed, a present rendered more pleasing and to him most truly valuable by its being the ingenious Work of so fair an Artist.

Mr. Pelham thinks the best way of apollogizeing for remissness in so long neglecting to return his thanks is by telling what is real Truth, that he was ashamed to see Miss Barrett before he had finished the enclosed which he has had so long in hand being prevented by buisn[e]ss and not knowing what she would like. Such as it is Mr. P. now begs Miss B. acceptance of it at the same time wishing it was better.

J. S. Copley and Susanna Copley to Henry Pelham

NEW YORK, 17th Octr., 1771.

DEAR BROTHER,

When I write you soon after my letter by Capt. Montresor you have neither reason to complain of my too long silence nor of remisness if I should not fill my paper. this Eveng. I have devoted to my Drawing, but a small request that you must grant calls me off a few minutes. it is this: if Smith sails by the first of Novr. Sukey would be glad to have the suit of Black that you[r] Mamma gave her sent by him. it is in the bottum of the Trunk that Contains her Linnen. She fears giving our Mamma too much trouble and think you may do it without troubleing her. as we are much in company we think necessary Sukey should have it, as her other Cloaths are mosly improper for her to wear, as she must put on some little mourn'g for her Sister.[1] but if Smith is gone when this come[s] to dont attemp[t] to send it by any other way, nor if he dont sail till the latter end of the first Week in Novr: for we propose Leaveing this place by the last of that month or beg[in]ing of Decr. so that She will do without it as well as she can.[2]

Mr Copley is Call'd of Desirs me to inform you that we are

[1] Mrs. Barrett.
[2] The remainder of the letter is in Mrs. Copley's handwriting.

Jeffries was this day to have accompany'd Mons.r
Blanchard in his Baloon the weather proving
unfavorable it is postponed to the next good Day, which
which I hope will be in season for me to give your
an account of his success before this leaves London

Our Circle being now all assembled in George
Street (and I am happy to add in good health, my father
remarkably so) desire to unite with me in best wishes
that every Blessing may attend yours as well as insin
cere affection to each of them, If ean it will not
be in my power to write to my sister by this oppor
tunity, nor to discharge my Debt to Miss Betsy, but
will take an early oppertunity to do it, I must beg the
excuse of my Friends if I am not so punctual as I ought
to be in this respect; I now that they will not impute it to
neglect —

Adieu my Dear Friend
and believe me to be yours
with much sincerity
J. Copley

well. I have nothing new to add but that I hope the time draws near when we shall have the Happyness of meating our Friends again. in the mean time please to present our Duty to our Mama, Compliments to Miss Maclavin,[1] and except of the Affecti[o]nate Love of your Brother and Sister,

SUSANNA COPLEY.

Henry Pelham to Copley

BOSTON, Octor. 22, 1771.

MY DEAR BROTHER,

I shall not take up your time nor my Paper in describing the Pleasure we take in having a line from you and in hearing that you and my dear Sister are well after an agreable tour to Philedelphia. As Mr. Flagg setts out tomorrow morning for your City and as my time is short I shall without further Circumlocution proceed to inform you that your severell Favours of Septmr. 20th and 29th and Octor. 12 came safe to hand. Captn. Smith did not arrive here 'till last Thursday so that your Letter by him was of an old Date.

I shall answer them in their Order. I have wrote to Coll. Putnam and Mr Payne. Mr. Payne informs me he shall pay the utmost attention to your Cause. your Other Directions respecting it I shall follow. I have endeavoured since you left Boston to be as perticuler as possable in following your Directions; but with regard to the Peazas, I have been obliged to depart a little from your Inclination. Captn. Joy informs me and I believe you will see it yourself, that if it is let alone till the next Season it will cost at least 10£ Lawfull if not 10£ sterg. more, and it will be impossable to do the Work so well. If they are not done now the House must be closed Boarded and Clap-

<hr>

[1] Miss Peggy McIlvaine.

boarded down to the Foundation and Water Tables put round.
The lower Windows must be capped and Cornished. The doors
either not cut out, in which Case it will make a great deal of
Work, or if they are cut out the[y] must be closed at top and
Caped, all which will be thrown away. he says it will not be
possable to unite them so well to the House. He further says
that he is quite disinterested in it, that he shall be but just able
to make days Wages by them, and had much reather (for his
own sake) that they had been left out entirely. As the case was
so situated, as the time was short, and as by your several Letters I found it was your intention that they should be done
some time or other, it left no doubt in my Mind but that you
would think it was best to have them done. I have accordingly
after the maturest Deliberation and advice given Orders for
their being done, hopeing they would meet with your approbation. The Passage to your great Room is very convenient and
worthy of the place it leads to. I don't think the Chinese you
sent by Smith is so hansome as Mr. Vassell's.

In yours of the 29th I have an Account of your Journey
to Philedelphia and a discription of some capitall Pictures. I
should be exceeding happy in having an Opertunity of contemplateing good Coppys after some of the best Artists that
have enriched Europe. I have not been able to ascertain at
what time Vandyck came to England. Fresnoy[1] and Depile[2] are
entirely silent. Walpole amidst all his exactness has neglected
to give us that date. I think it probable that the Pictures at
Brunswick dated 1628, must have been done before Vandyck

---

[1] Du Fresnoy, *De Arte Graphica*. It was translated into French with additions
by De Piles (1661). There are English translations by Dryden (1695), Wills
(1754), and Mason (1783), the last with annotations by Sir Joshua Reynolds,
and afterwards included in Reynolds's Works.
[2] Roger de Piles, *The Art of Painting*.

came to England, for Walpole says "Hearing of the Favour that King Charles shewed to the arts, Vandyck came to England, hoping to be introduced to the King," that "he was not," that "he went away Chagrined, but his Majesty hearing what a Treasure had been within his Reach, ordered Sir Kenelm Digby to invite him over he came and was lodged among the King's Artists at Black Friers. Thither the King went often by Water and viewed his Performances with singuler delight, often sitting to him himself, and bespeaking Pictures of the Queen, his Children and his Courtiers, and Confered the Honour of *Knighthood* on him at St. James's *July 5, 1632*"[1] 4 Years after the date of the Brunswick Picture. I think we may reasonably conclude that those Pictures were done before his arrival at the British Court. It seems very unlikely that so distinguished a Patron of the Arts and so eminent an encourager of Artists as Charles, should suffer Vandyck to remain in his Service four Years without Confering that Mark of his Royal Favour. Your's by Captn Montresor is upon moneyd Matters. by the next opertunity I shall send you a state of your Acct. I should have sent it now but have not time. I must take this Opertunity to make great complaints of Mrs. Dawson. after several delays she has given me to understand that no rent shall be paid 'till you come home, and that you cant be so unreasonable as to expect any till the Place is put into good repair. Mr. Green has got your Letter. he say[s] three quarters of it consists of Apologies, that no printer would undertake to print your Life and Conversation but that in some leasure Hour he will write it. He further desires his and his Ladys Love to you and my Sister. My Mamma is rather unwell has a bad Cold she desires her kindest Love and Blessing to you and my Sister and

[1] Walpole, *Anecdotes of Painting in England* (1762), II. 90.

longs to see you. My Brother and Sister Pelham were in Town a few days ago, present their Love and Compliments. I have heard little Betzey was well a few days ago. she is a fine Girl and is almost able to walk alone. Your things are arrived from London in 13 Weeks from the departure of the Orders. The Glass is very good but 3 Squares out of 184 Broak, and those will cut 10–8. The White Lead I have not opened. The Box contain'g Putty, Brushes, Chalks, etc., has gone down (by the Captns. Mistake) to Salem from whence I expect it every Moment. The Cloths are good. Inclosed is Copy of the Invoice and Letter. Would it not be best to send for some more Paint as 200 lb will not be neer enough to finish both Houses. The Potatoes are dug and a prodegiou[s] Crop. Woodward and I have divided 80 Bushalls between us, that is 40 a peice. I imagine that the Field produced about a Hundred Bushall and most excellent ones they are.

We had like to have had the Town blown about our Ears a few nights ago. A quantity of Oacum in the store Room of the Admiral's Ship adjoining the Powder Room in which was 500 Barrells of Powder, by some Accident took fire and was burnt. The new powder house at the back of the Hill goes on briskly. I believe the Town will be perfectly Secure from it in that Situation, it will be finished in eight Weeks.

The Question is, as Mr. Fayerweather says, shall you be at Home this Fall or shall you not? I am dear Sir with my Love and Compliments to yourself and my Sister, Your Affectionate Brother and Humbl. Sert.

HENRY PELHAM.

P S. I have just found myself in a great Dillemma. I applyed to several Painters for boyled oyl to paint the outside of the

Houses, but to my surprise found that there is none to be had. Mr Gore has but about 30 Gallons, and wont spare a drop of that without I take a proportionable Quantity of Colour. As the Stages are up I have been obliged to bye a hundred lb. of White lead with a proportional quantity of Oil, to carry on the painting. If there is any Linseed Oyl to be had at New York, you had better send a Barrell as soon as possable. Or I think the better way would be to send and bye it at Philedelphia. As this is the time of year that Vessels, come from Philedelphia to Boston, it may be easily done. NB. There will be no Oyle to be had here till the Spring. Yours as above.

H. P.

Copley to Henry Pelham

New York, 6th of Novr, 1771.

Dear Brother,

I have the pleasure to inform you your favour by Mr. Flagg came to hand, after a long silence of four months I had like to have said, but upon recollection find it to be four weeks. I am almost led to beleive you of a Revengefull Temper and that you mean to retaliate with interest. or do you Imagin it gives us no pleasure to hear from you? if you think so I assure you are much mistaken, for be assured it is a pleasure greater than I can express to receive a Letter from you, and as great a disappointment not to receive one when the post comes in. but I must leave this Subject or I shall fill my Paper, and I have a thousand things to say. it gives me much uneasiness to hear our Dear Mama is unwell, but I hope she is better by this time. pray present our most Effectionate Duty to her. We Long much to see you all. I work with extreem application to hasten that happy time which will be by Christmas at farthest, for I now see all my work before me. But it takes up much time to finish all the parts of a Picture when it is to be well finishd, and the Gentry of this place distinguish very well, so I must slight nothing. I beleive you will think I shall do very well to finish the amount of thirty Busts in 20 Weeks, besides going to Philadelphia which took up 2 Weeks of the 20; and this I shall do at least by the time I menshon, and you may be assured it is my determination to be at home at the time I menshoned tho much impertuned to stay. I have been obliged to refuse a great deal of Business here and in Philadelphia. I have done some of my best portraits here, perticularly Mrs. Gage's, which is gone to the Exibition.[1] it is I think beyand Compare the best Lady's portrait I ever Drew; but Mr. Pratt[2] says of it, It will be flesh and Blood these 200 years to come, that every Part and line in it is Butifull, that I must get my Ideas from Heaven, that he cannot Paint etc, etc. I am fatigued; must therefore draw to a close but say somthing first about my Lawsuit. the time Draws near when I hope there will be no impediment to its coming to Tryall. I am sorry you could find nothing on the Chambridge Records, but hope you have taken some thought about that, that is, if possable, by some means to assertain the fact, for it may be of great importance. as to Mr. Quincey I think it is rather Luckey my absence furnish's so good reason for the Lawyers settleing among themselves who shall speak, for you can with no propriety set any one aside to make room for a younger without my express orders, and I never gave you any. therefore they must do what is custommary, and if Mr. Q is so sett as to leave the Cause, you nor I can help it, tho in my

---

[1] Exhibited in 1772, and described in the catalogue as "a lady, half length."

[2] Matthew Pratt (1734–1805), who had studied under Benjamin West. Dunlap, *History of the Arts of Design*, 1. 98.

absence it will be treating me ill in a pecular manner. do you attend the Tryall and mark every point, observe every Surcumstance, and sit at the Lawyer's elbow to be ready to remind him if he should be at a loss.

The Peazas I would not have had done only on this acct, least they should not be done right. But if you are at a loss about any thing Capt. Montresor can and will sett you right with pleasure. one thing observe, that you make the boards of the floor run across, that is the end of the boards to but against the side of the house and let them have a decent of 4 Inches in 10 foot which is the breadth in the Clear of the Peaza. but there is one thing I should chuse different from what Capt. Montresor would make. he would have the boards of the floor at a small distance from each other, to let any warter run through; but I would have them quite Close and as neat as possable. I have been two much ingaged to send the Chinese but will as soon as possable. I am, Dear Brother, Yours Effectionatly,

J. S. COPLEY.

Copley to Henry Pelham

Novr. 24, 1771. NEW YORK.

DEAR BROTHER,

I duly recd. yours of the 17 instan[t] am sorry to find you have been so unwell. hope ere this time you have perfectly recover'd your health; also our Mama, whom we hope ere long to see in her usual health. pray give our Effectionate Duty to her as also Love and comp'ts to all our other friends and acquaintances, etc. We have just come from Mr. Verplank's where we have spent the Even'g; therefore you will I hope excuse my Brevity. you say of my Action it is to come on the 10 Day of Decr.; but why was it not try'd at the Novr. Adjournment? And suppose Coll Putnam should not be well anough, must I submit it to Mr. Pain and Josiah Quincey? I should be loath to, if it be possable to help it. if the Coart met this month I shall think hard of Coll Putnam for puting it off. I design to write to him by Wednesday Post, but dont let that prevent your writing just as if I did not. I have now been weiting upwards of 12 Months for his assistance and shall think myself not well used if I am finially deserted by him; but I will hope better things and weither to advise for tryall or not, if he cannot attend, I am totally at a loss. do give my comp'ts to Mr. Goldthwait and beg him to advise you herein. tell him all Surcumstances, also advise with him about the fees to Mr. Pain and the Quinceys. I think Mr. Paines need not be so much as the Coll's, and S. Quincey wont expect more than an ½ Johanees. Joh Quincey I suppose will not take any if he dont speak; and if Coll. P[aine] dont attend and you shall with advise of Mr. Goldthwait and my other friends bring it on, he was to have five Guineas as proposed by himself. But you must not Look on yourself Tied up by me in any of those matters. I am tired of delays. but I would do nothing rash, you will know more when you write to Coll. Putnam about the prospect there is of his attendance. do be attentive and let Mr. Goldthwait know I have rested the determination on him, and beg he will advise you in it. menshon the Danger of Losing Judge Cuishon and Linds,[1] who are boath old. perhaps my Antagonists wish for the Delay in hope to avail themselves of that advantage. You forgot the frame and Glass and to menshon Betsey. I am, Dear Sir, Your most Effectionate Brother,

JOHN SINGLETON COPLEY.

---

[1] John Cushing and Benjamin Lynde, judges of the Superior Court of Judicature.

P S: Sukey and myself are perfectly well. you have never menshoned in all your Letters Antonio. I am rather inclined to think it better not to have the Tryal without Coll. Putnam; although I know the consiquence will be lengthening out another year, yet I should think this the safest. Brother Startin promis'd me, if you stood in need of some Cash, 20 or 30 Guineas, to supply you. We had some hopes of living this Winter in the upper house ourselves, but you may let Stutson live there if you please.

Henry Pelham to Copley

BOSTON, Novemr. 28, 1771.

DEAR BROTHER,

. . . We have been most remarkably Lucky in Weather for carrying on the Works at Mount Pleasant. It has been and still continues very moderate Weather. The lower House was finished plastering yesterday. The upper House will be finished in a few days.

In your great Room, instead of the common manner of finishing with Arches at the side of the Chimnie I have substituted a Couple of Niches, which have a clever effect and are quite uncommon. They are so large as to receive a Figure 4 feet high. Politicks are reviving in full splendor. The Printer[1] of the *Spy* has fallen under the censure of the Governor and councill, who seem to be endeavouring to revive the justly exploded method of Tryal upon Information, and have arbitrarily ordered a Gentleman to appear at his Perrill before them

---

[1] Isaiah Thomas. In the issue of the *Massachusetts Spy* of November 14 he printed a piece signed "Mucius Scaevola" reflecting upon a clause in a late proclamation of the governor. Hutchinson ordered the King's Attorney to begin a prosecution.

to answer upon Interegatories. They have unfortunatly for themselves and the Publick ingaged Deeply in Measures that must end either in their own dishonor or be the source of the utmost Confusion to the Province. It becomes peculiarly necessary for the People to preserve inviolate what Laws we have already, as it is not likely we shall have any new ones, unless the House at the ensueing Sessions should, as a Writer in the *Spy* says, meanly give up every remaining Privilidge. Our commander in Chief has received instructions from his Lordship of Hillsboro' to consent to no Tax act or other Law, unless the Commissioners and all other Crown Officers are exempted from paying Rates.

We have had several sudden Deaths this Morng Mr. Sheaff [1] the D. Collector died of a fit of the Palsey. He was taken ill the last Eveng. I have not time to add further than that with my best Love and Respects to yourself and my Sister I remain Your most affectionat[e] Brother and Humble Sert.

HENRY PELHAM.

P. S. Every Body present their Compliments to you and beg that you would come home as they want to have their Pictures done. Lord William Campbell, Govornor of Nova-Scotia, was at your Room a few days ago. he says, he wonders, that you bury yourself in this Country and that he thinks you are the greatest Geniou[s] in the World.

Little Cousin Betzey was well and hearty a few days ago. I must now go and write a long story about Thomas Banister and his three Sons, Thomas, Samuel and John and their heirs forever. So I wish you a good Night.

[1] William Sheaffe.

Copley to Henry Pelham

New York, the 15 Decr., 1771.

Dear Brother,

I take this oppertunity of informing you, I have sent by Capt. Smith (who sails this Day) 51 Trees of the Best fruit this Country affoards, also some wild Laurell which I think a very butifull Flowering Shrub. the Laurell is in earth in a Barrell. also 3 Barrels of Newtown Pippens, and as many for Mr. Clarke which I beg you to inform him of, as I dont write to him by this oppertunity. and one trunk Directed to Mr Jonathan Clarke. Likewise the Large Box with the large Frames which I have not been able to Dispose of. your favour per Mr Glover came to hand. we are happy to hear you are all well, and that at last I can inform you this Week finishes all my Business, no less than 37 Busts; so the weather permiting by Chrismass we hope to be on the road; but you must not expect our journey will be less than a fortnight at this season, as we propose to take so much care of ourselves, and which we may very well do, as the Country is surprisingly settled between Boston and York. you scarcely lose sight of an house. you may omit writing any more as we cannot expect to meet another Letter here wrote after this reaches you.

Give our Effectionate Duty to our Hond Mama and except our sincere Love yourself. I am your most Effectionate Brother,

John Singleton Copley.

PS. please to Give our Duty to Mr. Clarke, Love, etc. to our Brothers and Sisters, etc., etc., etc.

John Hancock to Copley

Mr Hancock [1] presents his Complimts. to Mr. Copley, has just rec'd his Message, is extremely sorry it so happens, but the Lady to whom he Refers has been some days Confin'd, that she is not in a Situation to wait on him to morrow but the moment her health will admit, Mr. Hancock will with pleasure inform Mr. Copley. Mr. Hancock hopes Mrs. Coply and Connections are well.

9 Jan'y. 1772.

[   ] to [*Montresor?*]

[January, 1772.] [2]

MY EVER DEAREST COUSIN,

It has been a matter of great concern to me that I coul'd not send you the things I now do, by the Ships that went from hence the last Autumn; I did not receive your Letter dated 17 Augt. untill the 6th Novr. following. Captn. Stephens told me he had met with severe Gales, which had oblig'd him to put back to New York; at the time of his Arrival here all the Ships for America were gone. I must also appoligize for not having wrote by the Packet, which I shou'd certainly have done had I not been severely afflicted with the Rheumatism in my stomach and Bowels, under which disorders I still Labour tho not in so great a Degree and I have hopes of getting still better. I purchac'd a Lottery Tickett as you directed the No. 17 m 697, which I had secur'd as your property, by an Endorsment declaring it to be yours, and witness'd by two of your hearty well wishers, Henry Austen Esq., and Mr. Rd. Jones both of

---

[1] The name has been erased but the H and k are still legible.
[2] So endorsed by Henry Pelham.

the Searchers Office; it had not the Sucess I ardently wish'd, yet you have your Money again. after remaining in the Wheel of Fortune untill the last Day of finishing, it was drawn a prise of 20£, which I have sold for £17 : 16. Goverment deducts £10 per Cent on all prises, so that you are only a gainer of £4.6 by your chance. you will see by the inclos'd account and by the Bills and receipts which are pack'd up by my good Girl in one of the Boxes, that we have been obligd in several articles to exceed the price Limited, but we were under a necessity of doing so, or not getting the things in which we have so exceeded agreeable to the opinion of my wife, whose judgment on these occasions I never contest; she writes to your beloved, and I hope will give a good account of her self, if one can judge, by the alacrity with which she sets about it, and the pleasure which seems to animate her she will succeed. I am under some apprehension in respect to the Liverys, the Hat and Cap, as you did not give any demensions for them, I have them [made] rather of the largest size, as it is more easy to take in, than let Out, in other respects I hope they will be as you desire; I do not send you a Brawn as I imagine it wou'd not be in proper season; but if you please I will by the next Autumnal Ships send one which will be in Time for Christmas; I have several acquaintance in Oxfordshe which County is held famous for that meat. from thence I propose to send it. The picture frames are not of *Carlo Marratti* kind, they are at present not the Taste. the person I employ'd agreed to make them at the price propos'd, but with some hesitation. I insisted they shou'd be done very neatly and well Gilt or desir'd him not to undertake them, as I wou'd rather pay something more then have them clumsely executed, he promis'd they shou'd be well done. I hope they will prove so. Let me congratulate my Dear Friend on having employ'd so ingenious an Artist as Mr. Copley. our people here are enraptur'd with him, he is compard to Vandyke, Reubens and all the great painters of Old. I saw one of his portraits at Mr. Wests. it was of a Woman [1] and a very ordinary one, and yet so finely painted that it appeard alive. West was lavish in its praises, pointed out its beauties, the natural fall of the arm and hand, the delicate manner in which the light was carried thro the whole, and many other things which I forget; in short he said Mr. Copley wou'd make no small figure in the World of Painters, and told me that your portrait was admirably well executed, and I wish you joy of it. I receiv'd some time ago a Letter from Coll. Montresor, in which he tells me he laments the expence he has been at, for his Lands in America, that they will never be of any advantage to him (unhappily what he only considers) and desires me to try if I cannot let them for him to some Merchant adventurer, on Lease of 99 Years at 6*d* per Acre, I have been so Ill that I could not answer his Letter, neither did I intend, farther than to amuse him, untill I had consulted you. I do not apprehend any Person will give 6*d* per Acre for Lands in America that must be settled and Cultivated at great expence; but I am afraid that the same consideration which induces him to wish to Let these Lands will also prompt him to sell them, if he can get £100 or so by them; in which case they wou'd be lost to you and your family to whom hereafter they may be of the greatest advantage; therefore if what I conjecture shou'd take place what Method cou'd be taken to put a stop to it? and if they were to be sold, wou'd it be not proper for you to be the purchaser rather than a Stranger? or supposing you wrote to him, telling him there was a better chance of Letting them in New York

[1] Mrs. Devereux?

then in England; by which means you might gain time to deliberate what resolution to take. any instructions you can give me relative to it I will endeavour to execute, for I heartily wish he may not sell these Lands for the reasons I have men- tion'd. I have a strang piece of News from Denmark. The Article says that the Young Queen has long been suspected to have carried on an Intrigue with her Physician (a Scotch Man who went from England when she married).[1] The Populace suddenly broke into the Palace imprison'd the Queen, and (it is said) put the Physician to Death;[2] Time only can clear up this Matter; perhaps it may be an Intrigue carried on by the Queen Dowager,[3] who jealous of the legal Power being soley in the hands of the Young Princess, might wish to [*incomplete*]

Henry Pelham to [*Miss Peggy McIlvaine?*]

BOSTON, March 1st. 1771 [1772].

DEAR MISS PEGGY,

Your agreable Favour of Jany. 28 1772 came to hand but a few days ago. By it we have the Pleasure of finding that You, Your [Sister] Mrs. Billings and family were well. Had not Mr. Buttler told us that he saw you well at Falmouth, I should have been uneasy for you[r] safe Arrival at home. My Mamma who is tolerably well desires her kindest Love to [you] and Mrs. Billings and is exceeding glad to hear from you. We were really quite lonesome after you Left us, and much wanted your good Company. As my time is short I must briefly tell you some Peice of News. Brother and Sister Copley, have returned after seven Months abscence in Charming hea[l]th. they arived the

---

[1] Carolina Matilda, wife of Christian VII, and mistress of Struensee.

[2] He was beheaded April 28, 1772.

[3] Juliana Maria, widow of Frederick V.

Third of January. Left York Chrismass day, had a fine Season for Travelling and luckely finished their Journey, before the Weather sot in very severe. the[y] have spent a most agreable Summer abroad, and have been highly Carressed. they present their Comts. to all their Friends at Casco. While you was in Boston I think you was knowing to some of the difficul[ties] I underwent with regard to a Lawsuit my Brothe[r] had with Banis[ter]. I have now the Pleasure of informing you that the Tryall Came on Last Thursday when the Case was determind fully in Mr Copleys favour. The Houses at Mount Pleasant are not yet finished. My Brother expects to get into one of them the Begining of next Month. Your Friend Mr. Hancock drew the day before yesterday 1500 Dollars the Highest Prise in the Present Lottery. he had seven tickets; one is not yet drawn, two were blancks, the other four p[r]ises. this is the second tim[e] he has drawn the Highest Prise. By the Papers I suppose you have seen that he has given the most generous sum of 7500£ [1] towards rebuilding Dr. Coopers Mee[t]ing house. To tell you that We have had a most severe, Cold, and disagreabl[e] Winter will be telling you what I fancy you must know already. Little Cousin Betzsey is very well. Snap has behaved himself exceeding well. I have not time to ad further at present, than In my Mama's Name and for myself to salute you wishing you Mrs. Billings and Family all Health and Happyness, and hoping to have the pleasure of your Company in the Spring. in the mean Time we beg that you would let us hear frequently from you. I am Dear Madam your sincer[e] Friend and Humble Sert.

H. P.

[1] The records show that he gave £1000 and a bell. Lothrop, *History of the Church in Brattle Street*, 101.

Mr. Copley and Lady present their best respect[s] to you your Sister and Family.

We are exceeding sorry for Mr. Tyngs very considerable Loss.

Isaac Smith, Jr.[1] to Copley

[1772.][2]

Mr Is. Smith jr. presents his compliments to Mr Copley, and begs leave to inform him, that he has met with an extract, whh. he made from Sir C's letter in *Anderson's Hist. and Constit. of Masonry* (as it was not his own), but that the principal circumstance in it is what he has already mentioned to Mr. Copley, i.e. with regard to placing a pulpit, he observes, "a moderate voice may be heard 50 feet in front, 30 on each side, and 20 behind the preacher." Anderson's book may probably be found among some of the worshipful fraternity in town.

James Bowdoin to Copley

[1772.]

Mr. Bowdoin's respectful Compliments to Mr Copley.

He thinks wth. Mr. Copley the Pilaster cannot be objected to on account of its projection and if the Comtee. shd. not think the Entablature too expensive, it probably may be the best Method to finish the Front: concerning wch. Mr. Copley is the best judge.

Monday Eveng.

[1] Son of Isaac Smith, brother of Mrs. John Adams.

[2] Pelham had endorsed this note 48, the first one from James Bowdoin which follows, 49, and the extracts from the *Records of the Church in Brattle Square*, 50. The second note from James Bowdoin has no endorsement.

[James Bowdoin] to Copley[1]

Memo.   [1772]

Mr. Copley will please to delineate on the Plan eleven Pews
on one Side of the Pulpit and ten on the other; all of an equal
width viz: 3 feet and a little more than 3 Inches each.

The Brattle Street Church[2]

At a Meeting of the Committee for rebuilding the Meeting
House in Brattle Street June 11th, 1772. Present, the Honble
JAMES BOWDOIN, Esq. Chairman, the Honble JAMES PITTS, Esq.,
the Honble JOHN HANCOCK, Esq.

MR. SMITH	MR. PAYNE
MR. NEWELL	MR. BRATTLE
MR. GRAY	

The Committee had laid before them the plan and Elevation of
a Meeting House, with the Steple compleat, exhibited by Mr.
Copeley, which was much admired for its Elegance and Grandure;
but upon making an Estimate of the Expence that would attend
the carrying the Design into Execution, it appeared that it would
much exceed the Funds the Society depended on for the purpose,
and for that Reason it was laid aside. Whereupon, a Motion being
made and seconded, it was unanimously Voted, that Mr Storer be
desired to wait upon Mr. Copeley and make him acquainted there-
with; at the same Time to tender him the Thanks of the Committee for the great Pains and Trouble he had been at, and so desire he
would let the Committee know what would be an adequate Compensation for the same.

At a Meeting of the Committee August 3rd, 1772, Present the

---

[1] This note is in the same handwriting as the preceding one.

[2] These notes are not printed in *Records of the Church in Brattle Square*.

Honble JAMES BOWDOIN, Esq., Chairman the Honble JAMES
PITTS, Esq., the Honble JOHN HANCOCK, Esq.,

MR. SMITH   MR. GRAY
MR. STORER   MR. PAYNE
MR. NEWELL   MR. BRATTLE

The Committe being informed that by Reason of Mr. Storer's
Absence when they passed upon Mr. Copeley's Plan on the 11th
of June, he was not so fully apprised of their Determination, therefore Voted unanimously, that Mr. Storer, together with Mr. Gray,
be desired to wait upon Mr. Copley in Person, and present him
with a Copy of their Vote passed the 11th of June last, and to
thank him in the name of the Committee.

A true Copy, as of Record, Attest,

THOMAS GRAY, *Secretary to the Committee.*

William Carson to Copley

NEWPORT, 16th Augt., 1772.

MR. COPELY,

Mrs. Gibbes and Mrs. Carson are arrived in that good health
and beauty in which I wished to see them. The longer I look,
the better I am pleased. I discover new beautys every day, and
what was considered as blemishes, now, raises the most exalted
Ideas of the perfection of the Painter "and painting to the life."
Mrs. Carson's picture, which is by much the most natural and
just painting I have seen of yours, only shews, what you are
capable of executing. Your painting of the Squirrel was a
modest production, and your picture of Mrs. Gray in Crayons
could only testify, that in Boston there was one fine face, and
you, a man of some Genius. Neither, could point out your
Genius, qualitys or perfections as a Painter. You are unknown

to the world and yourself. Rise but in your own opinion, and you will attempt something worthy of yourself, and then every judge will bestow on you that applause which you justly merit. A painter of faces gains no reputation among the multitude, but from the Characteristick strokes in the outlines. Life and expression require judgement and knowledge. You really are and ought to consider yourself inferiour to no Portrait Painter in England.

I doubt much if there is your superiour in Europe. I use the term generally, as a Copier of nature, from any object, and I consider you can paint a Horse, Cow, Squirrel or fly as justly as a Man or woman from the life. Why do you not attempt it? Strange objects strongly strike the senses, and violent passions affect the mind. To gain reputation, you should paint something new, to catch the sight and fix the attention.

I must think, if you would paint such a piece, as a Child in the Cradle, sick. — the mother applying some remedy, her face and attitude expressing hope and fear, a Sympathizing nurse, officious in her duty, a Doctor standing by, of strong features, and wig in Character, recommending his Nostrums in a Vial, Bolus, or box, some female friend looking on with indifference. Contrasting the objects — Suppose your wife and child, the nurse old and black of complexion, the Physician long visaged, covered under a hideous wig, pale complexion and his baird two or three days old, and such a Young Lady looking on, eligantly dressed, as the youngest Miss Fitch; all, in a bed Chamber with such furniture as to show the mother and child of genteel rank. Such you could copy from the life and from such paintings, only, will your merit be known. Any piece of that kind, altho, it might cost you time and trouble will gain you more money and reputation than all you can get by face painting in Seven years. Send such a piece home before you go, it will be the best recommendation and you will be received there with Eclat. Be not afraid to make the experiment, for you will please and surprise the best judges, tho you may not immediately please yourself. You'll readily forgive me for my presumption in giving advice, knowing, that I mean well, however unqualified.

I wish to hear of your arrival in England; in the mean time would be glad to hear from you, and to render you every service in my power.

I am, Sir, Your sincere friend and hum. Servt.

WM. CARSON.

Mrs. Margaret Mascarene to Henry Pelham

SALEM, Sept. 14th, 1772.

SIR

My Sister told me some time since that she did not think you would be able to take a good likeness of my late Father, on so small a piece of Copper as I proposed to you. I write now to let you know that I had full as lives have it on a larger. the size enclosed I think a pretty one, I have one of this, that looks very well, and if a glass can be got for it I should prefer it to a smaller, but I submit to your Judgement in the Matter, a likeness is what I want, otherwise the picture will be of no value to me, save as a piece of paint. I was in hopes to have seen you before this, but it has not been in my power. I hope it will be finishd before Cold weather. My Complements to Mr. Copely. I am with regards your humble Servant,

MARGARIT MASCARENE.[1]

[1] Margaret, daughter of Edward Holyoke, president of Harvard College, married John Mascarene (1722–1778), comptroller of the customs in 1760. He was son of Jean Paul Mascarene (1684–1760).

Jonathan Clarke to Copley

LONDON, Decr. 20, 1772.

DEAR BROTHER,

I recd. your obliging Letter of Nov. 8th, the subject of which is so important that you'll excuse me if I put you to the charge of some shillgs for several answers; there will be no Vessell sail from hence directly to Boston in less than two Months and having heard that the [Jany.][1] Pacqt. is detain'd by contrary winds, I took the chance of sending a Letter to Falmo. last Evening and there being one bound to So. Cara. I intend this per her, as its probable she may have a good passage at this time of year. but neither of those conveyances will be safe eno' for Mr. West to send an answer to your Lettr. to him. he will write you by the Jany. Pacquet, and if this should come to hand first let me acquaint you, that Mr. West approves and commends your resolution of coming to Europe and confirms the advice given you by Mr. Palmer as to going first to Italy in one of our Fish Vessells to Leghorn. he thinks that there will be nothing in England that will require you to take this in your way. you may depend upon the most friendly and disinterested advice as well as every assistance in his power that will conduce to make your travels beneficial and agreeable to you. for this end he will send you a Letter to a friend of his at Leghorn, who will give you Letters to the other places you pass thro'. you will also receive from him a Lettr to a Gentleman at Rome who did him eminint services and who will be happy in doing the same for a friend of Mr. West's. he would advise you to tarry some months for a good conveyance to Leghorn rather than to take shipping for England, as it will save you a good deal of trouble

[1] Erased.

and some expence. Tho' I think this last article need not deter your comeing this way, if it is the only thing that will influence your bringing Sister with you. for besides your expences in London which will depend upon the time you tarry here, the charge of traveling from hence to Rome will be about 30 Guineas, and when you have got there you'll find it a very cheap Country. you and your wife may live there genteely for about one hundred pounds per Ann. it cost Mr. West about that Sum and he had a companion much less agreable and he thinks as expensive as a wife, I mean sickness, altho' it is in general a healthy place, except in the fall of the year at which time you will go to visit other parts of Italy, where you'll meet with entertainment and improvement. but Mr. West has an objection to your carrying Mrs. Copley to Italy with you, and that is the attention so good a wife will require from so good a Husband, and which it's probable will be so much as to retard you in the pursuit of the grand object. he says the eighteen Months or two years that he supposes you to be in Rome will be the most important period of your life, and will require a constant application, and perhaps your having a Lady with you will oblige you to cultivate such acquaintance in order to make it agreeable to her as will not be necessary on any other acct, or such as you would not if you were alone. for these reasons it seems to be his opinion that you had better go alone. perhaps Mr. West does not know what little trouble your wife will be. but however from him you will have a particular answer to your inquirys. When I first came to England I met with Mr. Hale[1] our former Collector, who I found was a friend of your's, and who spake highly of your Pictures and much encouraged your comeing to England, not doubting that you

---

[1] Roger Hale.

would meet with the greatest encouragement in this place where every thing gives way to the gratification of peoples fancy. When I came to London, I found Mr. West a great admirer of your Portraits. you seem to think by your Lettr to him that the one you last exhibited was not esteemed so good a one, but Mr. West thinks you was under a mistake, for Mrs. Gage's Picture was tho't a very fine one. only some of her friends who had never seen her tho't it was not like, because she had been represented as very handsome. Mr. West thinks you have a very good adviser in Mr. Palmer, as much so as if he was a great artist himself. he is spoke of with the highest respect, as having employed his time and money very judiciously, and whose improvement has been great and made him very ornamental to his Country. all the objection we can have to our friends traveling is that after they have been some time abroard and much improved themselves, and been used to the society of Men of Literature and attached to the polite arts, upon their return they find our young Country don't furnish a great number of the same relish and therefore are obliged to seek them in older Countrys where it is reasonable to suppose they more abound, so that our Country is check'd in its improvement. now I hope better things of you, than a disposition which is rather selfish. I hope Mr. Palmer will be so attached to his native Country as to settle there. Mr. West acquaints me that a Lettr. is about 16 days traveling from Rome, so that if you should leave Mrs. Copley at Boston she may hear from you as frequent as if you was in England, if there's no fault on your part.

If my discription of Manchester, etc. give you any pleasure I am glad and I would willingly increase it by adding that of Londo[n], but its magnificence and grandeaur discourage all attempts of that sort. I lodge in St. Paul's Church yard where

I have an opporty. to observe tho' not sufficiently to admire that grand and elegant Pile.

I am glad to observe the progress you have made in finishing the Buildings, which you'll wish you had not began before you had seen those in Europe as you have now a prospect of it: tho' perhaps it will make one more attachment to your native Country.

It will not be agreeable after having lived in Rome for about £100 to come into this Country to spend five, for Mr. West says it bears that proportion; but you'll doubtless consider that the more you save there the more you'll be enabled

to spend here; for here money will go and you Sons of Liberty will find some times without your consent. I am glad to find Sukey and your little family are well. give my love to them, and, Dr. Sir, pray accept of my hearty wishes for your health and happiness as well as success in all your enterprizes.

Please to give my Duty to Papa. I was favor'd with his Lettr: per Capt. Calef. I shall write him per Jany. Pacqt. my Duty and love to all and believe me to be, Your affectio. Brother,

JONA. CLARKE.

P. S. 22d: the weather has been very fine from my first arrival in England till this day which is the darkest I ever saw.

Endorsed: Charlestown, 4th March. Recd. under cover and forwarded by your most Humb Servt., ·

NATHL. RUSSELL.

Benjamin West to Copley

DEAR SIR,

Some days past Your Brother Mr. Clark delivered into my hands your letter of the 8th of Novr., Which informed me of your intended Tour into Italy, and the desier you express'd of receiveing my Opinion on that Subject. I am still of the opinion the going to Italy must be of the greatest advantage to one advanced in the arts as you are, As by that you will find what you are already in possession of, and what you have to acquier.

As your jurney to Italy is reather to finish a studye then to begin one; Your stay in that country will not requier that length of time that would be necessery for an Artist less advanced in the Arts then you are; But I would have that time as uninterrupted as possible. And for this reason I would have you make this Tour without Mrs. Copley. Not that she would be of any great aditional expance, But would reather bring you into a mode of liveing that would throw you out of your Studyes. So my Advice is, Mrs. Copley to remain in Boston till you have made this Tour, After which, if you fix your place of reasidanc in London, Mrs. Copley to come over.

In regard to your studyes in Italy my advice is as follows: That you pursue the higher Exalances in the Art, and for the obtaining of which I recommend to your attention the works of the *Antiant Statuarys, Raphael, Michal Angilo, Corragio,* and *Titian*, as the Sorce from whance true tast in the arts have flow'd. There ware a number of great artist in Italy besides thoss, But as they somewhat formd their manner in paint from the above artists, they are but second place painters. The works of the Antient Statuarys are the great original whare in the various charectors of nature are finely represented, from

Newman Street June 7. 1817 —

Dear Sir

    With this Note you and Mrs Adams will receive a Print and Medal of my likeness, the Print is for yourself and the Medal for Mrs Adams: they are considered by the admi= =ers of the Fine Arts, as Excellent in booth of the branches of Arts, as well as in likeness, and as such I request you both will honour me by accepting them as a small token of my high regard for my two American friends.

    On the reverse of the Medal are the Names of those Noblemen and Gentlemen who were solicitous of possessing my Picture of Christ in the Temple, as the commencement of a British Gallery; and your depositing the Print and Medal in your Family, will be considered an honour by Dear Sir

        yours with profound respect

J. Q. Adams Esqr   Benjⁿ West

the soundest principles of Philosophi. What they have done in Statuary, Raphael, seems to have acquiered in painting. In him you see the fine fancey in the arraignment of his figures into groops, and those groops into a whole with that propriety and fitness to his subject, Joynd to a trouth of charector and expression, that was never surpass'd before nor sence. Michal Angilo in the knowledge and graundor of the Human figure has surpass'd all artists. his figures have the apearance of a new creation, form'd by the strength of his great amagination. in him you find all that is great in design. Corragio, whose obscurety in life deprived him of those aids in the art which Michal Angilo and Raphael had,[1] and which prevented his acquiering those Exalances, which so charectoris'd them. But there are other beuties in the art he greatly surpass'd even those in and all others that came after him. Which was in the relieaf of his figures by the management of the clear obscure. The prodigious management in foreshortning of figures seen in the air, The greacefull smiles and turnes of heads, The magickcal uniteing of his Tints, The incensable blending of lights into Shades, and the beautyfull affect over the whole arrising from thoss pices of management, is what charmes the eye of every beholder. Titian gave the Human figure that trouth of colour which surpass'd all other painters. His portraits have a particuler air of grandour and a solidity of colouring in them that makes all other portraits appear trifling. I recommend to your attention when in Italy the workes of the above artists, as every perfection in the art of painting is to be found in one or another of their works. I likewise recommend your going directly to Italy by sea as that will carry you through in one voyage if you land in England first you will have to traval the Continant twice.

[1] The antique statues. [*West's note.*]

I have not time, by this oppertunity to write your letters of recommendation, but another will offer in a few days when Mr. Clark has undertaken to send them.

The Honor your workes have allways done you in Our Exhibitions is the very reason you should perservear in the Tour to Italy. the portrait of Mrs. Gage as a picture has received every praise from the lovers of arts. her Friends did not think the likeness so favourable as they could wish, but Honour'd it as a pice of art. Sir Joshua Reynold and other artists of distinguished merrit have the Highest esteem for you and your works.

I Wish you all Happyness and success, and am with great Friendship Your Obedt. Humble Sert.

BENJN. WEST.

LONDON, Jany. 6th, 1773.

Benjamin Andrews to Henry Pelham

Mr. Andrews presents his Compliments to Mr. Pelham, and would be greatly obliged if he could finish his picture in season to be brought home by Saterday; as Mrs. A, agreeable to custom, expects much company next week, and would be glad to have our vacant frames occupied.

The reason of this request is, on account of some Alteration in the Landskip which Mr. Copely said Mr. *Pelham* was to make; excepting which, Mr. A's picture was done, and Mrs. A's has been finish'd some time.

MONDAY P.M. March, 1773.

Henry Pelham to John Singleton

BOSTON, August 3d, 1773.

DEAR AND HONORED UNCLE,

The difficulty of Conveying a Letter to Ireland perticularly to that part where you reside has hitherto prevented my tendering you those marks of my Duty esteem and affection which the distance between us will permitt and the duty I owe to the Brother of an honored and most excellent Parent demands. But a Gentleman Mr. Auch[mut]y going immediatly to Dublin affords me an opertunity of presenting myself with my most affectionate duty before you, as a Nephew who is exceedingly solicitous of obtaining your favour and Corespondence. My honored Mamma has been (as well as myself and My Brother Copley) very an[x]ious at Not hearing from you for near four years past. Indeed within that time Brother Copley had one Letter from Aunt Cooper by which we had the inexpressable pleasure of hearing that all our Friends in Ireland were well. Distance of Place and length of time has not in the least abated that affectionate Concern she alwa[y]s entertained for a Friend so near and dear to her and for whom she expresses the most affectionate and tender Regard. For my self I can most truly say, that, till I can have the pleasur[e] of seeing my dear Fri[e]nds in Irel[a]n[d] and it would be my greatest happyness to cultivate even that imperfect acquaintance which distance of Place only permitts by a regular Corespondence.[1] H[e] proposes this fall or the next spring at farthest upon the recommendation of his numerouse Fri[e]nds both in Europ and

---

[1] What precedes and what follows were two widely separated fragments. There is nothing to show that they belong together except the context and the marked similarity in the appearance of the handwriting.

America to make the tour of Italy France and England. When he arr[i]ves he intends if possable to take a turn over and see you and his other F[r]i[e]nds in Ireland. I intended to have given you a Larger and more perticular Account, but not knowing of this Opertunity of writing till a few hours ago, and the Gentleman who favours me by taking the care of this setting out before Sun Rise tomorrow morning for Portsmouth, where the post Vessell sails from, obliges me by shortining this Letter to lessen the pleasure I take in thus imperfectly conversing with you, a pleasure which I propose resuming the very fi[r]st opertunity I can get to convey a Letter to you, and my other Friends. but before I conclude this I am to present My Mamma's most tender and affectionat[e] Love with My Brother and our most affectio[nate] regards [to] you, My dear Aunt Singleton, Uncle and Aunt Cooper, and all our dear Cousins, and permitt me to join them in most Earnest Entreaties that you would write and give us a perticular Account of your and my Aunt Cooper's family. Requesting your Blessing I conclude Wishing you and connections all Health and Happyness by subscribing myself your Most Dutifull Nephew and most Humble Sert.

HENRY PELHAM.

Henry Pelham to [Stephen Hooper]

BOSTON, Septmr. 9th, 1773.

SIR,

Agreable to your directions I have done your portrait in Minature and have had it sett in Gold.[1]

1 A fragment.

Stephen Hooper[1] to Henry Pelham

NEWBURY PORT, 19th Sept., 1773.

SIR

Your Letter, dated the 9th Instant, I did not receive untill last Evening; wherein I find you had compleated my Portrait in Miniature, and that it was ready to be delivered to my Order; for which I am obliged; and now enclose you an Order on Coll. Snelling, for the Amount, and should be obliged you'll deliver the same to him, to be forwarded. I could wish Our Friend Mr. Copely, had made equal Dispatch with Mrs. Hoopers[2] Picture, as we want it much; however, I suppose him much hurried, as I hear he has engaged his Passage, but hope he'll finish it ere he leaves his Native Place; Mrs. Hooper joins me, in our respectfull Compliments to him, his Lady and yourself; and believe me to be Your Friend,

STEPHEN HOOPER.

Henry Pelham to Charles Pelham

BOSTON, Novr. 5, 1773.

MY DEAR BROTHER,

Amidst the Noise and disturbance of a turbulant and factious town it is with pleasure that I contemplate those of my Friends, who far removed from all the busy Sceanes arising from the Ambition, the Envy and the Vices of Mankind, have opertunity and Leasure calmly to enjoy the rational Delights of a Country Life, where uninterrupted by the Idle and the vicious, an universal Freedom reigns and social Happyness and Domestic Felicity are only to be found in perfection. The transactions

[1] See Currier, *History of Newburyport*, II. 193.   [2] Sarah Woodbridge.

around me for several days past makes me wish[1] to taist the Happyness of that retired Life which I always pleased my self with the Hopes of being able at some future Pe[r]iod to obtain.

The various and discordant Noises with which my Ears are continually assaild in the day, [the] passing of Carts and a constant throng of People, the shouting of an undis[c]iplined Rabble the ringing of bells and sounding of Horns in the night when it might be expected that an universal silence should reign, and all nature weary with the toils of the day, should be composed to rest, but inste[a]d of that nothing but a confused medley of the ratlings of Carriages, the noises of Pope Drums and the infernal yell[2] of those who are fighting for the possessions of the Devill. the empty Noise, useless Hurry impertinence and Ceremony attendant upon a town Life are a perfect contrast to the felicity of a rural retreat, which Pliny elegantly discribes. There, says he, I hear nothing that I repent to have listened to. I say nothing, that I repent to have uttered. No person under my Roof vents any Scandal. No hopes deceive me. No fears molest me; no Rumours disturbs me. My book and my thoughts are the only companions with whom I converse. Welcome thou life of I[n]tegrity and Virtue! Welcome sweet and innocent Amusement! I am Led to these thoughts and these Wishes by the very disagreable situation of this Town in general and some of My Friends in perticular. I have been several days attentively observing the movements of our Son's of Liberty, which was wonce (like the word Tyrant) an honorable distinction. A short Sketch of their procedings may not be disagreable as nothing in the Papers is to be depended

---

[1] This was first written: "almost makes me wish myself upon some Desert Island."

[2] Erased: "of the Children of Satan."

[upon.] Last tuesday Morng. a considerable Number of Printed papers was pasted up, directed to the freemen of the Province inviting them to meet at Liberty Tree at 12 oClock the next day to receive the resignation upon Oath of those Gentle'n to whom the India Company have consigned their Tea of their Commission and their promise of reshiping it by the first opertunity. The above handbills were signed O. C. sec'y. The next morn'g incendiary Letters were sent at 2 oClock to those gen[t]ln. sign'd O. C. sec'y, commanding upon their Perril their attendance at 12 oClock at Liberty Tree. This summons the Gentlemen took no other notice of than by assembling at Mr. Clark's[1] Store, where a considerable Number of their Friends mett them. A little before one o Clock, a Committee consisting among others of Mr. [William] Molineux, Wm. Denny, [Gabriel] Johonnott, Henderson, Drs. [Joseph] Warren and I think [Benjamin] Church came down (attended by the whole body, consisting of about 300 People) with a Message in which [*incomplete*][2]

Thomas Palmer[3] to Copley

Mr. Palmer presents his Compliments to Mr. Copley, and sends him two Letters wch he beleives will answer his Purpose in Italy. He wishes him success, and cannot but say he wishes him gone.

Tuesd Morning.

[1] Richard Clarke and Sons.

[2] See 2 *Proceedings*, x. 79. The story of the notice served on Richard Clarke, November 1, is told in Stark, *Loyalists of Massachusetts*, 405. A reply prepared by the merchants is reproduced from a copy in the Massachusetts Historical Society.

[3] Thomas Palmer (1743–1820), a loyalist, died in London. He left his library to Harvard University.

TRADESMEN'S PROTEST

AGAINST THE

PROCEEDINGS

OF THE

MERCHANTS.

Relative to the New IMPORTATION of TEA.

Addreſſed to the TRADESMEN and INHABITANTS of the Town and Province in general, but to the TRADESMEN of BOSTON in particular.

☞ *AVOID THE TRAP.* *Remember the iniquitous Non-Importation Scheme.* ☜

BOSTON, Nov. 3, 1773

WHEREAS we have repeatedly been impoſed upon by the Merchants of the Town of BOSTON, and hereby incurred heavy Taxes upon us, and we ſtand unjuſtly charged with the ſame : And as it is now propoſed by ſaid Merchants to prevent the Importation of Tea from the India Company, whereby that Article may be ſold or leſs than half the Price they can afford it ; who now call for our Attendance for that Purpoſe at Liberty-Tree, you are hereby adviſed and warned by no means to be taken in by the *deceitful Bait* of thoſe who falſely ſtile themſelves Friends of Liberty.

THE

PROTEST.

We the TRADESMEN of the Town of BOSTON therefore PROTEST againſt ſaid Meeting in the following Manner, Viz.

I. THAT the preſent propoſed Meeting is illegal and underhanded ; and as it is our humble Opinion that it is ſubverſive of that CONSTITUTIONAL LIBERTY we are contending for, and that ſuch Proceedings will tend to create Diſorder and Tumult in the Town, it is earneſtly wiſhed every well-diſpoſed Member of the Community would uſe his Endeavors to prevent them in future.

II. THAT the Method of notifying ſaid Meeting is mean and deſpicable, and ſmells of *Darkneſs* and *Deceit*, as the Notification for warning the ſame was not ſigned, and was poſted in the Night.

III. WE are reſolved, by Divine Aſſiſtance, to walk *uprightly*, and to eat, drink, and wear whatever we can *honeſtly* procure by our Labour ; and to Buy and Sell when and where we pleaſe ; herein hoping for the Protection of good Government : Then let the *Bellowing* PATRIOT throw out his thundering Bulls, they will only ſerve to ſooth our Sleep.

THE TRUE SONS OF LIBERTY.

Printed by E. RUSSELL, next the Cornfield, Union-ſtreet.

Thomas Palmer to James Byers [1]

BOSTON, Novr. 10th, 1773.

DEAR SIR,

This will be deliver'd you by Mr. John Singleton Copley, who proposes spending a year or two in Italy, to improve himself in his Profession as a Painter. His Character as a Gentleman is unexceptionable, as an Artist, you will soon discover his Merit I have advis'd him to spend the most of his time at Rome, and I hope you'll be so obliging as to introduce him to some of his Brethren in the Arts. I am with great Regard your Friend and humb. Servt.

THOS. PALMER.

Au Chevalier Hamilton Bart. [2] *ministre Plenipotentitiare de sa majesté Brittanique à Naples*

Your known Love for the Polite Arts, and the Encouragement and Countenance you give their Professors emboldens me to recommend to your Protection the Bearer of this, Mr. Copley, as a person of very great Merit. he was born, and has been bred entirely among us, and for what knowledge he has acquired in his Profession, he is indebted to the force of his own Genius only; I beleive he has never seen a good Picture but of his own painting. His Character as a Gentleman is unexceptionable, as an Artist I trust his works will very soon speak for him. I hope, Sir, you'll excuse the Liberty I take with you.

Present my best Regards to Lady Hamilton and beleive me to be with the greatest Respect your much oblig'd, and most humble Servant,

THOS. PALMER.

BOSTON, Novr., 1773.

[1] See *Dictionary of National Biography*, VIII. 110. Now an architect at Rome.
[2] Sir William Hamilton (1730–1803).

Dr. John Morgan[1] to Copley

PHILADELPHIA, November 24, 1773.

SIR,

At the request of my particular friend Mr. Mifflin and of my Brother in law Mr. Stillman, I have taken the Liberty of writing a few Letters to some of my former friends in Italy, where I with pleasure learn you are going for the sake of endeavouring to make further Improvements in your profession. I hope these Letters may be of use to you. I have delivered them to Mr. Mifflin to forward to you. If you approve of delivering them, be pleased first to seal them. If not, you will be so kind as to destroy them.

That you may be enabled to form some Judgment how far they may be of use to you, it will be proper to acquaint You with the Characters of the several Gentlemen to whom they are written, and to explain on what footing they may be serviceable. Mr. Rutherfoord was a considerable Merchant at Leghorn, a Man of great Worth and politeness, and particularly civil to his Countrymen, the English. He can introduce you to Sir John Dick, Consul at Leghorn, and either by himself or friends procure you an Introduction to Sir Horace Man, the British Resident at Florence, which will be of great Use in obtaining easy Access at all proper times, to the Gallery of Paintings there, which contains one of the grandest Collections in Europe. Mr. Byers was bred to Painting, and reckoned a Connoisseur in Painting, Statuary, Sculpture, and very obliging in the charge he undertook of conducting Strangers to visit whatever was deemed curious and worthy of Observation in or about Rome, and in explaining the History of what he shewed.

---

[1] See *Journal of Dr. John Morgan, of Philadelphia, from Rome to London*, 1764.

The Abbey Grant was a Scotch Gentleman who, having followed the Fortunes of James to Rome, resided there. He was much esteemed by the English, and procured Access for the party I was with to Persons of the first Distinction at Rome.

Mr. Jamineau, the British Consul at Naples, was very friendly to me, during my Stay at Naples, and has since honoured me with his Correspondence. His Patronage was I beleive of use to Mr. West, and to Signora Angelica.[1] From his particular situation and disposition to please, I should think he might prove a valuable Acquaintance to you, in a great Variety of ways.

I wish you success equal to your warmest Expectations, and still greater, equal to the Opinion I have of your great Merit. Tho' personally unknown to you, I am, Sir, with great Regard Your most obedient and very humble Servant,

JOHN MORGAN.

Dr. John Morgan to Mr. Rutherfoord, Esqr.

PHILADELPHIA, November 24, 1773.

SIR,

I did myself the Honour of writing to you a few Months ago in favour of Mr. Bingham[2] a young Gentleman of this City, who purposed to pay a Visit to Leghorn, in his Way to see some parts of Italy. I now take the Liberty of introducing to your Acquaintance the Bearer Mr. Copley, who goes over to Italy for improvement in the Art of Painting. He is a Gentleman of exceeding good Character, and, without a Master, or Oppertunity of seeing the works of eminent Artists, has himself become highly eminent for his Skill in Painting.

I am perswaded there are many, who after all the improvements they have made from being conversant with the Works of the first

---

[1] Angelica Kauffman.   [2] William Bingham.

Masters in the World, when they leave Italy are not equal to Mr. Copley, at his first entering upon the study of those same Masters.

Depending on your great politeness to myself, and your known readiness to oblige Strangers of Worth, I doubt not but the liberty I have taken of recommending Mr. Copley to your Acquaintance will be taken in good part, and that you will have a pleasure in rendering him all the good Offices in your Power, by giving him advice how to proceed, and introducing him to such Gentlemen as may be most likely to have it in their Power to Promote the design of his coming.

With assurances of my great Esteem, I remain Dr. Sir Your much obliged and most obedient humble Servant,

JOHN MORGAN.

Dr. John Morgan to Mr. Byers

PHILADELPHIA, Novembr. 24, 1773.

SIR,

I make no other Apology for the Liberty I now take of introducing the Bearer Mr. Copley to your Acquaintance than to say the knowledge I have of your desire to cultivate a friendly Intercourse with worthy Artists, and to shew every Civility in your power to Strangers that go to Rome for their Improvement, makes me think you will be pleased with it. He is, I durst say, already known to you by report, as you are not ignorant of those who have excelled in the Art, or of the Works of those who have gained a reputation by their Exhibitions of Painting at Spring Garden. Be that as it may, Mr. Copley is generally esteemed here to be the best Painter that has ever performed in America, without excepting our American Raphael, as I have often heard Mr. West called, if we confine his Character to the Period of his being in America. Without other means of Improvement than what his own Genius has furnished Mr. Copley may be truly allowed, in my weak Opinion, to be a Master of his Art. Yet not content with that skill he has already acquired by dint of his Application to copy nature, he is fired with the laudable Ambition of studying the Works of those who have excelled in the same Employ, to discover what Lights they have struck out, and to avail himself of their Improvements, from which tis to be hoped he will derive great advantage.

After what I have said, I need not use many Arguments to induce you to cultivate an Acquaintance with him, and to shew him every Civility in your Power.

In a visit I lately made to Charles Town, South Carolina, I saw Mr. Bambridge, who is settled very advantageously there, and prosecutes his Profession with Reputation and sucess.

Your Friend Mr. Powel[1] is well. With great Regard I am, Sir, Your most Obedient and Very humble Servant,

JOHN MORGAN.

A Monsieur L'Abbé Grant[2]

PHILADELPHIA, Novr. 24, 1773.

SIR,

Tis now a long while since I did myself the honour of writing to you. tis much longer since I have had the honour of hearing from you.

The Bearer Mr. Copley intending for Italy will probably see you. Glad am I of an Oppertunity of introducing him to your Acquaintance as an Artist in Painting. I put him on the same footing with my Country Man Mr. West, in which I believe it will be found I have not disparaged that now justly celebrated Painter.

I think it an Honour to America that such an illustrious Pair have been produced in this Country; who by the strength of their own Genius, and without the assistance of able Masters have deservedly acquired Reputation amongst the first Rate Painters in the Mother Country.

Mr. West has already enjoyed the benefit of improving himself since his Genius shone forth, in the Schools of Italy, and in Studying the best Models, and works of the first Masters. This is what Mr. Copley is now in persuit of. Time will make manifest whether

---

[1] Samuel Powel.

[2] Peter Grant (*d.* 1784). See *Dictionary of National Biography*, XXII. 400.

he is as capable of improving those advantages. For my own part I have an exalted Opinion of his Genius, and think him even superior in that respect to some of those whose works he is now gone to study, tho' I am perswaded his Genius will receive great helps from the Works of Art, those almost super-natural Exhibitions to be met with in Italy of Raphael, Angelo, Corregio, Titian, Guido, Dominicino, Guerchino and others.

I perswade myself you will be much pleased with Mr. Copleys Acquaintance, and that you will chearfully assist him, as far as lays in your power, to procure Access to whatever is most worthy of his Study, Observation or Pursuit.

I have lately been on a public Mission from the Trustees of the College at Philadelphia to Jamaica to extend the knowledge of this Institution, and the advantages it may be of to such of the youth whose Parents may think proper to send them here for education, and to procure some Assistance towards establishing it on the most extensive and permanent foundation. I was there but about ten Months, in which time, I procured Subscriptions for carrying on the Design to the amount of between four and five thousand pounds sterling, and a Number of their Children are since come over to study at the College of Philadelphia, and others are preparing to follow.

My fellow Traveller Mr. Powel is well and joins me in the warmest Wishes for your Wellfare. I am with unfeigned Regard, Dr. Sir, Your much obliged Affectionate Friend, and most obedt. humble Servt.

John Morgan.

Dr. John Morgan to Isaac Jamineau

Philadelphia, November 24, 1773.

Sir,

I did myself the Honour of writing to you about four months ago by Mr. Bingham from this place, which I hope came safe to hand. This will be presented to you by Mr. Copley a very celebrated Painter from Boston, who proposes very shortly to sail for Italy, with a View of improving himself in that art, from the helps that are to be met with there, and from studying the works of those immortal Genii who have shone forth so illustriously for their skill and Imitation of Nature.

Mr. Copley may justly be looked upon as the greatest Painter we have ever yet had in America. I do not mean to except Mr. West, who was doubtless far short of Mr. Copley at the time he left America, however considerable his improvments were after he had the advantage of Studying in Italy. Perhaps History cannot furnish a single Instance of any Person, who with so little Assistance from others, and so few Oppertunities of seeing any thing worth studying has by the force of his Genius and by close Application to study Nature, arrived to such preheminance in Painting as Mr. Copley.

Although I have not the least acquaintance with Mr. Copley, nor ever seen him in my Life, yet from some paintings I have seen done by him, and Accounts of others who are no mean Judges, and have seen more of his performances, as well as from his excellent moral Character, I am perswaded you will be much pleased with his Acquaintance. Several of Mr. Copleys friends and my own have apply'd to me, without his knowledge, for Letters of Introduction to some Gentlemen of Weight and Character in Italy whose acquaintance might be the means of making his Merit better known, and thereby securing to him the greater Advantages and procuring him the best Oppertunities of gaining information of and access to what may be most worthy of his Study and Persuit.

Knowing of none to whom I can with so much propriety recommend him on these Acc'ts as to you, I have taken the Liberty, my good Sir, of begging the favour of your Countenance and Patronage of this worthy person, from whose Acquaintance I doubt not you will derive great pleasure. I should not wonder to hear some time hence, that others who resort to Italy to study the Labours of those departed for ages past, should be very ambitious to be made acquainted with this living Artist; and if some who are esteemed Masters, should condescend to study a little the works of one, appearing under the Character of a Student or Novitiate. But I leave it to yourself, who are so good a judge of Merit, to decide for yourself. Wishing you all possible Happiness, I remain, Dear Sir, Your most obedient and much obliged humble Servant,

JOHN MORGAN.

Copley to Jonathan and Isaac Winslow Clarke[1]

[December 1, 1773.]

DEAR SIRS,

On my return to the Meeting (after making an apology for so greatly exceeding the time propossed by me when I left it,) I made use of every argument my thoughts could suggest to draw the people from their unfavourable oppinion of you, and to convince them your opposition was neither the effect of obstinacy or unfriendliness to the community; but altogether from necessity on your part to discharge a trust commited to you, a failure in would subject you to ruin in your reputation as Merchants, to ruin in point of fortune your friends having engaged for you in very large sums; that you were un- influanced by any persons what ever, that you had not seen the Governor that Day (this last I urged in answer to some very warm things that were said on this head in which You were charged with acting under the Imediate influance of the Governor which in justice to you and him I undertook to say from my own knowledg was not true.) I observed you did not decline appearing in that Body from any Suspicion that your Persons would

---

[1] Sons of Richard Clarke and brothers-in-law of Copley. See Sabine, *Loyalists of the American Revolution*, I. 316.

not be intirely safe. But as the People had drawn the precise Line of Conduct that would sattisfy them, You thought your appear[an]ce in that Meeting would only tend to inflame it unless you could do what they demanded from you, which being impossable you thought they aught not to insist on; that you did not bring your selves into this Dificulty and therefore, aught not to be pressed to do an Act that would involve you in Ruin, etc. I further observed you had shewn no disposition to bring the Teas into the Town, nor would you; But only must be excused from being the Active instruments in sending it back. that the way was Clear for them to send it back by the Political Storm as they term'd it, raised by the Body as by that the Capt. could not unload it, and must return of Coarse, that your refusal by no means frustrated their plan. In short I have done every possable thing, and altho there was a unanimus vote past Declaring this unsatti[s]factory yet it cooled the Resentment and they Desolved without doing or saying any thing that showd an ill temper to you. I have been told and I beleive it true, that after I left the Meeting Addams[1] said they must not expect you should Ruin your selves. I think all stands well at present. Before the temper of the People could be judg'd of, we sent Cousin Harry to your Hon'd Father to urge his Imediate Departure to you. You will see him this Day. I have no doubt in my own mind you must stay where you are till the Vessel sails that is now in, at least; but I beleive not Longer; Then I think you will be able to return with Honour to Town, some few things in the mean while being done on your part. I had a Long and free conversation with Doc'r Warren, which will be renued this afternoon with the addition of Col'l Hancock. Cousin Benj'n Davis is to be with us. I must

[1] This is doubtful. [*Note by Copley.*]

advantageous, both to Mr Pearson and to you. It gives me no small satisfaction, to hope that my Grandson will be so near the worthy Gentleman who took so kind a care of the early part of his education, and I flatter myself with the hope that Mrs Pearson will favor him with his further attention, to prevent his falling into any mistakes, that persons of his age and situation are exposed to—

I hope and pray that you may have the happiness of having Sister returns to you in as good health as She has been favored with for some time past—

I am greatly obliged by your affectionate wishes for my Welfare; through the Divine Goodness I enjoy a comfortable state health, considering my very advanced stage of life, but what may be allotted to me, is known only to the Sovereign Disposer of all events; To His most holy Will may I ever be resigned; and I desire to join with you in humble and fervent prayer that I may be enabled to follow the example, and if it may be the Divine Will be favored with the supports and comforts that my dear Daughter was blessed with—

I wish my affectionate regards to your Father; I acknowledged his last favor by a Vessel that sailed for Nantucket some time since which I hope he received: please also to remember me affectionately to your Brother and Sister. I intend if I can to write my Grand Daughter by this opportunity if I should not I will be mindful of it by the next—

Adieu Dear Madam. I am

Your affect'd & faithfully,

Richard Clarke

conclude with recommending that you avoid seeing the Govournor. I hope he will not have any occasion to go to the Castel; if he should do not converse with him on the subject. this, I think is the best advise I can give boath as a friend to you and Him. my reasons for it I will tell you when I see you. Mrs. Copley and my self went at 9 o'Clock to Mr. Lees and return'd so late that I have no time to do any thing [but] Scrawl; but I hope you will be able to read this. I will see you as soon as possable. I am, Dear Sir, Yours

J. S. COPLEY.

Wednesday noon.

Copley to [*Richard Clarke*]

[BOSTON *ca.* February 15, 1774.][1]

HON'D SIR,

I received your Letter of 11 Inst, incloseing one for Col'l Worthington which I have not Delivered, thinking it best to see Mr. [Joseph] Lee first, and after waiting till yesterday without his coming to Town I went to Cambridge and had a full oppertunity of converseing with him on the matter; but being detained all night by means of an unruly horse which gave Sukey and my self some trouble I could not get to Town this Morng time anough to write you by any oppertunity of this Day.

The matter of a Memorial had started in my mind more than three Weeks ago but I had many objections to it which I could not get over, the most meterial was this, that however Clear the

---

[1] See postscript at the end of this letter. Mrs. Thomas Hubbard died February 15, 1774. Hill, *History of the Old South* (Third Church) II. 150. Mrs. Thomas Boylston died February, 1774. *N. E. Hist. and Gen. Register*, VII. 148. Copley's portrait of Thomas Hubbard, who was treasurer of Harvard College, from 1752 to 1763, is now the property of Harvard University.

facts may be yet they may be controverted, your conduct mis-represented, and what ever you either have or shall say mis-construed by the prevailing party in the House and a tryal brought on in which the House with the other Branches will be the Umpires and their desision should it be against you will confirm great numbers in their oppinions who are but too much disposed to beleive the Worst of you and are not at all solicitious to look into the facts and vew them with candor and impartial-lity: and this Judgment of the Court will stand on Record and conclude every thing against you, and render it more dificult than ever to bring People to think of you as they aught, not only in this province, but through the Continent and in Europe. Should this be the effect, as I really think it may, your principal intention would be defeated, that of doing justice to your Injured carractors, which, however, I think will be well effected in the way you propose. if it could be asertained, that the lead-ing Members in the House would take hold of such an opper-tunity to reinstate you, their ends being answered and having no advantage in prospect from keeping you at the Castle or Banishing you your Country, having taken up this oppinion and an oppertunity presenting itself when I was in Town on Tuesday I improved it to the purpose finding out the Senti-ments of some of the Heads and hope very soon to be able to asertain what the fate of a Memorial would be should it be persued. Should it [be] unfavourable it appears to me a News-paper Publication signed by the Agents would answer all the purposes of doing justice to your Injured carracters, that a Memorial would, without the disadvantages.

I have no doubt that some of the many Callumneys in the Newspapers aught to be contradicted. This has been my oppinion ever since the dispute commenced; After I had fully weighed the whole of your d[e]sign the above was what struck me, and being the only sentiments I could adopt I saw your friend Mr. Lee who agreed in every perticular, only he thought me almost romantick in supposeing it a possable thing that the Leaders would countinance a Memorial in the Coart; but I think it may be tried. I own I think the prospect of success very small, but I dont dispair neither. Mr. Lee observed to me that although his own Sentiments were against the Memorial yet as they stood connected with yours he should be for your trying it, as he has often found your judgment better than his own where you had differed in oppinion. Should you on the Whole conclude to prefer a Memorial rather than publish in the Newspapers your justification, be pleased to let me know and I will deliver the letter to Coll W—— imediately. Mr. Green I would not see till I had been with Mr. Lee, but will see him to morrow. As it now grows late I must conclude with assureing you I shall not neglect any thing that will have a tendancy to remove every obstacle to your return and that will do justice to your Carracters as far as may be in my power. I am, Hond Sir, Your Most Dutifull Son

JOHN SINGLETON COPLEY.

P S I have jus heard Mrs. Hubbard is Dead and Mrs. Boylston.

John Singleton to Henry Pelham

BALLYGERREEN, Jany. 27, 1774.

DR. NEPHEW,

I recid your favor of the 3d augt. Last and am hartley Consarned to find my Dr. Sister is still in a declining way and hope the gret God will prolong her days till she sees you all well provided and setled to her sattisfaction.[1] I hope you will present my warmest Love and Sencer affections to her, and asure her the lenth of time and gret Distance has not abeted my love and sencear Regards for her and all her famaly, and belive me nothing but the Difacolty of Conveing lettrs. to you hinders My not writing oftner to you all, as I am serten maney of my Letters Niver Coms to your hands.

I sincerly Congratulet you and your Brother on his Mator-amonall State and on the blesing God has given him by the increase of his famaly which is Sertenly a gret blesing when they are blesed with sence and the feer of God and dutey and love to their perants. Your acct. of his marrige is the first I hard of him. You mentioned in your letter that he intended to make the tour of Europ; if so I hope he will be so kind to Com to this Kingdom. I asure you It would give all his frends heer Infinet plesur to see him or aney of my Dear Nephews.

pre what is becom of yr Br Charles? I have not hard of him sence he was in London and then I reci'd to Lettrs. from him the Last of them was Dated 27 Decr., 1759. I hope in your next you will give me an acct. of him and all the rest of my relesons in ameraco and that you and my Name sake will Continue a More Reglaur Corespondance with me as nothing would give me more rell plesur then heering from you all. I now will give you a shart acct. of my famaly. I have but four Child'n, two Dauters and two Sons — the youngest is mared 7 years ago to one Edwd. Palmer; he was bred to the Law and has a good Estate he has 3 Dauters and is very hapley setled in Birr in the King County. I gave him £1000 pounds Stg. with her. My Eldist dauter was mared 13th Instant to Antoney King, a man Bred to the Law who has a good Estate In Dublin. I gave him

[1] Mrs. Pelham died in 1789.

£2000 pound Stg. his fathe[r] is an Alderman In Dublin and was Knighted by the Lord Leftnant for his actifety and Clifornes when he was Sherif; I asure you I am gretly fitteged from the horey of this weding by receveing and paying visets which was finesed Yester Day; My Br. Cooper and his wife[1] are all well and wants for nothing but Childer to make them happy. My Eldist Son is 19 year ould; me Second Son a bout 10 year ould.

I send this by Cap'n Kley who is bound to Lond'n and promises to forward it to you by som safe hand.

[the youck you ware to be sadled with and tron of by the brafe Bostons is now the Stamp act past in a Law and to take place the 25 of March next, besides severall other Vilonos taxes lead on Yous by a Most Vilors and Coropt Parlement whos prinsoble part are bribed to sel there Contrey.][2] plese to present my sencer Love to my Dr. Sister, yr. Brother and Sister In Law, and all frends, and belive me to be Dr. Hary, Yours Most Sencerly and Affly,

JOHN SINGLETON.

Copley to Isaac Winslow Clarke[3]

BOSTON, April 26, 1774.

DEAR SIR,

The Ladys after the pleasure of spending a most agreable day with you, got home about half past eight oclock all well, and at the usual hour retired to bed; about 12 oclock a number

---

[1] Ann, sister of John and Mary Singleton.

[2] The words in brackets have been erased so effectively that it is almost impossible to decipher them. There is nothing to indicate whether this was done by Singleton or by Pelham, to whom they must have given offence.

[3] From the Collection of Mr. Denison R. Slade.

of persons came to the house, knock'd at the front door, and awoke Sukey and myself. I immediately opened the window, and asked them what they wanted; they asked me if Mr. Watson[1] was in the house. I told them he was not, they made some scruples of beleiving me, and asked if I would give them my word and honour that he was not in the house. I replied yes. They than said he had been here and desired to know where he was. I told them he had been here, but he was gone and I supposed out of Town as he went in his chaise from this with an intention to go home; they than desired to know how I came to entertain such a Rogue and Villin, My reply was, he was with Coll'l Hancock in the afternoon at his house and from thence came here and was now gone out of Town; they seemed somewhat sattisfied with this and retired a little way up the Street but soon returned and kept up the Indian Yell for sometime when I again got up and went to the window; and told them, I thought I had sattisfied them Mr. Watson was not in the house but I again assured them he was not and beg'd they would not disturb my family. they said they could take no mans word, they beleived he was here and if he was they would know it, and my blood would be on my own head if I had deceived them; or if I entertained him or any such Villain for the future must expect the resentment of Joice. a great deal more of such like language passed when they left me and passed up the street and were met by a chaise which stoped as in consultation by Mr. Greens, which in a little time turned and went up with them, by this you must see my conjectures with regard to you are not ill founded, nor my cautions needless. I hope you will be continually on your gaurd when you are off the Island; what a spirrit! what if Mr. Watson had stayed (as I pressed him to)

[1] Colonel George Watson, of Plymouth, a mandamus counsellor.

to spend the night. I must either have given up a friend to the insult of a Mob or had my house pulled down and perhaps my family murthered. I am, Dear Sir, Your Affectionate Brother and Humble Ser't,

JOHN SINGLETON COPLEY.

Addressed; For Mr. Isaac Clarke at Castle William.

Joseph Webb to Henry Pelham

SIR,

Your's of the 26th Ulo. I Recd. per last post, and am much surprizd at the Contents. I wish you wou'd take the trouble to call on Mr. Hyde, the Hartford Post Rider, to whom I paid the Mon[e]y on the Receiving the Picture, which was last fall. I was in Boston last February and shou'd hardly have come out of Town, had it not have been paid; and was sorry that I was in such hurry as not to be able to wait on Mr. Copley out of Complisance. for I found Him vastly polite and genteel when He did the Work for me. I can't say but I am much displeased with the post, for of all debts, I shou'd never consent to one like this. I am, Sir, with compliments to Mr. Copley and His Lady, and to Your Self, Your most H. Servt.

JOS. WEBB.[1]

Shall be much Obliged to know what Mastr. Hyde says. You shall soon have the Affair put to rights as I Expect to be in town in the Course [of] 4 Weeks.

WETHERSFIELD, June 3d, 1774.

[1] Brother of Samuel Blatchley Webb.

Henry Pelham to [Helena Pelham] [1]

BOSTON, June 8, 1774.

HON'D AND DEAR AUNT,

A diffidence of appearing in a proper manner before you has hitherto prevented me from tendering you those marks of duty, Esteem and Affection which the distance between us will permitt and the Regard I owe to the sister of an Hon'd and dear Father demands. By so favourable an oppertunity I take the liberty of presenting myself before you with my most affectionate duty as a Nephew who is exceedingly solicitous of obtaining your favour and Blessing.

This will be delivered you by my very dear and tender Brother Mr. Copley who I hope will obtain your favourable Notice. He is a Gentleman possessd of all those endearing qualities which are respected by the Virtuous and good and adornd with those accomplishments that attract the notice and esteem of his Friends and Acquaintance. In his profession he is very capital, the many testimonies of Respect he has received from abroad evincing his fame to be very extensive. *To him* I am under the greatest and most perticular Obligations for the early and continued Mark of his kindness to me. *By him* I am fixed in a Buisness which by the blessing of Heaven upon Industry and application will render my future Life easy and happy.

The difficulty I find in speaking of myself forms the propriety of my refering you to Mr. Copley for a more perticular Account. My hon'd Mother begs your acceptance of her best Wish[e]s for your Happiness her kindest Love and Regards.

[1] See *Copley to Pelham*, August 5, 1774, *infra.*

Affections she has always bore you, and hopes for your excuse in droping a Corespondence with you[1] which her very ill state of Health[2] has prevented her many years from continuing with her nearest Fri[e]nds.

My Brother Chas. Pelham I had the pleasure of seeing this Morn'g. He and my other Fr[i]end[s] with him are well, except my sister Pelham, who has not yet entirely recovered from the violent Disorder with which she was some time ago attack'd but which I hope time will Eradicate. Requesting your Blessing and asking the favour of a line from you which be assured will much add to My Happyness, I conclude with wishing you health and every felicity. I am with regard Your very Dutifull Nephew and Humble Servt.

H. P.

Captain John Small to Copley

DEAR SIR,

Your father in Law Mr. Clarke told me you are at the Eve of Departure for England; and that Letters of Introduction would be agreable to you. I have therefore troubled you with the inclosed to a Gentleman whom without Partiality I can venture to say you'll find a most worthy Benevolent sensible Judicious regarder of Men of Merit.

I have only time to wish you a good passage and to assure [you] I am, Dr. Sir, Yours very Sincerly,

JOHN SMALL.

DANVERS near SALEM, June 9th, 1774.

[1] Erased: "owing to trouble and Illness occasioned by the death of the dearest and most affectionate friend."

[2] Erased: "renders very difficult and painfull to her."

Captain John Small to Alexander Small

DEAR BROTHER,

I left New York so suddenly I had no time to apprise you by the last Mail (I mean that of June) of my departure for this Country.

I have at present every reason to suppose that my coming here will be of some Service to myself and of no loss to the Publick Service; my extensive acquaintance with the People of New England enables me to be so far of use, as to distinguish those who are well dispos'd, from those that are otherwise (and of course Enemies to their Country;) and I doubt not from the general appearance of Tranquility at present, that the Province from having been consider'd one of the Least; will soon appear one of the most Loyal, (and of course one of the most happy and flourishing) in America. I hope I shall soon be able to confirm this assertion and shall be truly happy if it can be in any shape in my poor power to contribute thereto.

I herewith beg leave to introduce and recommend to you a most ingenious and deserving native of this province, Mr. Copely the Gentleman I have frequently mention'd to you of so high merit and distinguish'd a Character as a portrait Painter. He is in my oppinion one of the first Geniouses of the Age; and as such I'm very sure you'll take great pleasure in protecting recommending and introducing him to People of Taste of knowledge and of Judgement of which your extensive and Valuable accquaintance and Friends chiefly consist.

Mr. Copely drew a portrait in *Crayons*, about six years ago; which you are now possess'd of. He has hardly us'd his Pencil where the Performance has not been universally admired; so that his own works will speak far more in his favour than any thing [that] can be said by, Dear Sir, Your most dutifull and affectionate Brother,

JOHN SMALL.

SALEM the residence of Genl. Gage, June 9th, 1774.

[*Addressed:*] *To Alexander Small, Esquire, in Villars* [*Villiers*] *Street York Buildings, in the Strand, London.*

A Bill for Portraits

Boston The Honble Thomas Fluker Esqr.
      to Jno. S. Copley, Dr.

1774
June To his own Portrait................... £14..0..0
   To his Sons. Do.................... 14..0..0
                £28..0..0
  To two black and Gold Frames at £1.8 2.16..0
         Total £30.16..0

Copley to his Wife[1]

DOVER, July 9th, 1774.

My ever Dearest Sukey,

Through the Divine goodness I am now in safe at this place and shall take my departure for London where I hope to be to morrow, it being but one Days ride from this, it is not possable to have a better passage than I have had, the weither during the whole time being very moderate and winds fair except about six hours calm. Capt. Robson has been his whole life passing the seas and never knew any thing like it. however after 29 Days at Sea the land is a most greatfull sight. I was two Days very sea-sick, ever since which I have my health very well and I trust in the Mercys of God that it will be continued to me to yourself those dear little Babes (and our other friends) and that we shall long enjoy a happy union when this blank in life for I can call it no other is passed. in the mean time remember you cannot shew your love to me in a stronger manner than by takeing the utmost care of your own health. I am very ancious to hear from you how you all are, and what state the Town is in, and how Brother Harry has proced'd in my affairs. I hope my

[1] Chamberlain Collection, F. 4.10, in the Boston Public Library.

Hon'd Mother did not take it hard: that I did not see her, or Brother or Sister Bromfield before I left em. I hope you have taken care to let them know how it happened that I did not. do let me know if my Dear Betsey missed me much. be very perticular when you write at all times. give her and the other dear babes a tender kiss for me and as soon as I can I shall send some pretty things to gratify them. give my Duty to my Dear Mother, love to Brother Harry, and love to Brother and Sister Bromfield, Couzin Nabby, Sally, Betsey, etc., and best respects comp'ts. Love etc. to all my friends as you shall judge fit and proper, To your Hon'd Pappa my Duty, love to Sister Lucy, Brother Isaac, when you shall have an oppertunity. if Brother and sister Startin are yet with you remember me to them in the Most Effectionate manner. My best Wishes ever accompany you, my Dearest life, and my prayers for your happiness health and safety shall at all times be offer[ed] up to the throne of Divine mercy for you and our Dear little ones, and trusting in Gods goodness that we shall not long be seperated I conclud with assureing you I will make the time as short as it is possable, and am My Dearest love forever most Effecly your tender and Loving Husband,

JOHN SINGLETON COPLEY.

I forgot to tell brother Harry when Mr. Startin came to town to see Mr. (I forget his name, he to whom the bill on Mr. Startin was sold to) and see if the overpluss money can be recoverd. he must well remember he took the Bill in Ster'g, purely as he said that I might not suffer by the Difference of Exchange, Guineas being at twenty one shillings. this he did to oblige me. the Bill Drawn on Mr. Mifflin was for fifty two pounds ten shillings sterling, and that shurely aught to admit of my Drawing for the same without loss.

Copley to Henry Pelham [1]

LONDON, July 11th, 1774.

DEAR BROTHER,

I am now begining that corraspondance from which you will no doubt receive much pleasure, and altho you will not find much to entertain you in this first Letter, yet that defect will be amply supplyed by its giveing you certain intelligance of my safe arrival in this City after a most easy and safe passage, and that I am in perfect health. through the Divine goodness I have been so ever since I left Boston except two Days of sea sickness. I landed at Deal, not at Dover, as I informed Sukey in my first Letter, that Letter being wrote on board and left with the Capt. to send if he should find any Vessell in the River as he went up. at that time I was in expection of a boat from the shore, of which I was disappointed, and so saild in the ship to Deal where I landed and took a post Chaise and came to London through a most enchanting Country, of which no part of North America that I have seen can give you the least Idea of. my Post Chaise and Horses were as genteel as any Chariot that roals through your Streets, with a Postillon well Dress'd as any you have seen in the service of the first gentlemen of fortune with you. My living on the Road of the best kind, Double refined Shugar, best hison Tea, and all things in proportion. no gentleman with us has things better or more Genteelly served than is in all the Houses where I stoped to be met with, and this Journey of 72 Miles cost me but three Guineas, when with us the Carriage would have cost more money. Sunday Even'g I arrived at the New England Coffee House, and soon

---

[1] An extract from a letter of the same date to Mrs. Copley is given in Amory, *John Singleton Copley*, 27.

found Brother Clarke,[1] who is very well. this Morn'g at his Lodgings I devote to write to Mrs. Copley and you, as a Vessell will sail in a Day or two and I cannot go abroad till I have procured some things to be Decent in.

July 15th. I have been to see my friend Mr. West, and find in him those amiable quallitys that makes his friendship boath desireable as an artist and as a Gentleman. on Wednesday he introduced me and Brother Clarke to Sr. Josha. Renolds's, where we saw a very large number of his portraits, and a fine collection of Other Masters. yesterday, or Thursday, for I think it better to pursue by the Days of the week in my Cronology than by other Dates, I had the superlative pleasure of Visiting the Royal Accademy where the Students had a naked model from which they were Drawing. the front of this pallace, designed by Inogo Jones, is Very magnificant. The Collection of the Statues Bassorelevios, etc., is very fine. I have seen Mr. West's Death of General Wolf, which is sufficient of itself to Immortalize the Author of it. there is a fine print of it ingraveing,[2] which when done you shall see. I find the practice of Painting or rather the means by which composition is attained easier than I thought it had been. the sketches are made from the life, and not only from figures singly, but often from groups. This you remember was have often talked of, and by this a great dificulty is removed that lay on my mind. Mr. West proposes to Carry me to the Queen's Pallace to Day. I must not be very perticular in my Acc'ts of what I see in this place yet, for they come so thick my time will not permit me to be so at present. this Mor'g I have to deliver most of my Letters of Recommendation which will encrease my Acquaint-

---

[1] Jonathan Clarke.
[2] By William Woollett. The plate was not issued until January, 1776.

ance. this is really an astonishing City; many parts of which, I mean, the buildings, are so exactly what I had conceived that I am surprized at it. I find I am like to have a companion to go to Italy with me, a Gentleman who is about forty lately ingaged in painting and our pursuits will be the same.[1] he has the french and Italian Langage and only weits for the best season. that will be in about three weeks. in this I think I am happy. I have from Mr. West, that I need coppy very little, that fifteen Months for me will be equel to as many years to young Students, so that my time will not exceed what I talked to Sukey, and desire you to tell her so. the last night I slept in my new Lodgings. I have the first floor, very Genteel, for which I pay a Guinea a week. it consists two Chambers, with small room to powder in. I find my breakfast and have an invitation to dine always with Mr. West when not otherways ingaged; Capt. Scott sails in about a week, when I shall write more at leasure than I am at present, and hope to send your things by him. Give my love and Duty to my Hon'd and Dear Mother, Comp'ts, etc., etc., to all Friends. observe this letter is several Days later in the Date than Mrs. Copley's, which I put into the bagg least it should be taken down. so you must communicate (if you can read it) to her, I never had my health better. I am sorry Brother Clarke and I are so distant from each other, but he is in the City and I at the Coart End of the Town, about two Miles or somthing more from each other. I am within a few Doors from Mr. West's,[2] but shall see Mr. Clarke every Day; for two Miles here is not what we think them with us,

[1] Carter was the artist's name, and his companionship is shown in the extracts from a diary kept during this journey. Printed in Cunningham, *Lives of British Painters*, and in Dunlap, I. 112.

[2] West lived at 14 Newman Street for forty-five years before his death in 1820; before that he was in Castle Street, Leicester Fields.

and I might as well have stayd at home as in the City. Lord
Gage[1] is out of Town this Week, so have not seen him. so is
Lord Dartmouth, to whom I shall be introduced when he
returns. but I must break off. remember to be Active to do
with Spirit what you have to do. I long to hear how things go
with you. I am, Dear Brother, Most Affecly your

J. S. COPLEY.

July 15, 1774. Direct to New England Coffee House.

Henry Pelham to Copley [2]

BOSTON, July 17,[3] 1774.

MY DEAR BROTHER,

A Vessell sailing tomorrow for England from Dartmouth[4]
affords me an oppertunity of presenting you with my most
sincere and hearty wishes for your Happyness and welfare.
The weather since you sailed having been remarkably fine,
your affectionate Friends here felicitate themselves in the Idea
of your having before this arrived in England after a safe,
quick and ple[a]sant Passage. I hope this will meet you placed
agreably to ours and your own wishes in health Peace and (as
far as possable) in the enjoyment of all Earthly Happyness.
My Honor'd Mamma desi[r]es me to present you with Blessing
and kindest Love, and to assure you that you shall allways have
her prayers at the throne of Heavenly Grace for your temporal

---

[1] Thomas Gage, first Viscount Gage in the peerage of Ireland.

[2] There are two drafts of this letter, with numerous corrections in both of
them. The first draft is shorter and has nothing about the dispute with Edward
Green.

[3] June 25 changed to July 17.

[4] First draft: Providence. Second draft: Providence changed to Dartmouth.

and eternal welfare. I am happy to inform you that her Health is rather better than when you left us.

My Dear Sister and her little family are well. she has wrote you by the Admerals' Ship, which sailed a few Days ago. I must make an apollogy for not having wrote myself by the same Conveyanc[e]. I fully intended it but the Vessel sliped away before I was apprised of the time of her Sailing. Mr. and Mrs. Bromfield, my Sister and myself, spent a day or two lately[1] at Salem where we had the Pleasure of se[e]ing Mr. Clarke and our other Friends with him in health and Peace, once more enjoying the Blessings of social and domestic Life. By this Oppertunity I propose writing to aunt Cooper, Uncle Singleton and my Cousin King. I received a few days after you sailed a most tender and affectionate Letter from my Uncle, a few extracts of which I beg leave to incert. it is dated January 27, 1774 . . .[2]

I must now leave a pleasing to enter upon a disagreable Subject, a Subject I sincerely wish I had no accasion to mention, Viz. the Conduct of Mr. Green[3] with respect to the settlement of hi[s] Account. I shall not repeat what passed previous to your sailing, for that cant but be recent in your memory. I think it was to[o] remarkable to escape it. shall therefor[e] confine myself to what has since occurred. The 4th of July I went in to him and told him I came from Mrs. Copley, with her request that he would settle his Account, as she was in want of Money to support her Family. he told me that he had not got the Accou[n]t and cou'd not get it from you, tho he was very solicitous to for a month before you went away. I gave him the

---

[1] First draft: "spent the last Sunday."
[2] The whole letter is printed p. 213, *supra*.
[3] Edward Green (1733–1790), who married Mary Storer.

Ac[c]ount. He read it, and objected to the price of his Brother's Picture, spoke largely of Mrs. Copley's solicitude to get some articles of Ferniture from him, said he did not care for the Pictures being paid for two years before hand, woud not have objected if it had been three, would not mention these things only to give me an Accou[n]t of how the matter stood. he said you had charged 25 per Cent upon the glass. I told him no that I had paid for that very Glass 16/. well, sais he, these are mere trifles. The Rent is the main article, your Brother has over charged that. I was to give but 40£. I told him I was much surprised to hear him say so. That It had been always understo[o]d that He was to give 46£ 13/4 a year and that you had refused 40£, which was what Mr. Startin had offered you. here he gave me an Explination which as well as I knew the man I must Confess astonished me coming even from him. that was, that He was to give 40£ for the House and 6£ 13.4. for the barn, if he chose to occupy it. but, sais he, I never had the barn. the Key of it indeed was sent into me, with a Desire that I might make use of it if I had Ocasion; but in two Days after it was sent for again and I have never had it since. to this I exp[r]essed my great Wonder, ánd told him that the barn was certainly occupied by him, that you had frequently put yourself to Inconven[i]en[ce] rather than trouble him for the Occasional Use of it. No, he said, so far from it that you had let the Barn to other People. He asked me what Directions you had left respecting a Deduction for the House not being finished etc? I told him that you had left directions about it, but that it was proper for him to say what he expected. he said he mentioned one Article of Damage, that of his wood. He was obliged to give 20/ a Cord for 30 Cord, by which he lost 10£ Lawfull Money for want of a Wood House being bu[i]lt in season. How in nature he got 30 Cord of wood into a place that can hold but 20 is beyond my sagacyty to find out. After a long harrange in which he spoke of breach of engagement and not being well treated he told me that he had not made out his Accounts, which he promised to do the next day and send it in, and expected to receive some bills from Salem that Even'g, or at farthest the next Saturday, when he would settle the acc't some how. upon the Whole I collected that he did not mean to pay for the Barn, and that he means to have a very large Deduction for the other things.

A few Days ago I again called upon him and asked weithe[r] he was now ready to settle. the only answer that I got from him was that he had not drawn out his account owing to want of time, he being engaged in very important buisness; that he did not know when he should, perhaps next week, or the week after that, he must first post up his Books, etc.

There are several Gentlemen of the Army solicitous to get the House, among others Coll. Wallcot,[1] who bears a good Character, has a Wife and one child. he is to see the House this day. I am in expectation that he will give 50£ L. M. for it, as he wants it very much. Thus at present stands the matter respect'g Mr. Green and his house. upon his Conduct I shall not remark. to you it wants no Comment. I would observe respecting the Barn that it is very remarkable that he should not have mentioned the matter before you left Boston, especially as he knew long before what rent you charged. It is also worthy of notice that he should have lent the Barn to several People, perticularly Coll. Hancock, to keep his Chaise in, to Mr. Fenno to keep fowls in, to Redman for the same use, and his constantly calling it his Barn. I shall pursue the matter

---

[1] William Walcott, lieutenant-colonel of the 5th Regiment of Foot.

with him till I bring him to some explicit Determination, and
shall constantly give you the Earliest Information of what
passes, and should be glad of your Advice respecting him, as I
find It is not lik[e]ly to be settled soon if at all. I find it very
difficult collecting money. I have not yet made the progress
that I could wish or that you expected. Coll. Hancock I have
not yet been able to gett an audience of, tho he is so well as to
talk of Heading his Company in a few Days. I have always the
misfortune to go there [1] when he has a Violent Headack, or
when he is laying down. I am very sorry I have not collected
money eno to make you a Remittance, but hope to do it before
you have Occasion for it. I was in hopes to have been able by
this time to inform you that this Town was restored to its
former flourishing State.[2] But alas! delusive hope still spreads
its fascinateing Charm over the minds of a once happy but
now too fatally deluded and distressed People. A Congress
of the Colonies is to meet at Philadelphia the 1st of Septem'r.
This and the large assistanc[e] the other Colonies affords to the
Poor of this place keeps up their Spirits, and has hitherto prevented the Town from doing any one thing towards a removal
of those Difficulties, which sooner or later will be most severely
felt. Four Regiment[s] [3] and the Artillery are quietly encamped
on the Common. They behave very peacebly and well. The
Common wears an Entire new face. Instead of the peacefull
Verdure with which it was cloathd when you left it, it now
glows with the warlike Red. The fireing of Cannon, the Rat-
tling of Drums, the music [4] of the fife, now interrupt the pleasing silence which once rendered it so peculiarly deligh[t]full. But

[1] Erased: "(which has not been seldom)."
[2] First draft: "its former Reason."
[3] Erased: "two Regiments."   [4] Erased: "shrill."

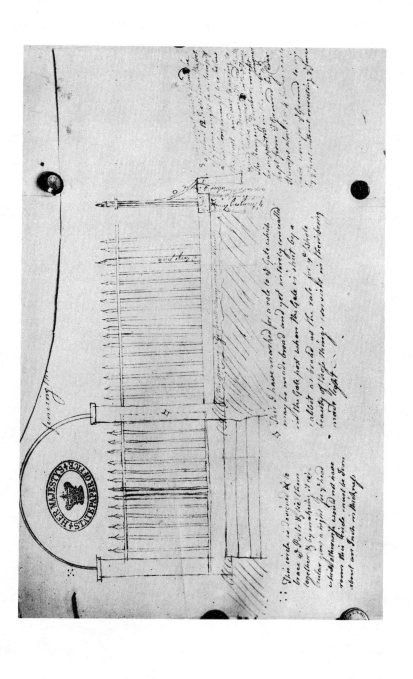

still all this Noise all this confusion are incomparably to be prefered to the infernal Wistle and shout of a lawless and outragious
rabble. The strictest disciplin[e] is kept up in the Army and the
greatest order preserved. After nine oclock in the Ev[en]ing
there is not a Soldier to be seen nor a whisper to be heard in the
Camp, Excepting the Centries. The solemn League and Cove-
nen[an]t which has been issued out by our Committe of Core-
spondenc[e], and for Which they have been sever[e]ly handled
in some of our Papers, I would give you some account [of], but
It would exceed the Compass of my Paper, [and would] probably be as disagreabl[e] to you in the reading as it would be
painfull to me in reciting.[1]

I have only time to again express my ardent Wishes that
every happyness may attend you and to assure you that with a
grea[t]full Since of your Kindness I remain immutably your
affectionate Brother,

HENRY PELHAM.

P. S. I beg you would present my affectionate Regards to
Mr. J. Clarke, of whom I entertain the most pleasing Remembrance, and to whom My Mamma desire[s] her Compliments.
We beg you would write soon and often. A Gentleman, a
Captain in the 43 Regm. told me yesterday that Sir J. Reynold[s] said to Him I would give 1000£ Str. that I could paint
white equal to Mr. Coply, and that Mr. West told him that he
was asshamed to have one of your Pictu[r]es placed by his as
they intirely eclipsed his Performances. I would just caution
you about Coll. Hall's Letters, for he has been crasy and I
beleive is not now intirely well.

---

[1] It was framed in June and circulated for signatures. Copies are in the Massachusetts Historical Society's collection of broadsides.

Copley to Henry Pelham

DEAR HARRY,

I have sent you on this leaf an exact plan of part of those Iron fences that is in front of all the Houses in this City, that in case you should be obliged to plan one for Mr. Green's house you will have nothing to do but have recourse to this. for I think it will be strong anough if the pales are made of Oak or some tuff wood, with the Addition of thickness to the peace the pales go through has given to it, in the Draught which I have made with Read chalk. by this you will see that it is only the hollow I have marked with Chalk that you may know what my addition is, and not confound it with what I meant to give you, Viz. the Iron Fences generally used here. those pales are about five foot high to the poin[t] at the top from the Bottom; the bottom is let into stones which are neatly laid together, and ranged so that a peace of ranging timber of about 9 Inches broad on the Top and 4 Inches high on the side would well Imiatate, as I have Sketched on the inclosed paper. this timber will not be more subjected to rott than the cant that the pales are incerted into in all the open fences in your Town. I think I like to have the pales all of a length, and those here drawn are a good distance from each other. you are to take notice about every 18 or 20th or at highest 25th, there should be one barr larger, perhaps ½ as large again. I have markd it with Chalk. mind I do not mean to add this to each side: it would make them too thick. They must have some support as drawn in the plan. this must be on the Inside and of Iron, and not thicker at most than the small pales. as to these large pales the house must regulate their Distance from each other as it would the Posts of a Piazza; that is, one opposite each peer, or any way that they will be made to turn out regular. if you should think oak would be strong anough, but I think it will not, it would be much Cheeper than Iron for the braces that support the fence. Certain I am all the other parts will be strong anough if made with Oak, and if Mrs. Copley should think proper to have any fencing done, I should chuse it exactly of this kind, I mean front fence, and the barrs of this thickness. as to the hight of the fence you must determin by the eye what will be best; and the hollow I have added (to give the barr through which the pales pass, more strength) I do not determin the size of, only, I would make it as small as possable. nothing can be cheeper than this kind of Fence. indeed in this place they do not make any object of their fences. if they are sufficient to keep Creatures out, they do not consider the fences as giveing any beauty to their building or gardends; and since I have been in this place I have not seen such a thing as a showey fence, neighther in town or Country. But I think the Post and the Gateway must be about 10 or 12 Inches thick, and only about 6 Inches higher than the pales with a flatt peace like a Cap on the top, as I have sketched it on the inclosed plan. this fence aught to be painted a light Lead Colour, all but the Gatepost[s] and Ranging Tim[bers]. I think should you exicute a fence of this kind you could not mistake any part, I have been so exact. I hope if you must do Mr. Green's you will follow every perticular, and be not afraid that the Stuff will be weak for I am sure of its sufficient strength and its neet look. I have sent you Colours for Painting the Houses, and Directed them by this oppertunity to Mr. Clarke at Salem. I send you your Cloaths and fine Colours, pencils, tools, paper, Chalk, etc. I shall send them under the care of Mr. Wheatly, who will see that you have them. I shall put them in one box, if I can; I inclose a note of them altogether. I cannot give you any perticular Acc't. of the things that I see for want of time. you perhaps think it strange I should want time when I have nothing to do, but I am constantly imploy'd one way or other, and find so much Civility in this place more than equil to all I have ever received in Boston in my whole life, if I except what a few friends have shewn me, which I shall ever retain a greatfull remembrance of. I shall have business when I can engage in it. several have spoke to me, but I am determined not to do any till my return from Italy, for any one less than the King's or Queen's. such a thing as that might tempt me to stay a month longer than my time. Lord Gage has been very polite to me, and on my return to this place will imploy me. he would have done it now, if I had been willing to take up the Pencil. I dined with him last week and was very much urged to take his Country house[1] in my way to France in such a manner that I am constrained to think it more than mere compliment. at this season all the Nobillity is out of Town, so that I have not seen many of them, and this End of the Town is said to bee quite Dull, though I think it brisk anough. There has not been more than 2 or 3 Days since I came here that I have not had perticular invitations to Dine, tho it is now 3 weeks since I came here a stranger. many persons have desired Brother Clarke to bring me to Dine, tho they had never seen me nor I them. Mr. West when I first came would have had me to lodge at his House, but was just prepaireng to move to his New house and could not accomodate me; but had this not been the case I should have declined it;

---

[1] Furle or Firle, in Sussex. "Lord Gage has a noble seat; the house was built by a Sir John Gage (in the reign of Henry the 8th), the first ancestor of whom they have any memorial. Of him there is a very fine picture." *Diary and Letters of Thomas Hutchinson*, I. 223. This portrait was painted by Holbein. On Sir John Gage, see *Dictionary of National Biography*, xx. 351.

but he desired I would always come to dinner when I was not ingaged, with the same freedom as I should at home. indeed, he is extreemly friendly and I am under great obligations to him. I have the same invitation from Mr. Rook, an old Gentleman, father to General Gage's Aid de camp;[1] and I assure you those are not mere peaces of ceremony, but from a real Desire they should be excepted of. so I am never at a loss, tho I have not yet improved Mr. Rook's general invitation. but when I dined there the last week he made me promise that I would come the first Day that I was not ingaged, and that I should always find a Dinner at 4 oClock, and when I went out, his Son, who I think a very polite Genteel Man, told me his Father was hurt that I had not gone in that friendly way and taken a Dinner with him before, and that it would give him great pleasure if I would without the least ceremoney, and made me promise that I would certainly do it. I mention this so perticular to show you how friendly those people are into whose acquaintance I have fallen, and that when they had made a Dinner, they do not think it a trouble they are glad to have done with, but wish to see me with a rriendly freedom that precludes all suspision of incincerity, or mere ceremonial complisance. you cannot Immagine how much it adds to my pleasure having Brother Clarke here; he is so used to the place that I am already allmost inneciated into all the manners and Customs of the City. Yesterday I dined with Gov'r Hutchinson, and I think there was 12 of us altoge[the]r, and all Bostonians, and we had Choice Salt Fish for Dinner.[2] I have not yet been able to see your Aunt,[3] for I beleive I shall be obliged

---

[1] Harry Rooke, a captain in the 52d Regiment.

[2] He had already dined with Hutchinson on July 30. *Diary and Letters of Thomas Hutchinson*, I. 198.

[3] Helena Pelham was living at Chichester at this time.

to go on purpose to Chichester. I am very sorry you did not give me a Direction by which I might have seen the person that transacts her business. you intended it but forgot it. however, I will do the best I can. remember me in the most tender and Affectionate manner to my Dear Mother. I intend if possable writing to her by this Vessell. Love to Brother and Sister Pelham, and All others as they stand connected, and beleive me your Affectionate Brother,

J. S. COPLEY.

LONDON, August 5, 1774.

Nathaniel Hatch to Henry Pelham

SIR,

Be so good to let the Bearer have a sight of your plan, in order to lay out the street called Sewall street through Captn. Erving's ground,[1] which he has consented to.[2] I am your most Obet. Servt.

NATHL. HATCH.

BOSTON, 15 Augt., '74.

Copley to Henry Pelham

LONDON, Augst. 17, 1774.

DEAR BROTHER,

This Evening I devote to you and Mrs. Copley. I shall therefore not write you a long Letter, as the evenings are very short and it is now time to go to bed. you will perhaps think it strange I did not give some of the Day to this business, but you have no Idea how time is filled up in this great City. I get

[1] John Erving, whose property lay between Copley's and George Street.

[2] Sewall Street, thirty-five feet wide, was laid out from George or Belknap, now Joy Street, to Coventry, now Walnut Street. It ran through Sewall's "Elm Pasture" and the Copley property. The street was discontinued at an early date.

up in the morn'g, dress, go out see such a variety of objects, that the Day is spent before it seems well begun. I am invited to dine allmost every Day. since the Day I arrived in this place not more than three or four Days has passed that I have not had a perticular invitation to Dine, and from Mr. West and Mr. Rooke I have a general invitation at all times that I am not otherwise ingaged. I am fallen into a much larger Circle of acquaintance than I could have expected. at this season all the Nobillity are out of Town, or I should no doubt be known to more of them than I am at present. I have been treated with great politeness by Lord Gage. Lord Grovesnor has been very polite to me, also. I dined with him last Sunday week, at his house in Town. the next Day he went into the Country. Lord Gage is also gone to his seat at bright Hamsted, where his Lordship pressed me to go in my way to France. he told me the stage came within 4 miles of his seat, and if I would write him a line to acquaint him with the time I should be there, he would send a Servant to fetch my baggage and desired I would bring any Gentleman I might have as a companion in my Tour, to his house. there is a great deal of Manly politeness in the English. there is somthing so open and undisguized in them that I can truly say exceeds rather than falls short of my expectation. Sr. Thos. Rich is married. he came to Town a few Days ago and called on me. on mon[day] I breakfasted with him went to see some Pictures and than Dined with him on the same Day. To Morrow I have an invitation to breakfast with Sr. Joshua Reynolds, than go with him to see the Ceiling of White Hall, Dine with a Mr. Watson, etc., etc. I menshon this to give you some Idea of the politeness of my Friends in this place and the manner of my Life while I am thus Idle: I might have begun several Pictures if it would have consisted with my plan, but I must see Italy first. I am therefore determined not to take any one subject the King has got till I visit that place. if nothing meterial should prevent me I shall very soon leave this place. I wish I could have a letter from you first. Sukey says in one I have had from her that you wrote by the same oppertunity, but it has not come to hand. you must Direct to be left at the New England Coffee House. I suppose you expect I should say somthing on the Pictures I have seen, but the field is so large I cannot yet begin it. I see so much that it is impossable to know where to begin, but do you go on as you are in your practice; but observe one peice of advice, to turn as much as possable Delicate Womens faces so as to have as little shade on them as may be. dont make it faint, but let it fall from the front of the face into those parts of less importance, as you will find it in Bentivoglio's portrait, and I think it is so in Mrs. Sidley's Picture at Capt. Phillips's, which by the way I believe the face to be painted by Van Dyck's hand by what I have seen here. I would have you very carefull to preserve as much as possable broad lights and shadows, only turn the face so that it shall be all aluminated, or as much so as possable. at the same time let the shade fall some where else: what if you should try somthing for an Exhibition? I would have you also observe to get into your Picture an hew of Colours that is rather gay than otherwise, at the same time rich and warm like Bentivoglios. but be carefull that you intersperse some cool Colours of the Green and white with yellow, etc., so as to give it the Colouring (when the whole mass of the Picture is taken together) of the Rainbow and be carefull as you go towards the bottum of your Canvis to mannage your objects that they do not take the eye. Scumble them down so that when you Vew the Picture the Center shall predominate. I think in Diana's figure in your Room you have an Example. observe her leggs how they seem to run out of observation, from her head and breast Downwards how gradually her figure seems to lose it self. but I must wish you a good night. in the Morn'g I will add a little more if I can.[1] I would send you Sir Josha. Reynolds's Lectures if I was sure you had not them; but if you have not they are well worth your possesing. I think them the best things of their kind that has been wrote. in my next I will send you a receipt for making a retouching Varnish, and wish you to send mine for making Spirit Varnish by the next oppertunity. I have not seen your Aunt, but shall to morrow write to her and send your letter. I am sorry you did not give me a Direction to the Person that transacts her business. She lives 72 Miles from this and I have been loath to take such a tour unless I could take it in my way to somthing else at the same time. however I will write and shall hear from her no doubt in a few Days. I will not neglect your Interest any more than my own and hope you remember what I left in Charge with y[ou] and will conduct your self agreable to it. I have your well being as much at heart as you can possable have it yourself. be very Active, Study incessantly, and practice continually, and you will find your advantage. remember it is [not?] anough to be a painter; you must be conspecuous in the Croud if you would be happy and great, and you must learn to rid off work. Inclosed is some Acct. which you will take care of. I have not been able to write to our Dear Mother but will do it soon, tho I consider my Letters to you the same thing only differing in name. I beg she will accept my most Affectionate Duty and Love. I am, Dear Harry, your Affct. Brother,

J. S. COPLEY.

---

[1] The handwriting changes.

Copley to Henry Pelham

LONDON, Augt. 25, 1774.

DEAR BROTHER,

Please to send enclosed to Gov. Hutchinson the drawing I took of him with a pencil some years since. you may if you please keep a copy of it.

I shall set out in about four hours for Brighthemstone and from thence take shipg. for Diepe in France etc., etc. God bless you. Your affect. Brother,

JOHN SINGLETON COPLEY.

Copley to Henry Pelham

PARIS, Sepr. 2d, 1774.

MY DEAR HARRY,

I have now the pleasure to inform you of my safe arrival in this City that I am in Spirits, am grown much fatter than you have ever seen me. I know not how it happens, but I beleive there is somthing in the Air of France that accilerates or quickens the Circulation of the fluids of the Human Body, for I already feel half a Frenchman in this respect. I left London on the 26 of Augst. and reached Bright Helmstone in the Evening of the same Day, and was there detained by bad weather till the 29th, when I and my companion imbarked on board one of the Packets, and in about 11 hours we arrived at Dieppe in Normandy. from thence we set out Imediately and reached Torst [1] at noon, from thence to Rouen where we Slept. Rouen is the Capital of Normandy, and you might expect I should give you some account of it; but we did not reach it till dusk, and at four oClock the next morning left it to pursue our rout. so I can only say the Streets are so narrow and the buildings so

[1] Tôtes.

high, all of Wood and in the Gothic or rather no stile, that in passing through the streets it seem'd like going through an Arch. for the Houses seem almost to meet at their Tops their oposites; But we pushed on our Way, resolved to lose no time and reached Vaudrieul[1] to Breakfast, and for the first time missed the Tea. we were served with Eggs, Chese, and Wine, etc. from this place we went on to Gaijon[2] where we dined in the true French stile, or we would have Dined if we could; but the Victuals was so badly Dressed that even Frenchmen complained of it. however this did not move us in the least. we went on after Diner to Vernon, there made a short Stop. thence to Bonnières, where we had a good Supper and good Beds. We now live altogether in the French Stile. Deserts are brough[t] after meals as regular as the Table is laid. at 4 oClock next morning we went on to Roboise,[3] from thence to Mentes,[4] than to Meaulen[5] where we dined, than began our last Stage to this Great City where we arrived in the afternoon. we passed many Towns which would be tedious to mention. all Normandy through which we passed is very fertile and full of delightfull Landscapes. The hills are covered with Vines. I think from Normandy to Paris not so rich a Country, though it is rendered more butifull by the many Towns and Seats that are interspersed through out it, and the fine River Siene, by which we rode many miles, adds much to the beauty as well as convenience of the place. We provided a Knife and fork for our Pockets before we left London, for the People always Carry a knife about them in this Country. so none are laid on any Table. Wine is drank out of Tumblers; but you must know those French Wines are not so strong as our Cyder. no other liquor except a little Warter is drank sometimes mingled with

[1] Vaudreuil. [2] Gaillon. [3] Rolleboise. [4] Manset. [5] Meulan.

Wine. The Peaches are Very good in this Country and very plenty. We are now in very *Clean* Lodgings in this place, which we reached the 1st of Sepr. I beleive you will think we made Dispatch to go from London to Paris in 4 Days and 3 Nights which we did, allowing for 3 Days detention by bad Weither. This Day my first in this place, I have seen the Church of St. Sulpice. it is rather grand from its quantity than the Eliganc of proportion, and the Pallais Royalle, in which I saw a very fine Collection of Paintings. and this Evening went to the Opera. the Subject was Orpheus serching for his Wife in the Infernal Regions. I was much entertained; tho a strainger to the Language, the Musick Charmed me. but it now grows late, so wish you a good repose and an earley attention to business in the morng., and a Care to Cultivate your knowledge of the Languages. this will make your future Life happyer than any thing in this World. do let me from my own feelings intreat of you not to Idle, or misapply, one moment, for they are Innestimiable. I feel what I Now write and Injoy the effects of my application in such a manner as no words can express; and this you will feel yourself if you will purchase it with Industry, as I know you may and you have a pleasure above me in having such a foundation for the Languages which will be of great use to you when you come abroad. my wishes for your happiness carrys me beyond my intention at this time, but it is so momentious a thing to you that I could not excuse myself, if I should let any time pass before I pressed it on you; lest by my delay some of those precious moments might be lost that this earley advice might have saved. let me just recommend to you to keep the faces of your portraits, perticularly your Weomens, as Clear of Shade as possable, and make broad Masses of Lights and shade. practice continually. Draw Landscapes, Dogs,

Cats, Cows, horses, in short I would have you keep in your Pocket a book and Porto Crayon — as I now do — and where ever you see a butifull form Sketch it in your Book. by this you will habituate your Self to fine formes. I have got through the Dificultys of the Art, I trust, and shall reap a continual Source of pleasure from my past Industry as long as it pleases God to give me health and life, but yet I lament I had not saved more of my time than I have done. you have it now before you and if you are determined you will accomplish it. Study those Works of Raphael which you can procure, the Cartoons in perticular. Draw them not in a finished manner, but to habituate yourself to the manner of combineing your figures. I trust you will take this in a manly manner and feel its force. I write under a Kind of impu[l]se, and would perswade you from inactivity as I would a near friend from plunging into certain destruction. Adieu, good night. I again take up the Subject (this morning) of my Observations on what I see in this place and hope you will excuse my long digression, as I think it is so important to your happiness. I shall return to the Pallais Royalle, which We saw yester Day or 2d Sepr. In this Pallais there is a very great Collection of Pictures by various Masters, some very fine, some indifferant, some bad. In the Chamber of Poussins are his seven Scacraments. the prints you have seen in Mr. Palmer's Vollumn of Italian Masters. they are very Dark, much more so than his Scipeo at Smibert's, and about the same size of that. these are however esteemed his best Works, but I should have liked them better if they had been coloured in a more brilliant manner. he has been somtimes very beautifull in his colours, light and warm in his Shawdows somthing resembling the Light of the Sun, his Shadows broad sharp and transparent. you possess an Accademy figure or two much stumpt. I think there is two on one paper, one on each side, much in his manner of treating his figures. you cannot mistake them, as you have none like them. one of them I think is puling a rope or in such an action; add to this kind of musseling the colour of Shade you see in the Camera which are in some parts very blew, in some a kind of readish or sandy tint. The out lines of his figures are not blended with the ground, but Sharp and determined, his expression is charming. his Men, Weomen, and Children, laugh, Cry, Grieve, and indeed express all the passion of the Soul surpriseingly well. I would have you draw some of his heads, that you may lern of what forms and Lines they are composed. I wish I could convey to you a more perfect Idea of what I see, but study the Camera for human figures and in short every Peice of Nature if possable, and you will go on in the way you are in and Diligence will make you an Artist. as you proceed invent Historical Subjects. possess Sr. Josa. Renolds lectures as soon as you can, — some of the Book Deallers will send for them for you — and they will tell you how to proceed in the management of those great Subjects. I dont mean to alter your pursuit in portraits, but you aught to be capable of treating every Subject. you have some Draw[ings] of Albonius's in bister which show how much is to be done from Imagination. only when you have got thus far, the Life is to be made use of for hands, feet, heads and for each figure Drapery sett on the Layman, broad and eligant. in this Way you make your finishd Drawing, which when done the Difficulty is over. There is several Titians in this collection, but shall forbear remarking on them till I see others that I am sure will give me a just Idea of his merrit in all respects. I am your Affecte. Brother,

J. S. COPLEY.

Robert Hooper to [P. Thomas?]

Call on Mr. Copeleys Brother up above the Orange tree, and desire him to put my son Stephens Picture into this Case and bring it without fail.

ROB HOOPER.[1]

Endorsed: Receid. the within

P. Thomas, Boatman,

Sepbr. 5, [1774?]

Copley to Henry Pelham

PARIS, Sepr. 7, 1774.

MY DEAR HARRY,

I was obliged to break off my last Letter somwhat abruptly as I found the Post was to go sooner than I expected, and I was loath you should miss of the most earley inteligence of my safe arrival in this place and of my health. I have given you the best Idea in my power of the Works of Poussin which I saw on the 2d Sepr. the same Day and in the same collection I saw many of the Works of Raphael, Corregio, Titian, Paul Veroneise, Guido, etc., but as I do not think I have yet seen their most perfect Works I shall suspend my remarks upon them till I have that pleasure. I do not think it is important to send you catalogues of the Pictures I see, but such an account of the Masters as will give you the best Idea of their Works in General and their merrit. as I write to one who has not seen any Works of Art I shall indeavour to adapt my Language to answer that end in the most effectual manner. In my way to the Palace Royalle I stoped at the Church of Notre Dame where I saw many Paintings, and much Sculpter. the Church is a very

---

[1] Of Marblehead, and known as "King Hooper."

beautifull Pile of Gothick Architecture, and perticularly menshoned by Mr. Addisson. it was founded by Robert one of the Kings of France in A.D. 1010, but a perticular disscription of every peice of Art would take up too much time. I shall only mention one peice of Sculpter which I think very fine. It is the Alter behind the High Alter. it is in form of a Niche and composed of four Figures; in the middle sits the blessed Virgin Looking towards Heaven with an Air of Holy Grief, if you will allow me the expression, her Arms extended, her Drapery flowing, and supporting on her Lap the head and part of the Body of a dead Christ. the Christ lays partly on the Ground and is very fine, behind is the Cross from which the Christ has been taken down, with a flowing peace of Linen hanging over it which makes the whole more pleasing in its form than it would have been without this continuation of the Mass of Art. it plays off from the Group and as a flame loses it self insensably first into a readish soft colour than tapers into many serpentine streaming points and gently steals unperceived into reaths of Smoke, so in this manner the mass is melted away. And observe, all lights in Pictures aught so to be mannaged. the first great ligh[t] ought to be followed by some suxceeding ones less powerful than the first that let the eye off by gentle degrees. this is effected by Colours as well as lights and shades. for instance read Will lead the eye from bright yellow, and black from Read, Green from White, etc., etc. but to return to the Alter. on one side is a figur of an Angel Kneeling, his Wings partly extended, holding the Crown of thorns in his hand. another Angel on the other side supports the hand of Christ. there is a great sublimity of expression in the whole Group. the heads perticularly that of Christ is very lovely and of a divine carractor perhaps not to be surpassed by any thing in Art.

This Group is of white marble much larger than the life and exicuted by Coustoux the Elder; in 1723. In this Church is the Royal Vault.[1] There is many Paintings by Cheron,[2] Ant. Coypal, etc., as large or larger than life. but I do not mean to give catalogues of the Pictures, for it would be an endless thing, and tend but little to your profit. my intention is to give you as just an Idea of the Works of the first Master[s] as I possably can without giving the Carracter of those that are inferior. nor shall I labour to Discribe perticular Pictures even of the first Masters, unless it is some of exalted Merrit, such as the Transfiguration. for this reason I shall not say any thing of Coypal or his works, nor shall I observe on Lebrun till my return to France for his Capital Works are at Versails which I shall not Vissit till my return from Italy. But I will endeavour to convey to you a just Idea of Raphael from the body of his best works taken collectively. the same of M. Angelo, Corregio, etc. I have now inform'd you of my plan and shall proceed without more preface. there is Building in this City a Colledge for Surgions. I think this will be a very beautifull building. there is a fine Corinthian Portico Wonderfully beautifull. in the Pidiment is a fine Bass releif of Sergery joining hands with learning cross an Alter, on one side some boys bringing forward Books, etc., on the other another group of boys inspecting a Dead body. the whole is built of free Stone.

Sepr. 3d. Vissited the Luxemberg. this Gallery is intirely Painted by Rubens, but I think the Pictures very unequel in merrit. you have seen the prints; they give you the design, so I shall not enlarge on that; only observe, that it is of a great car-

[1] Erased: "In it will be depossited in a few Days the body of the late King."
[2] Chéron.

ractor. you must take notice how he combines his objects, with what an easey flowing out line he Draws his figures, smooth and easey as the flow of Homer's Verse. all this you have before you, but you have not the colouring. it is very brilliant, rich and tender. when you vew Poussins Sippeo you must have observed one general tint runing over the whole Picture, as if the Painter when his work was done had immersed it in a brown Varnish. but when you see one of Rubens's you cannot say his Picture is of any one Colour, so happily has he divided his Colours over his Picture, that it is neither read, blue, yellow, or Green, but one agreable whole, pertakeing of many tints so well proportioned to each other that none predominates. The head at Mrs. Hancocks give[s] you a tolerable Idea of his men's flesh, only I think it a little too Raw. When he paints a River God, or Satire, Or an old man, such as Lot in the Picture you have, he colours the flesh very yellow and makes the half tints very green. these carractors I think he makes a litt[l]e of the Gumbouge copperry Colour. in the Dark shadows of those complections he puts almost pure Vermillon, expecially if a Read Drape[ry] should come in contact with it. I think the Shoulders and back of Pan in the Pan and Sirinks at Mr. Chardon's comes neigher the mark than any I can think of; only if I remember right the tints in that are more Grey and broken than Rubens's and darker. I beleive those figures in the Deluge at Mr. Chardon, I mean the Group that is most principal, that is clambering up the bank, may come nearer the mark than pan, especially if a little yellow is added to the tints. Rubens is very carefull not to let any part of his Pictures look sad or heavy, nor does he make them gaudy, but brilliant Clear and harmonious. his Weoman are very clear, but I know not what to refer you to by which you will form to yourself the Idea I wish to convey to you. I think the head of Bentavoglios comes the nearest to it. he seems to me to have mixt his tints first very clean and Rich in colour, than to have lay'd on his lights as they were mixed on his pallet, than the next pure tint in like manner and all the little musseling in the light parts of the body is only express'd by tints somthing reader, avoiding the gray tints. he only darkens with read those soft mussels and lines that fall in the mass of Light. even the extremitys next the back ground ar[e] carried off as much as possable by those clear Readish tints. I mean on the light side of his figures, for when he carrys his flesh into the shade, his first tint, after he leaves the pure carnation or the second tint above menshoned, he lays on one that pertakes of the blew, than follows his warm shade. but observe, the Demi or blew tint must be so far rendered harmonious by pertakeing of the Read and yellow that it makes an agreable whole. I think when he comes to the feet and hands he seems loath to Dray the fingers or Toes but scumbles them as much as possable in to a readish mass. this management is esspecially in his feet, tho somewhat so in his hands or rather fingers. the head of the Nimph in your Picture of Dianna has a great deal of this management, I mean her in the fore Ground. he never divides the Toes by any Dark lines so that when you are near the Picture you can scarcely make them out. The tone of his flesh, take an whole figure together, of one of his Weomen, and it is full and rich, about as much so as the head of Vandyck at Mrs. Hancocks.

I think it would be worth your while to paint a Picture from one of his prints to try the effect from this Acct. of his Colours. I would further add that when the musling is so deep that read would Appear too flaming and make the flesh look fleed, he puts between the read in the bottum of the hollows and the Second tint above menshoned the blewish tint. this keeps the mass of flesh soft and harmonious in its Whole body.

Sepr. 4. Vissited the Church of St. Roch, Hospital for Invalids, Place Victoire, the Collisee, etc., etc. I saw many paintings and much Sculptor, but shall pass them without any perticular remarks, as I can say nothing that I think will be important to you. only that the Chappel in the above Hospital is a most Magnificent peace of Architector. the Richness as well as purity of Stile is amasing. I shall now end my Letter to you — I beleive you think it a pretty long one — unless somthing should occur to fill the paper before I send it off.

Sepr. 7. I have just returned from takeing a second Vew of the Luxembourg where I and my friend spent the afternoon, and I find my above observations all confirmed with respect to Rubens's colouring. only that somtimes, he has thrown some little dashes of blewish tint (to take off a rawness that might otherwise arrise). I mean in the Light masses of his flesh. he has been however very sparing of all but the pure Carnation. Mr. Carter thinks this Account I have given you is so just that it is equel to your seeing the Pictures, and that you cannot mistake his Colouring. the Day after tomorrow we set out for Lions. you cannot imagine the pleasure that this Tour affoards me, but I miss the Language extreemly. I find was my stay here any length of time, I mean 2 or 3 Months, I should possess a great Deal of it. but Adieu, Dear Harry, and believe me yours,

J. S. COPLEY.

Copley to his mother

PARIS, 8th of Sepr., 1774.

DEAR AND EVER HOND. MAMMA,

I did not think it would have been so long be[fore] I should have wrote you, but I know you will excuse me in this when I inform you I have found it dificult to write those letters to Brother Harry, it being necessary they should be the result of great attention and Study, and that although I painted nothing in England, being resolved on making the tour first, yet I had a great deal to do in attending to the Art. by which means on my return to London I shall not have this to do, knowing at the same time you received every inteligence by the Letters to Harry and My Dear Sukey relating to me, for I have been very perticular to them, and have let no oppertunity of Wrighting to them for your Sake as well as theirs. for I consider'd my letter[s] wrote for you as well as them though addressed to them. I arrived in this City the first of Sepr. and shall leave it Tomorrow. We had a very fine tour to this City. we left Bright Helmstone on monday afternoon, and reached this place the Thursday following. Mr. Carter [is] well versed in traveling, has the languages, boath Italian and French. this makes [it] very convenient and agreable. he is a very polite and sensable man, who has seen much of the World. it is most probable one house will hold us boath at Rome, and the same Coach bring us back to England in a twelve month from Our leaving England. I desire to bless God I never had my health better in my [life], and I am really grown fatter than you ever saw me. I find this a great City containing many Superb Buildings. altho I do not like the Architecture in General in their Old buildings, yet there is a Chappel in the Hospital for Invalids, beautifull, grand and rich, allmost beyand disscription. There is a number of New Bui[l]dings arecting of a very magnificient Kind. I am assured there is a Capital Architect in this place. We are fixed in very Clean lodging. this you may think strange in this place for Paris is generally thought to be a Dirty place; but tho that may be true, yet people may live Clean and well if they please. there is Hotels in Paris in which there is appart's, that let for 50 and 60 Luisdores per Month. these are very grand. my Companian and myself give but a Guinea per Week for the Appartments we have. they serve us boath and we find a great saving in being together, in many things. we dine at a publick house, which is the best in Paris. I am told they lay tables for an 100 People per Day. the Cumpany are very genteel. they lay Table in differant Rooms; at each there may be about 15 Persons or 20. I think seldom more sit at the same Table. sinc[e] I have dined there several Knights have been of the Cumpany; none but Gentlemen of Carractor dine in this House. The Tables are mostly served with plate. Soupp is the first thing brought and this in Silver Turenes; than is brought the Bully; that is the Beef of Which the Soupp is made; than the Tables is served with two Courses of everything that is in season, and of the best kind; than a Desert. a pint of Wine is set to each plate, and is I think sufficient for one person. there is a Roal of bread of a very good quallity containing as much at lea[s]t as a 15 penny loaf. this is for one person. a Silver spoon Silver fork and knife and Towel. at each Corner of the Table a large Decanter of Warter. I think their bread far better than the London, or than any I have met with any where. in this House they never bring any thing a second time to table (not even the Linen) without Wash'g; but what is left is given to the poor. it is said the fragments feed 50 poor per Day. the attendance is excellent and the order of decoram of the Table so well preserved that you would rather think it a select cumpany of private friends met at a private House, than a mixed cumpany in a publick House. now I have given you this Acct. of the fare, what should you think is the Charge for this? not more than two shillings Sterling. I am sure you think this very Cheep indeed, but it is really no more, and I have not enlarged in the least. As it was my intention to stay in this place place but a week, so I did not think it worth while to seek for any acquaintance or introduction to any persons. Mr. Carter thought it not worth while. he has no acquaintance here, tho he has been two or three times before in Paris. The Pallaces are open, so We Vissit them; and the Churches. I have now seen all that is worth seeing, so shall lose no time but push forward towards Rome. it [is] curious to observe that in all the places that I have [been] in, Men seem to be the same sett of being rather disposed to oblige and be civil than otherwise. I can scarsely reallise it that I am now in this City, as it has seem'd so like a Dream to me when I have though[t] of coming to it; but I find all the Dificulty is in seting about such business. I have enjoyd a fund of Delight in this excursition and hope it will fix me in such a way as will ennable me to provide for my Dear Children in such a way as to bring them into the great World with reputation. as it now grows late I shall close this letter, with my best respects to all those Friends who shall inquire after me, and with my constant wishes for your health and happiness, and desires of your blessing constantly to attend me in all the moments of my life. I am, my Dear and ever Hon'd Mother, your Dutifull and truly Affectionate Son,

JOHN SINGLETON COPLEY.

P. S. I hope Snap continues to behave himself well. if he Does I shall be glad to hear it, and shall certainly reward him for it. I shall be very Glad to hear from Boston. I have received only one letter (which was from Mrs. Copley) since I lift it. it gave me a pleasure I cannot express when I received it, and shall be very constant to write to some or other of them every oppertunity, because I know they will receive the like pleasure from my Letters.

Copley to his wife [1]

Lyons, Sepr. 15, 1774.

My Ever Dearest and beloved Sukey,

My constant attention to your happiness, induces me to improve every oppertunity that offers to inform you, of my health; and that I know nothing irksom (as yet) in my tour but the painful seperation from those friends I so tenderly love, being sure of your sincerity, when you wrote me your happiness so greatly depended on mine. you are in return to receive the only best and surest testimonies that is in my power how much mine depends on yours, that is, releaving your anciety as much as possable by constantly writing to you, and being as soon as possably I can, in London again. I am as certain as I can be of any thing, that if it pleases God to bless me with Life, and health, I shall not exceed the time I menshoned, that is, I shall be in England the next Sumer. If you knew how great my desires were to be with you, you would not think it necessary to say one word to hasten that happy time; I am sure I shall think that an hour of happiness that brings us together beyand any I shall enjoy till it arrives. I feel myself epsorb'd, in those tender

[1] Chamberlain Collection, J. 3.8, in the Boston Public Library.

feelings to that degree that I must restrain myself till the time of Banishment is expired; yet, my Dear life, I assure you such a fund of pleasure attends me in all the sceens through which I pass, that it is an ample recompence for all the time, and expence, that attends such a Tour. I do not find those dangers, and dificulties, in the exicution of such a Voyage and Journey as this I am now prosicuting from America to Rome so great as people do that sit at home, and paint out frightfull Storys to themselves in their Imaginations. their is no part of the way from London to this City, but what is so traviled, that the number of people one must associate with is rather burdensome than otherwise; tho it is very genteel Cumpany one meets with, and no other, as there is a subbordination of People in this Country unknown in America. We left Paris last friday at four in the Morning and reached this City last night. it is reckened three hundred miles and we performed it in five Days. we came in a conveyance called a Diligence; it is like one of our Coaches only large anough to contain ten persons with conveniance, tho we were but seven, with four or five without side. we set out by four o Clock every morning and at certain stages stop to dine at 11 or 12 o'Clock; at those Houres there is always a Diner provided for the Cumpany that are in the Coach and no one else, unless that Cumpany chuse to invite any that may be at that time in the House. we were all exceeding sociable, tho I felt some degree of mortification in not having the Language, so as to join in the conversation. we were drawn by eight Horses; and what with the size of the Coach, the bagage before and behind it seemd a moving House. I cannot say much in favour of the Country through which we passed the four first Days, but the fifth Day such it was as was really inchanting. I forgot to tell you that the last Day and half we came by warter. the price is paid at Paris for a seat in the Diligence, and for that you are fed on the road and very well indeed; but when we got as far as Chalon, a City on the River sone, which is within a Day and an half of Lyons, the proprierters of the Diligence, have a Vessel into which they put us with our bagage. in this Vessell or boat there is two Rooms, one of which is very comfortable, seats all round with Cushons, and very neat indeed; so that we were as comfortable as in any Room. this Room is always reserved for the passengers that come in the Coach. than by a long roap from the mast Carried to the Shoar and fixed to Horses she is Drawn down the River (which is as Smoath as Glass) and on each side [we] were delighted with such fine prospects as no pen can discribe. the vast variety of Towns, Churches, Villas and castles, together with the lovely variety of the Hills on each side, covoured with Grapes and Gardens, and the beautifull windings of the river which is very narrow and gave us a very perfect vew of the smallest objects on boath sides, the warter so shoal that I think in general it did not exceed two or three feet take one part of it with the other. The Principal Villages and Towns by which we passed and that lay on each side of the Soan[1] are, Essaune, Fontain bleu, Moret, Villeneurs la Guyare, Sens, Villeniuve le Roy, Joigny, Auxerre, Vermenton, Rovere' Auxere, Arnelduc, Challons, Tournett,[2] Macon, and a Multitude of others that inriched the prospects and varied them so continually, that it is vain to attemp to give you an Idea of it. in this way we reach this City, tho not large is from its natu[ral] situation very lovely. it lays

[1] Seine, Yonne and Soane.
[2] Essonnes, Fontainebleau, Villeneuve la Guyard, Villeneuve sur Yonne, Pouilly en Auxerre, Arnay le Duc, and Tournus, are conjectured to be the places not easily recognized by his spelling.

on each side the River Soan, over which there are several Bridges. on the south side of the City is the famous River Rhoan menshoned by many Historians and Poets. this afternoon I passed the Street that is bounded on one side by this River, and saw its windings a considerable way. On the north side of the City the Hills are very high and bound it. we assended in going on this high ground a flight of Stone Steps, the number about 120. those Steps lead from [one] of the Streets. when we had got to the Top of the Steps we still assen[d]ed till we reach the Summit, where there is several [buildings] one of them a Church. But such a prospect my eyes never before beheld; such an extended Country so rich and beautifull! and at the utmost reach of sight could see the Alps riseing like Clouds above the other Hills, we could see from this the Mountains of Savoy and Switserland very Distinktly, and the City of Lyons right under our feet with the two beautyfull Rivers one on the Side the other running through the midst of it. Brother Harry can convey a very perfect Idea of our rout by my maps. I design staying in this City only two Days to rest and see what there is to be seen, and than with Diligence go on. I believe you must think we have not loitered on the road when we have go[ne] so far in so short a time, but we want to get on as fast as we can, and the sooner will be the return that I trust will put me in possession of my Dear Family. I am very Ancious for you, my Dear, and our lovely Children, for I know not what state you are in, in Boston; but I pray God to preserve you and them. I beg you will not be uneasey for me, for I take all imaginable care of my self and find it an happy event the having a companion. by this everything goes on easy. We shall I trust soon be at the utmost distance from those I so tenderly [love] that I propose, after a few months tarry there, every remove will bring us nearer together. O my Angel! had it been convenient for you to have been with me, how happy should I have been! I am ancious to know how my Dear Mother does, and [whether] she is easey or not. I know she must be ancious for me, but I hope it does not make her unhappy. do give my tenderest Love and duty to her. I wrote to her to you and Brother Harry from Paris, which I hope you will duly receive. you must continue to Direct to Brother Jackey[1] at the New England Coffee House my Letters, and he will forward them to me. Give my Duty and Love to our Hond. Papa, and to all my friends remember me in such a way as you shall judge proper. I hope you meet with no dificulty in the settlement of those Accts I left in your hands. I shall be much distresed if you are put to any dificulty of that kind. do write by every oppertunity. I am impation to know how things go in Boston. if my Brother wrote by the Vessell that brought your welcom Letter to me, it is lost. I have never seen it. give my blessing to my Dear Babys, and a thousand Kisses. tell my Dear Betsey not to forget he[r] Papa. I finish this 16 tho I began it 15 of Sepr. it give[s] you one Days later inteligence. But I must bid you Adieu, my Dear life. I shall write to you from Marsells as soon as I arrive there if the[re] be any oppertunity; if not do not be ancious. I shall watch every oppertunity. in the mean time may the good God keep you and your little one[s] in continual Peace, and beleive [me] your Most Affectionate Husband,

JOHN S. COPLEY.[2]

---

[1] Jonathan Clarke.
[2] The omissions in this letter, indicated by brackets, are due to the writer's haste, not to defects in the manuscript.

Copley to Henry Pelham

MARSEILLES, 25 Sepr., 1774.

MY DEAR BROTHER,

From this place I write you, altho I have so lately sent you a long Letter, for I assure you I dont know a greater pleasure than writing to my friends. But I should if it was possible fill my letters with matter that diffiered, so that each should contain somthing percular to itself. for I consider those I write to you not only yours but belonging to our Dear Mama, and my Dear Sukey; but it is dificult, as we take only a cursory vew of those places through which we pass. however I shall as much as possable avoid repetitions. I arrived at this place yesterday afternoon, and now begin to see the end of my long but most pleasing Tour, big with pleasure of various kind and instruction. You must think we have made great Dispatch to reach this place not less than eight hund. and fifty miles from London in four weeks, and made a week's stay at Paris, two Days at Lyons, and four Days and an half at Avignon; but I assure you there is no more Dificulty in traviling th[r]ough this Country than in your going to Cambridge; nor is there any dangers attending it but those to which human nature is exposed at all times and in every place. my last Letter was Dated at Lyons. from thence went to Avignon and reached it in 2 Days and an ½. we went down (in a kind of Vessel) the River Rhone carried by the currant, which although rapped is for the most part like a Glass. the River is not wider than that of Cambridge full of winding, many small Islands in it, and on its borders many Vilages and the most romantic Country on each side that you can conceive. Quite from Lyons to Avignon there is one continued range of hills which are very high, and in many places there is ruined monestrys, Towers, Castels, etc., which give such an effect that it exceeds all Discription. those kind of Boats or Vesells is continually Stoping boath to Land and take in passingers. it is so safe and so easy a mode of conveyance that people go in them, if it is not more than two or three miles they want to go. there is certain places where they Stop to Dine, and there is allways an eligant Diner provided of three Coarses, consisting of Fish, Fowls, Beef, Mutton, small Birds, etc.; and after this a Desert of Grapes, Peaches, Almons, Wallnuts, figgs, Cakes, Chese, etc., and as Genteely served as you can Imagin. the forks are all Silver and at every plate a Napkin neetly folded and lying on it. these Napkins are never brought a second time, no more is the Table Cloath. I must do the French the jus[tice] to say in their Table Linen they are very nice. I suppose you will wonder if I tell you I never wish to live more eligant than I do at those Houses. the Linen of their Beds is also very clean, their plates are a kind of earthan but quite white, and I think very Clever: their bread is very good; and to every plate a Roal is laid; and a Tumbler set with a silver Fork and spoon; and you would wonder to see with what ease the Cumpany is tended and how very genteel every thing is. however it is to be observed we have lived in the first manner that France affoards. there is a Vast variety of made Dishes brought besides the above mentioned. their suppers are just the same that their Diners are. Through the agreable windings of the Rhone we passed till we arrived at Avignon, where we had a little English Colony which was compossed of Gentlemen and Ladys to the number of fifteen, and at the play we made no small Figure. we spent 4 Days in this place very happily indeed, in this English assosiation. Avignon is a very pretty place, and I beleive may contain as many Inhabitants as Boston. it is in the Pope's Dominions and divided from the French Kings only by the Rhone, which is very narrow as I before menshoned. there is on the other side of the Rhone, two Convents, one of Benedictines situated very high and commands a very noble prospect, the other at a little distance in a small Vilage of which I have forgot the name. it is surprisingly rich in painting, Guilding, etc. it is very Clean throughout and Eligent. from Avignon we came in a Chaise to this Seaport, which is a very fine one. yesterday as soon as we arrived, we weited on Mr. Burbeck the British Consul, Who treated us with the greatest politeness Imaginable, Kept us to Tea, called on us this morning, carried us throughout the Town, which he thinks contains an hund. Thousand Souls. I prefer this place to any I have seen sence I left London. the Harbour is a very fine one, secured from the Ocean every way; the Buildings very good. We were at the play the last Eveng. and have been this also, but I sit up to write, as the Consul will send this Letter for me, and must have [it] by 9 oClock in the morning. he intends carrying us to the Concert to morrow Evening, and the next Day we set out for Antebes in a Chaise which we have taken for that purpose. Allow me before I conclude to intreat you to get the Languages. it is of the greatest consiquence to you Imaginable. I have lost a vast pleasure in not having the french but am surprised to find I have got so many words in so short a time. was I to stay 3 Months I should be able to speak a little. I can now ask for many things, but I shall soon be in the midst of Italian. as I have now trespassed on the las[t] page I shall be oblige[d] to inclose it in Sukeys and I shall not put a Covour, because there is nothing but what your Sister may see and I shall save some postage. this I know you will excuse. pray give my Effectionate Duty to our ever Dear and

Hond. Mama, my love to Brother and Sister Pelham, and to all Friends. I find an amaising fund of Pleasure and improvement in my Tour and feell no other anciety but that of being so far from my Dear friends. remember my injuntions of Dilligance and unremiting Ardour in the Pursuit of your Art.

I am, my Dear Brother, Your Most Affectionate Brother and Sincere friend,

JOHN SINGLETON COPLEY.

Charles Reak and Samuel Okey[1] *to Henry Pelham*

SIR,

It wou'd have given mee singular Pleasure to have seen you on my Excursion when wou'd have explained my Intention of scraping some Plates in Metzotinto from Desines of yours or Mr. Copeleys. I have carried with mee A Picture of Dr. Cooper by Copley but cou'd have wisht it had been that, that is in Mr. Hancocks Collection. I have likewise A Picture of Mr. Addams

[1] Stauffer mentions three plates published by Reak and Okey, "Printsellers and Stationers on the Parade, Newport, Rhode Island." 1. October 28, 1773, a mezzotint of Feke's portrait of Rev. Thomas Hiscox, late pastor of the Baptist Church in Westerley; 2. November 2, 1774, a mezzotint of Gaine's portrait of Rev. James Honeyman, late Rector of Trinity Church, Newport; and 3. April, 1775, one of Mitchell's portraits of Samuel Adams. A fourth, without name of publisher, of Joseph Warren, he believes to have been made by Okey, and a plate of Hals' Burgomaster is known to have been his. Okey was the engraver and Reak a printer, and the two were associated in London before coming to the United States. See *Dictionary of National Biography*, XLII. 80; Stauffer, *American Engravers*, II. 391. An advertisement of Reak and Okey in the *Newport Mercury*, January 30, 1775, offers the "Much Admired ROYAL CLOVE DROPS," and "NEW BOOKS, among which are the Vicar of Wakefield, a work highly esteemed by the learned, Evans's poems, Macaronic Jester, Amorous Buck, being a collection of jocular songs, with a variety of curious watch-papers, etc. Prints and pictures neatly framed and glazed, portraits taken in chalk, miniature painting, and every kind of drawing, as usual."

wich I purpose Imediately on my return to put on the Copper.
I saw yours at Mr. Reviers which I admire. how unlucky for
mee I cou'd neither have the Pleasure of seeing you or him.
I cou'd have wisht for the best Picture of Mess. Hancock and
Addams. you have A Fine Picture of A Lady in Car of a
Sheperd or Nymph. it wou'd make a Good Metzotint. at
presant wee cou'd not undertake it. we shou'd beg your Interest
some time hence to get Mr. Hancock's and interim shall venture to work from this Picture of Mr. Addams by Mr. Mitchell.[1]
tho shoud be glad if Mr. Revier wou'd send us Imediatly the
small one of yours from which wee wou'd scrape the Face. I
wish to have this Plate done in about Two Months when will
send you A Proof. in Interim am your Most hum. sets.

CHAS. REAK and for
SAM. OKEY.

BOSTON, Octo. 5th, 1774.

beg you'l let Mr. Heard have the Proofs I think Seventeen
left I beleive in your hands and Mr. Mumford of our Town will
forward them to us.

Henry Pelham to Copley

PHILADELPHIA, Novr. 2d, 1774.

DEAR BROTHER,

A letter filled with appologies would perhaps as much require
an excuse as the long silence it was meant to extenuate I shall
therefore leave the subject hoping your candour will attribute
the omission to any cause but neglect or want of Regard for be
assured that not a day passes but I think of you with the most
tender and grateful Remembrance.

[1] J. Mitchell.

Your *welcome and pleasing Letter* of July 15 is now before me; *welcome*, as it gives me the happy account of your Safe arrival after an agreable Passage upon which I congratulate you, and *pleasing*, as I find I have a distinguish'd Place in your Regards. When in that Letter you say "you begin a Correspondence from which I shall no doubt receive much pleasure" you judged Very right, tho' had you substituted Happyness instead of Pleasure it would have given a truer discription of those feelings which I enjoyed upon the commencement and expect in the continuance of that Correspondence.

The Account you give of your Health and agreable Journey, your interview with and Character of Mr. West, your having a Companion with you in your tour, etc., give all your friends in this part of the world infinite satisfaction. I promise myself much pleasure in a Sight of Mr. Wests print of the death of Gen'l Wolfe. You will doubtless want to know why this is dated from Philadelphia. Alass! I wish I had a more satisfactory account to give than that I have taken this Journey in search of lost Health; but still Happy should I be could I say I had entirely recovered it. I have been for near 10 Months past very subject to nervous complaints which shewed themselves in an almost continued Dizziness, Headack, Loss of Appetite, Trembling of the Nerves, and Lowness of Spiritts. for these I early put myself under the Care of Doct'r Perkins, who ordered me a course of Steel and frequent Riding, and recommended a long journey in the fall which my friends much advised too. Mr. and Mrs. Startin returning home, I thought it a favourable time for the excursion, and have come thus far in Company with them and Judge Lee and Lady, our Cambridge Friends, who propose passing the winter here. In a few days I intend to sett out for home, stoping for about a fortnight at New Haven, where Mr. Babcock[1] has engaged me to do two or three minature Pictures. The effect my Ride has had is a great lessning of all the symptoms except the Headack and lowness of Spiritts; they still seem to continue inveterate.

I left my Friends as well as usually they are, my Mamma anxious for my Health and solicitous for my taking this Journey.

The State of Publick Affairs in Boston you are desirous to know. How pleasing would it be could I inform you that Peace and mutual Confidence, Mercy and Law had resumed their Sway. but Alass! my Dear Brother! Discord and Distrust, Cruelty and Anarchy, have banish'd them from this unhappy Land. I am glad My Paper will plead an excuse for not decending to Perticulars in a subject to me so Distressing. From the fatal publick Movements of the last Winter I date my present Disquietude, and much fear that will be the Æra of my future Unhappyness.

Buisness of a private Nature next claims attention. here likewise they are far from being as I could Wish.

My own entirely Stopped, yours not in that forwardness that you expected. Money people are very loth to part with. Our *Common* Friend Mr. G[reen] has entirely dropped the mask and by his conduct avows himself to be that finish'd Scoundrel I always thought him. He will neither pay his Rent nor remove out of the House, so that it is continually increasing, and Heaven knows there is now no Law to compel him to either.[2] We take no more notice of each other than if we were perfect Strangers.[3] Your Hon'ble Coll.[4] that was, for he is now dis-

[1] Adam Babcock.

[2] Erased in first draft: "Not the least Civilities pass between us now."

[3] The letter thus far has been neatly copied. What follows is from a very confused first draft, which has here the following erased sentence: "He has treated Mrs. Copley and myself in a base and unhansome Manner."

[4] Hancock, who was colonel of the Cadet Corps.

missed, has scarc[e]ly behaved better than Mr. G., tho much
more Complesantly. 3 times a day for a Week together have I
attended him upon his appointment, as often Disapoint[ed],
either by his absence or buisness or having lost the Account, or
some such trifling excuse. here again the temper of the times
forbids my doing other than taggle after his plagey heels whenever he is pleased to appoint it. my tongue of[ten?] itches[?]
to tell him that I think he is a very trifling Fellow. I should
certaintly do it was he a less Man, or I a greater, or the times
more favorable.

My Crazy Coll'l[1] has left me without settling with me and I
find he has nothing to settle with.

I shall not attempt a discription of this City or New York,
where we spent 9 Days. Such a Discription to you who have
seen them would be unnecessary, and had you not, would after
your English and Italian Tour be totally uninteresting. I have
been lucky in forming some very agreable Acquaintanc[e]s and
valuable Fri[e]nds in Both Citys, perticularly in Mr. Curson[2]
and Mr. Seaton[3] in New York, and Doct'r Morgan in this City.
from them I have rece'd great Civ[il]iteys and find them much
disposed to promote my coming among them as an Artist.
most People with whom I am acquai[n]ted are desirous of my
exercising the Pencill, and I have half promised to make another
tour in the Spring, but this is a matter that will entirely depend
upon contingancies. Those Gentlemen have promised to find
me some Buisness, and Kindly offer to introduce me to more.[4]

[1] Elihu Hall. See *Proceedings Col. Soc. Mass.*, v. 199.

[2] See *Mass. Hist. Soc. Proceedings*, XLVII. 232.

[3] William Seton, a merchant, with a store on Cruger's Dock. He was afterwards in the Bank of New York.

[4] Erased: "I saw those Pictures at Mr. Lows at Brunswick and was really
charmed. your discr[i]ption by no means gave me an adequate Idea of their

I have only Room to add that a continuance of your regard is the Wish, And that the almighty would bless you in Health, Peace and Content, is the Prayer of your ever affectionate and Obliged

H. P.

You are much talked of here. I was really surprized at finding you so well known. Scarc[e] a person but has your name as patt and speaks with a[s] much fluency of you as of Mr. West. Mr. and Mrs. Startin from whom I have rec'ed the polites[t] marks of attention and Regard, present their kind love to you as do also Mr. Lee and Lady. I am with affection as above,

H. P.

I just heard that our Friends at Boston are all well, and that a letter from you was arrived with my things etc. I also hear that Mr. Molineaux[1] was dead after 3 days illness of an inflamation in his Bowels.

Novr. 2d., 1774.

Henry Pelham to John Singleton

PHILADELPHIA, Novr. 10, 1774.[2]

DEAR AND HON'D UNCLE,

I am at last happy in an Opertunity of acknowledging the recei[p]t of your very welcom[e] and kind favour of Jan'y 27, which is now before me. accept my gratefull thanks, for the

Bea[u]ty. Doct'r Morgan has a few clever Coppys, and an Original Portrait of Angelica painted by her self. This I was so pleased with that I have taken a coppy of it in Minature."

[1] William Molineaux, a "noted merchant" of Boston, and an ardent defender of the liberties of America. A tribute to him is in the *Essex Gazette*, October 25, 1774.

[2] This letter was first dated Nov. 2, then Nov. 4, and finally Nov. 10.

Pleasure you have given me, and for the tender regard you ther[e]in express towards me. The Gratification I experienced upon receiving a letter, from so near and dear a Fri[e]nd, makes me sincerely Regret the uncertainty and frequent miscarriages attending a Correspondence, to so remote a part of the globe as yours is from this. I must appologize to you, for not answering your affectionate favour before, but doubt not your excuse, when I inform you that this is the first Opertunity I have had, since the receipt of yours, which did not come to hand till the middle of Last June. Your kind Congratulations upon my Brother Copleys Marriage I receive with greatest Pleasure, and return the Compliment with the most heartfelt Satisfaction, in wishing you joy of the marriage of my Cousin with a Gentleman of Mr. King's Fortune and Character, and hope you will find in the Connection every possable Satisfaction and Happyness. I pray Heaven you may. The Acount you give of your family is very pleasing to me, as is your kind wish for a more regular Correspondanc[e] with me. this be assured is what I most ardently desire, as what would add much to my Happyness and seem to shorten that distance at which Providence has placed us. those Letters you or my other Fri[e]nds in Ireland, may do me the Honor of writing, if Direc[t]ed to me in Boston, New England, and put on board any Vessells (of which I am told there are many continually sailing from Limeric and Cork) bound to Philadelphia, will come to hand in the directest and speediest manner. A Gentleman of this City,[1] who married a Sister of Mrs. C[opley], and in whose perticular Friendship I am hon'd takes the Care of my Letters, both to and from Ireland. So that I now Hope I have found a Channell of Conveyance that will afford me the Greatest

[1] Mr. Startin.

Benj.ᵗ West

Master Shelly & his elder Sister.

Pleasure and Happyness, the Happyness in your Correspond-
ance. You desire some account of your friends in America.
My Hon'd Mother still continues in that declining way she
was in, when I wrote you last; she still retains the warmes[t]
Regard for you; And I fullfill her (often repeated) desires, in
presenting her kindest Love and most sincere affection to you,
and our other dear friends in Ireland. Her Heart ever glows
with undiminish'd tenderness for those whom nature has placed
nearest it. She much interests herself in her Neice's Marriage,
and unites with me, in my Congratulations, and in wishing that
every felicity thro' time and Eternity, may attend you, the
new married Couple, and all your and their Conections. My
Brother Cha's [1] Alass! unhappy Man! sailed from Boston for
Carolina, where he arrived abov[e] 8 years ago, since which I
have not heard the least thing concerning him, and am entirely
ignorant where he is, or weither alive or not. My other Brother
your dear namesake I had the Pain of Parting with the begining
of last June when he embarked for England, on his way for Italy
where he proposes spend'g 15 or 18 Months for his improvement
in an art, for his excellence in which he has already received
from Gentlemen in England the most distinguishd marks of
applause and Friendship. His Wife, a most amiable and fine
Woman, remains in Boston with the[i]r three Children, Named
Elizabeth Clarke, John Singleton, and Mary, three as noble
Children as are in America. I have not room in this to give you
any account of my tour to this place, 350 miles from home,
which I left about 2 months ago for the recovery of my Health;
impaird by Nervous Disorders, with which I have been for
some time troubld. By the middle of Decm'r I hope to have a
happy sight of my Hon'd Mother in Boston. I conclude with

[1] Peter.

requesting your Blessing and Prayers, and a Contin[ua]nce of your Regard and Correspondenc[e]. I am, Dear and Hon'd Uncle, your Dutiful Nephew and Humble Ser't.,

H. P.

P. S. My Dutiful regards attend my Aunt S[ingleton] my Uncle and A[unt] C[ooper], my Love to my Cousins. I write to aunt C[ooper] but am at a loss for a direction. I have directed to her at Coopers Hill near Limerick. I pray you to favour me with a perticular direction for yourself, as also for her, for fear my Letters to her in which I request it should miscarry.

Nov. 10, 1774.

Henry Pelham to his mother

DEAR AND HOND. MADAM,

In my last to you from Philadelphia I informed you that I should sett out in a few days, when I expected soon the Happyness of seeing you and my other Fr[i]ends in Boston in Health and Peace. Mr. Mifflin[1] a Gentleman of great influence in the City upon my arrival there was so ingaged with the Congress of which he was a Member as this precluded him from giving me (which he was much inclined to do) an introduction to Governor Penn[2] and his Collection of Paintings, which is very great and Eligant, and to Governor Hamilton's[3] and Judge Allen's[4] Family. These Gentlemen [are] the first in America for fortune and Character, and highly distinguish'd for their love and Patronage of the Polite Arts and Artists, and who have it very much in their power to do me a Kindness either here or in Europe. I thought it imprudent not to be introduced to, espe-

---

[1] Thomas Mifflin. [2] John Penn (1729–1795).
[3] James Hamilton (*c.* 1710–1783), of Bush Hill.
[4] William Allen (*c.* 1710–1780).

cially as it was offered[1] for these Reasons, and at the earnest solicitatio[n]s of Mr. and Mrs. Startin, and by the advice of Doctor Morgan, who much interests himself in shewing me every mark of Civility in his Power, I have been induced to make my tarry at Philadelphia a fortnight Longer than I at first intended. now I have the Happyness of presenting you with my duty from this place[2] which is abov[e] half way between Philadelphia and Boston. Yesterday and today I have begun 20 Guines worth of Buisness here, the Heads and hands of which only I shall finish here, and send the Pictu[r]es home to finish the other Parts. I have found it extremly difficult to procure meterials here for oil Paint'g, but have after some time got them. I have only time as the Post is just setting out to recommend myself to your Blessing and Regard, and after present'g my Duty to you, and Love and Compliments to my other Friends and Acquaintanc[es] to subscribe Dear and H. M. Your dutifull Son and affection'e Servt.,

H. P.

I dont expect to remain above a fortnigh[t] in this Place. indeed am certain I shall not, and am pleased in having Company a Son of D. E. home with me, which is very pleasing upon the Road, Especially this season of the year.

Nov. 18, [1774].

Henry Pelham to Charles Startin

N[EW] H[AVEN], Novr. 21, 1774.

DEAR SIR

The very solitary ride I have had for a few Days past forms a very disgusting Contrast to the amusing Scenes I have for

---

[1] Erased: "and could not well be refused."   [2] New Haven.

some weeks past enjoyed, and makes me remember with
redoubld ardour and Regard the agreable Company I left at
Philadelphia, in whose Conversation and Friendship I recently
took so much Pleasure. The kind manner in which It was
desired prompts me to take up the Pen with peculiar readiness
to acquaint you of my arrival here, but Gratitude more immediatly commands it to return you and Mrs. Startin those thanks
which I shall ever think due for these kind polite, and very
friendly marks of attention and Regard I have experienced from
your Family since I left home. accept my sincere[s]t thanks,
and believe I shall ever seek and ever think myself happy in
Opertunities of shewing the gratefull sence I entertain of your
civilities and of retur[n]ing the Obliga[tion] I am under. I have
had six of the most disagreable days I ever spent in my life.
But of this I dont complain. considering that a motley Mixture
of Pain and Pleasure is Mans lot, how unreasonable how absurd
would it be to repine at four [six] unpleasant days when I have
just finish'd as many Week[s] which I shall ever rank among
the Happyest of my Life. The weither was very fine and pleasant during most of my ride. the last day it clouded up, and I
had not arrived here half an hour before it rained very smartly
and so continued for 24 hours. a Days confinem't upon the Road
would have made me quite Malencholly. News I can collect
none, in Boston; every thing Remain[s] quiet, but God only
knows how long they will continue so. in New York people
are very uneasy at the Proceedings in Your City. nobody can
find the reason of the Carolinas Exporting Rice.[1] many there

[1] In its "Association," October 20, the Continental Congress pledged its
members to export, after September 10, 1775, no "merchandise or commodity
whatsoever to Great Britain, Ireland, or the West Indies, except rice to Europe."
Journals of the Continental Congress (Lib. Cong. ed.), I. 77.

th[i]nk it will oversett the whole scheme, and be productive of general Murmering and discontent. Some late procedings in this place are the subject of altercation but it would perhaps be deemed improper in me a Stranger here to enter into a Detail of Perticulars; but if proper might be unsafe. for tho this Lett[e]r is directed to you and intended soly for your perusal, there is no knowing who may take the very innocent Liberty of peeping, and then we well know they claim unbounded freedom of Publishing. further that it can not be justified upon any principles that so far from distressing Great Britain it is entirely calculated to ruin the town of Newport by throwing that valuable Branch of trade into the Hands of the Merchants at Liverpool and Bristol. While I am writing this I hear that the town of Newport is in the greatest Confusion owing to the proceedings of Congress, perticularly the part respecting The African[1] Trade. many of the merchants seem much inclined to refuse obedience to their determinations. nay say they will if York should, tho they dare not be singular; say that their Deligates[2] have sold the Town to gratify the Quakers of Philadelphia. this is intelligence you may rely upon and which considering all Circumstances gives me much uneasiness. Should the Continental Association be broke thro it will still tend to prolong that unhappy dispute which is so subversive of the publick Tranquillity of this Country, and is so inimical to the private Peace of its Inhabitants, will deprive us of a fair trial of

[1] Erased: "the slave." The "Association" further pledged the members of the Congress: "We will neither import nor purchase any slave imported after the first day of December next; after which time, we will wholly discontinue the slave trade, and will neither be concerned in it ourselves, nor will we hire our vessels, nor sell our commodities or manufactures to those who are concerned in it." *Ibid.*, 77. Newport was the leading port engaged in the trade.

[2] The delegates from Rhode Island were Stephen Hopkins and Samuel Ward.

its utility, and will not save us from any disagreable Consequences which may arise from the Resentment of Britain to
that measure.

The smallpox is among the Troops in Boston. this calls to
Remembranc[e] the pleasing event of Mrs. Lees recovery from
that disagreable Disorder, and from the as disagreable apprehension of it, of which I sincerely congratulate her; to whom and
Mr. Lee I beg my respectful Compliments may be made. I shall
ever think myself Honourd in Your Friendship and Correspondanc[e]. my affection[a]te Regards ever attend you and
Mrs. Startin. I conclud[e] with requesting a line from you.
wishing you and Connections every Happyness attendant
up[on] the Happiest, I am, my Dear Friend, your affect. and
oblige[d] Hum. S.

[No signature.]

[Charles Startin] to Henry Pelham

PHILADA., Decr. 3d, 1774.

DEAR SIR,

I duly receiv'd your much esteem'd favour from New Haven
of the 20th. Ulto. and should have answer'd it sooner, but have
been confined with a severe Fit of the Asthma. You much
overrate the trifleing Civilitys shewn you here. believe me
sincere when I say that much more was due to your merit and
the esteem I hold you in. it will always give me real pleasure
to render you any acceptable Service, and I hope you will
command me with the Freedom of a Friend.

I wish I could send you any News but we have none here
worth relating. Politicks run extremly high indeed. Our Lords
and Masters, the high and mighty Committee Men, have now
enter'd upon their department to put the Non Importation

agreem't in force; So that as a witty writer observes, instead of being devour'd by a Lion, we are to be gnawed by rats and Vermin. Mr. and Mrs. L[ee] are both well, and nothing further has transpired in

the Squib way. they with my wife Join me with proper Respects, and good wishes for your health and welfare.

I shall always be happy to hear from you, and remain with real regard, Your Sincere and Affectionate Friend and H'ble ser't.

P. S. As I have wrote with some freedom on Publick affairs I thought perhaps, the Signature might be as well Omitted.[1]

Henry Pelham to Dr. John Morgan

N[EW] H[AVEN], Decr. 4, 1774.

SIR,

To the many favours already confered on me I must beg you to add one more if consistant with your time and inclination.

A little minute of the Ladys name, who painted the charm'g portrait in your Possesion which I so much admire, and of which, by you[r] kindness I have a Copy, with he[r] age and the time when and the place where she did it, and any other perticulars you may pleas[e] to add, will (by putting it upon my Copy) ennable me to gratify some antiquary into whose hands time may threw it, some future Walpole who may think its want of meritt happyly attoned for by being the Portrait of the justly celebrated An[gelica], and being an authentick tho deficient Copy from an original painting of that truly ingenious and

---

[1] This letter is in Charles Startin's handwriting.

Capital Artist. The Perticulars you did me the favou[r] to relate of that Picture and the Lady have so far sliped my memory as to preclude my giving with certa[i]nty that information I could wish.

I am induced to trouble you with this request from recollecting the regret Mr. Walpole warmly expresses in his Anecdotes of Paint'g at the Artists' neglect of giving on the back of their Portraits the name and other perticulars of the Persons for whom they are done; an Indeferent Artist he observes by doing that may often stamp a considerabl[e] Value upon an otherwise indefere[n]t Picture.

Your Letters to Doctr. Jones and Mr. Bossley I had the pleasure of delivering to those Gentlemen. A few days I hop[e] will give me the Happyness of seeing Mr. Stillman and deliver'g his Letter.

My thanks are due for the many Civilities I recd. from you in Philadelphi[a] and for the Hand of you[r] Friendship accept them with my respectfull Com[pliments] to yourself and Mrs. M——, and believe me to be with Esteem Sir, You[r] Obliged and most Obdt. humbl. Sert.

H. P.

P S. Mr. Startin will take the Care of and transmitt me any answer you may Honor me with, but whi[c]h I beg may not intrude upon you[r] time and important Buisness.

Henry Pelham to Charles Startin

New Haven, Decmr. 12, 1774.

Dear Sir,

I am highly pleased in having a place in your memory and friendship. Your very kind and esteemed Letter of the 20

Richard Clarke
From the original painting by Copley
in the possession of Mr. Copley Amory

Decem'r is an addition to the many favours already Rec'd and a fresh Instance of your politeness, and of the agreable manner in which you render your friends easy and happy. Could I find words adequate to my Ideas to thank you with, I would use them. as I cant I must content myself with simply saying that I highly value your Friendship, and am honord in the enjoyment of your good Opinion and Regard. I am too well acqua[i]nted with you in the least to doubt your Sincerity. But even my Vanity raised as it is by the Politeness and marks of attention I have experienced since I left home, cant prevent my denying your assertion that I much overrate the Civilities shown me at Philadelphia and that much more was due to my Merit. I am willing you should think I have more than I really have as I reap a material benefit from your mistake.

Some of the inclosed Letters are to me of considerable Consequence. you will do me a great kindness if you will forward them by the first Vessell sailing for Ireland.

I must solicit your and Mrs. Startins Interest to induce Mr. Clark[1] to sitt for his Picture. I consider this as the only chance of doing it. Brotr. C[opley], it is very probable, will remain in England, and where I shall be nex[t] Summer Heaven only knows. I pray it may n[o]t be a worse place than Boston. I shall be much restrained from urging Mr. C., fearing he will think me differently interested from what I really am. I wish sincerely wish to gratify myself in having an Opertunity to please some of my perticular friends, and to preserve the likeness of a Gentleman whose distinguish'd Merit has attracted my Veneratio[n] and Respect. Can I but admire the man whose Virtues have silenced the envenomed tongue of

[1] Richard Clarke.

party Malice, and whose Character in every shape has remained unempeach'd by the Gall dipt pen [of] Faction?

I inclose a rough sketch for a picture frame, which I think would be very pretty and neat if made of metal washd like some of the washed buckles. I have seen one in Gold of exqu[i]site Workmanship nearly like this, that pleased me very much. Those who are used to things of that kind might possably invent a neater pattern. They must be Well finishd, well gilt and be very neat, or they will not answer the purpose of orniminting a minature picture. It would be best to have two differe[n]t sizes, as I have drawn them. I would be glad to have half a Dozen of each, and doubt not I should want more. Should only one size be made I would chuse the largest, and that exact to the pattern which, if you app[r]ove, please to send it to Birmingham.

I conclude in a great Hurry, as I am just setting out for Boston. my Disoblegiant[1] now waits at the door. God Grant you and Mrs. Startin Heaven's choicest Blessings Health and Peace: Remember me kindly to her, and believe me my dear Friend to be yours entirely and afectionately.

H. P.

N B. two or 3 Request[s] mor[e], and then I have done. Be carefull of your Health. Please to present my respectfull Comp's to Mr. L[ee][2] and Lady. Be kind eno when you favou[r] me with a line, which I hope will be soon, to mention what Postage you pay for this Pacquet that I may pay you as you denot.

---

[1] "Carrage," erased. [2] Joseph Lee.

Adam Babcock to Henry Pelham

NEW HAVEN, Decr. 24th, 1774.

DEAR SIR,

The Business at Town-Meeting was so very arduous that I could not leave it a moment to take leave of You the Day You left us. I hope You will be good eno' to excuse me in this n[e]glect which was unavoidable. the main Point in View—the demolition of Liberty-Pole-Committee, — we could not come to, on that Day, and the Town-Meeting was adjourned to the Tuesday of this Week. and with great perseverance and not without some noise on their side, we obtain a Vote from the Town to dissolve that meeting, so that I hope matters will go on quietly with us for some time at least.

I designd to have given You money eno' to have bot. me 76 Coper plate Tiles for my Chambers, and 5 ps. of neat paper, blue Ground with a proper proportion of Bordering for one Chamber. I beg You would buy me these things and send them by one of the Providence covered Wagons, directed to the Care of Docr. Jabez Bowen at Providence, to be forwarded by him to Mr. John Bours at New-Port. if You are so good as to send these the Day after You recieve this, they will doubtless come time eno' for my Little Sloop to take them at New-Port; but if it puts You to any inconvenience, I beg You would omit it, as I shall hardly make use of them till Spring. the Glass for the little Picture You will please to forward to me at any Rate, and in that way that You judge best, and an accot. of all with the Case for the pictures. I shall embrace the first safe hand to send You the Money.

I hope You had an agreeable Journey, at least as much so as the Season would allow of, and that You found Your Friends and Connections well. Mrs. Smith presents Her Compliments to You. be pleased to accept those of the Season from me together with my best Wishes, and when You write Mr. Copeley don't forget mine to Him, nor to his amiable Lady neither, when You see Her. and believe me to be most sincerely and cordially Yours,

ADAM BABCOCK.

P. S. Mrs. Smiths Picture I shall send You by my Sloop.

I should chuse the Tyles all of different Figures — and not one side of the Fire Place like the other, if there is variety eno'.

Dr. John Morgan to Henry Pelham

PHILADA., Decr. 27, 1774.

SIR,

In answer to your favr. of the 4th Inst. I am to inform You that the Portrait in my Possession which I lent You to copy is an original Portrait of the justly celebrated Painter Angelica Mariana Kaufman, done by herself at Rome, at the Age (as nearly as I can recollect at this distance of time) of about 19 Years. It was done by her and sent to me at my own desire. She had been labouring for some time under an Indisposition for which she was pleased to take my Advice. The seat of her Disorder was in her Stomach and proceeded from Indigestion. I believe it arose from her sedentary Life and close Application to Painting, to which she was so attentive, that sometimes, when employ'd in copying the Paintings of Great Masters that were hung up in the Palaces at Rome to which she was admitted, she would not eat the whole day.

I suppose her to be at this time about 28 or 29 Years of Age. On my leaving Rome she wanted to pay me for my Advice.

I refused taking any Money from her on which she insisted on making me a present of a piece of painting, of her doing, and desired I would pitch on some piece of any of the great Masters that she could conveniently copy, and she would execute it for me. I thereupon begged her own Portrait, as of an Artist I greatly valued, and on asking her Father's[1] permission, which he readily granted, she promised to send it to me, which she did about a year after when she came to London[2] with a Letter accompanying it, — being induced to visit England from the great Encouragement given to her by the english Nobility and Gentlemen then at Rome.[3]

Other Particulars of her History since she came to London may be better learned from Mr. Copley. Thus I have gratified you in what you requested to know of this most valuable Lady.

At the Age of 10 Years, she spoke English and French as familiarly as if they were her Native Language, which she learned chiefly by conversation. She could read Spanish with equal ease, tho' for want of Opportunities to practice it, did not pretend to be Mistress of it; but she was quite Mistress of the Italian, and of German which was her native Tongue. She had an agreeable person, a sweet and open Countenance, of a very modest engaging Deportment, and was no small proficient in Musick. At her first coming to England she was soon presented to the Queen[4] and employed to take her Majesty's Portrait. In short she was in a fair way of rising to fame to honour and fortune, but an unlucky Marriage was a great Clog to her.[5]

[1] Johann Josef Kauffmann.   [2] She went to England in 1766.
[3] This portrait is probably that in the Pennsylvania Academy of the Fine Arts, deposited by Miss Elizabeth Powell.
[4] Queen Charlotte.
[5] To Count de Horn, an impostor of many aliases.

As she is an Acquaintance I highly esteem I do not expect, by satisfying your request, You can think I would have these particulars known to any but Persons of Merit, Prudence and delicate sentiments. Should it be known to Angelica that I had thus attempted to sketch her Character, it might be taken amiss, as it could not fail to hurt her delicacy, of which you will be pleased to take Notice, nor let any person Copy a feature of her Character from this Letter, which in every particular falls infinitely short of her. With this caution I conclude, wishing You all Happiness and remain, Sir, Your Most Obed't humble Serv.

JOHN MORGAN.

A Bill for Portraits

Boston   The Honble. Isaac Royall Esqr. to J. S. Copley Dr.[1]

	£	s	d
To a packg Box omitted in former Acct...........	0..	9..	4
To a portrait in Crayons of Miss Polly Royall.....	5..	12..	0
To gold carved Frame for Do....................	4..	4..	0
To London Crown Glass for Do...................	19..	12..	0 [2]
To his Lady's portrait half Length	19..	12..	0
To his own Do Do	19..	12..	0
To portraits of Mr. Mackintosh & Lady	14..	0..	0

Henry Pelham to Copley

BOSTON, Jany [27], 1775.

MY DEAR BROTHER,

With eagerness I embrace each Opertunity to testify the pleasu[r]e I take in your Remembranc[e] and Correspondanc[e] and to give you those assurerances of affection and Esteem which this imperfect mode of intercourse will allow and which

---

[1] In Pelham's handwriting.   [2] Obviously an error in copying.

I flatter myself you will accept, as flowing from the sincerest Emotions of a tender and greatefull Heart. I cant omitt this Conveyance tho' it is very Circuitous to wish you the greatest Joy upon the pleasing and most happy Event of my Dear Sisters being safe abed, and upon the enlargement of your family by the Birth of another Son, who I pray Heaven may be a Blessing and a Comfort to you. Certain I am, was it possable by Words to give Ideas of material Objects, you would expect a discription of your little Son. Be assured, for I can with safety affirm it that when you see the finest Child ever animated by the Pencill of Guido, it will give but an imperfect Idea of the fineness of my new Cousin.

I ardently Wish this Letter may have a speedy Passage to you as I am perswaded its contents will make you very happy and releive many and anxious hour, and prevent many a disagreable Thought. My Sister was brot to bed the 13th Inst. has been and is now as well as could possably be expected for a person in her situati[on.] The weather has been remarkably favorable for her, being very warm and pleasant, one of the finest Winters I Remember. I was honord by her appointment with presenting in Company with Mr. Clarke and Miss Lucy, the infant at the font, a Candidate for Baptism in which Mr. Walter officiated and named Him Clarke.[1] I must now, my dear Brother, return you my most greatefu[l] thanks for the great Happyness you have afforded me by your very tender instructio[n]s and entertaining Letters. It makes me really feel asshamed that I have reced 7 Letters from you since I wrote to you last; and have been fearfull you might take it amiss and

---

[1] This child, left in America when Mrs. Copley embarked in May for England, being too young and feeble to bear the passage, soon after died. The child was named Clarke Copley.

think me neglegent; but I console myself, that as impossabilities are not to be effected you[r] candour will attribute it to some material Difficulty. There has been no oppertunity that have come to my knowledg[e] since I left Philadelphia. Indeed I have been much out of the Way of the London Vessels, as none sail from Connecticut w[here] I spent a Month, and the Boston port Bill still continues.[1]

I sincerly Congratulate you [upon your] Arrival at Rom[e] and please myself in the expectation of soon receiving your discription of that seat of Scienc[e] with an Account of the Pa[i]nting of Raphael, Michael Angelo, etc., which [with] you[r] discription of places of less consequenc[e], assure me will be very entertain'g and highly instructive to me. Whenever I think of your Letters I cant but feel the most gratefull sensat[i]ons, for the great Kindness you show me. I want word[s] fully to express myself upon the subject.

As the limits of my paper shortens I must omitt till my next, which will go in Cap'n Robson, who sails in about a fortnight, an Acount of Publick Affairs, Replys to some parts of your several Letters, an Acct of my Phila'a tour etc. But before I conclude mu[s]t not omitt acqua[i]nting [you] that Dear Hond. Mamma[2] continues in her usual Health. She desires me to present you her Kindest Love and Blessing, and to assure you she takes part in the Joy arising from Mrs. Copleys present

---

[1] The sheet containing the first part of this letter has been folded as though for wrapping — and upon it is written *Messalenious Medals*. What follows, together with the first draft of the note to Jonathan Clarke, January 28, 1775, is written upon hand-ruled music paper bearing the date "Sepr. 30, 1747," probably in the handwriting of Peter Pelham, the artist. There is a third small piece of paper with phrases to be inserted in the two fragments, which is the only indication that they are parts of the same letter.

[2] Erased: "has been rather unwell for some time past but has again recov[ere]d her usual Health."

Happy Situation and desires her congratulation upon the Event, as does also Brother and Sister Pelham. I have spent a couple of Hours this Even'g very agreably at Mr. Bromf[iel]d['s] chatting upon vario[us] points, Pollitick[s], etc. He desires me to tell you that he continues of the same principles in politicks, and she begs me to assure you that she has not in the least altered her Sentiments. They, with their very amiable Miss Sally and Mr. Harry, desire their kind Love etc. We all unite in prese'g the Compliments of the season to you and you[r] fellow traveller.¹ In my last I informed you that my Health was rather indiferent. I am happy now in inform'g you that my journey by God's Blessing has had the wished for good effect in perfectly restor'g it. It grow[s] late. I wish you a good Night.

May each gracious Wing from Heaven of those that minister to erring man Near Hovering Secure [?] thy slumbers with present [?] Sun [?] Of Britest Vision; whisper to thy Heart that [*unfinished*]

Henry Pelham to Charles Startin

BOSTON, Jany. 31, 1775.

DEAR SIR,

My Fri[e]nd Mr. Russell going for your City affords me a convenie[n]t opertunity of acknowledging the rece't of you[r] agreable Letter of the 13 Inst. and of thank'g you for the care of the Letters I troubled you with. The affair of sitting has been mentioned to Mr. Clarke, and his answer is such as flatters me he will grattify the desires of his Friends. I shall take the first Opertunity to press the matter I hope to effect. You have doubtless before this heard of Mrs. Copley's being

¹ George Carter.

safe abed. I present you and Mrs. Startin Congratulations upon the birth of another Nephew, a fine Boy, Baptized by the Name of Clarke. We have just Rec'd the King's Speech. I inclose it with A[da]ms Commentary upon it. The Dye seems to be cast! How entirely must the spirit of Madness possess those who stake their Happyness their all again[s]t nothing upon the cast of a Dye. Our Sons[1] tho affect very much to redicule it, and say its only a thing of cou[r]se and what they expected. I also inclose you a pamphlet wrote by a young Gentleman, a Lieutenant in the Army here.[2] I believe it will please you as a sensible dispassionate and polite answer to another filled with invective attributed to Gen'l Lee. I was rendered very happy upon my return hom[e] to find myself much wanted, and to meet 8 Long Letters from my Brother Copley, giving a very entertaining account of his Journey from London to Mersailles and a perticular discription of all the Citys of note thro which he pass'd. Mrs. Copley has recd. one from him dated 28 Octr. at Rome Where he had just arri[v]ed. . . .[3]

Henry Pelham to Benjamin West

BOSTON, N. E., Feby. 13, 1775.

SIR,
    In a late Letter from Mr. Copley he wishes me to send something to the Exhibition; but Not having time to paint a Picture expressly for the purpose, I had declined all thoughts of it 'till finding one of my Pictures in Minature which I had lately done was going to London, it occured to me to Request Mr. Ingra-

---

[1] Of Liberty.
[2] *Strictures on "Friendly Address" Examined*, by Henry Barry, lieutenant in the Fifty-second Regiment.
[3] In Armory, *John Singleton Copley*, 37, is printed one of October 26.

ham in whose possession it is, and who favours me by being the bearer of thi[s] Letter, to permitt its going to the Exhibition, should you think it has merit sufficient to entitle it to a place in that collection. which if it has, and not be inconsistant with their Rules, I beg the favour of you to send it, or inform Mr. Ingraham who it must be given to for that purpose.

The Fri[e]ndship that subsists between you and my Brother Mr. Copley I hope will plead a sufficient excuse for the trouble I now impose upon you. By his More than fraternal Kindness I have been led into the path of Science and excited by the extensive and growing fame of two of my Countrymen in one of the most elegant Arts of polished Life am solicitous of meriting a share of publick Notice. Diffident of my abilities I have hitherto declined obtruding myself to the view of a diserning People distinguish'd for their Taste in the polite Arts, nor should now have adventured had I not been encouraged by my Brothers advice.

Not longer to intrude upon your important time, I conclude wishing you may long exercise those talents which have so deservedly rendered your work Orniments to the Old and yourse[l]f an Honour to the new World. I am Sir with the greatest Esteem your most humb Servant,

H. P.

Henry Pelham to Copley

Boston, Feby. 16, 1775.
My dear Brother,

I [take] the opertunity of Capt. Robson to amuse myself in scr[i]bling to my deare[s]t Frie[n]d a few random thoughts, some trifling anecdotes, and some serious facts. among the last I beg you would place those emotions of my love and

Gratitud[e] for your kindness and fr[i]endly attention which I want words fully to express. I have just finish'd a high regale, the Reperusal of all your Instructive and affectionate Letters. I never read them, never think of them without the liveliest sence of my obligations to you for the unaffected and endearing marks of your Love and regard for my wellfare with which they are replete; I always feel myself Happy in recollecting the agreable Situation you are in, far removed from the din of civil discord and faction, uni[n]terrupted by the tumult and cunfusion of licentiousness and anarchy, contemplating the works of the ingenious and great and cultivate'g the charming arts of Peace and Fr[i]endship. I would not have you suppose from this that we are altogethe[r] in a shock'g State ne[i]ther, for I really thin[k] we are in a better one than we were some time ago. Certain I am this town is incomparably more peaceab[le] than it was when you left it, and I flatter myself that the time is approaching when Reason will aga[i]n recover her empire over the turbalant Passons of an enthusiastic and misguided People, and that jarring and hatred, jealosies, distrust and mutual revili[n]gs, will give place to the long Cataloge of exiled Virtues; that Peace with her swe[e]t Voice will again hail this the Happy Land, once more the seat of Plenty Justice Security and Fre[e]dom. Your several Letters require no perticular Remarks. I shall pass them with observing that your discription of you[r] journey is very entertain'g and the Civilities you mention having rec'd are very flatter'g to your Friends.

I now propose giving you some accou[n]t of my Journey to Phlda. the motives for it, my Health, I have already mentioned. I purchasd a Horse and disoblegiant, and on the 18 of Septm'r, in Company with our Fr[ie]nd[s] Mr. Lee and Lady, Mr. and Mrs. Startin, set out upon the tour about two hours before day, hastned by an expected Visit from the County [Country?] Mob, Mr. L. having offended them by adjorning the Court which they said was a carrying into execution the regulation Bill. We mett with noth[in]g remar[k]able except Very fine Weather which we had the whole journey, till we ar[r]ived at Springfield. here an unlucky Visit from a Ge[n]tleman, one of the new mandamus Councellor[s], who had resigned a few days before upon being most severely threatned and ill treated, affixed the name of tory upon us and was near springing a mine which would have entirely marr'd our journey. This Occurance, tho it much disturbed me, afforded me some amusement. I had often seen the proceedings of a Boston Mob, but never of a Country one. I will give you the perticulars, know'g from Experien[ce] the pleasure arrising from a minute detail of the most trifling Occurrances our distant friend[s] meet with. We had not been long at the Tavern wher[e] we put up at for the night, when a party of four and t[w]enty who had been out that day shooting Squerels, mett there to divide their booty, which raised a quarrel among them. this with the plenty of Liquer they had made them noisy and Riotous. The landlord willing to have his hous[e] clear of this Confusion requested they would depa[r]t, acqua[i]nting them that he had travellers who wanted Rest, and with more zeal than prudence declared they should not have a drop more of drink. This made them outragious, and Coll. Worthington and Mr. Bliss, two Fri[e]nds of Government, coming out of our Room and passing th[r]o theirs, drew all this Resentment against us. They said He had a damn'd pack of Torys in his House and they would have us out.[1] Resistance on [our] pa[r]t incre[a]s[ed] the tumult on

---

[1] Erased: "and make us make an acknowled[g]ment of our offences aga[i]n[s]t the Libertys of the People."

theirs. They loaded and fired their musketts, for they were all armed, in the House and at the Windows. This you may well suppose created much noise and Confusion which continued near two hours. At length one more peaceably disposed than the Rest pe[r]swaded them to disperse for the night, and in the morn'g insist upon our mak'g an Acknowled[g]ment of our offences, and recant our principles. This with the landlord's asking their pardon in a very humble manner, co[o]lled them down, so that we had our nights rest. In the morn'g early we set out leaving those Sons of —— to find recantations where they could. From Springfield to Newyork we met with nothing extrordina[r]y, now and then a small affront which use made us disregard. We were 13 days between Boston and York, which afforded us ample time for seeing the several of agreable Town[s] which ly upon Connecticut River. At Newyork I saw a number of clever houses. the Kings Statue pleased me much. round this I saw one of those Iron fences which you have disscribed to me. We tarried here 10 Days, during which I mett with much Civility from Mr. Curson and Mr. Seaton. I was very unlucky here, Major Bayard, Doctor Auchmuty, and two or three Gentlemen, being out of town to whom I had Letters. From York we had a most delightful Ride through the Jerseys which took us 4 days. The 14 of O[c]tober bro't us to Phila. The regularity, the neatness and cleaness of this City, Its excellent and well regulated police, and the simple plainess of its Inhabitan[ts], struck me very agreably. Here the Letters I had procured several Valua[ble] and Ingenious Acquaint-anc[es], from whom I recd many marks of politeness and atten-tion, for which I shall always think myself Obliged. Doctr. Morgan I found a polite sensible Friendly Man, a great Lover of and a judge of Painting, and a perticular Friend of yours.

I would recommend your writing to him as he is a man of Consequence in the Literary World, a Fellow of the Royal Society. Mr. Mifflin shewed me much Civi[li]ty. I had another oppertun[ity] of viewing with pleasure their admirable Portrait[s]. I was introducd to Governor Penn, where I saw and admired the several Copies of which you gave me a very just discription, when you was at New York. I was at Mr. Hamiltons, the Late Governor, who rec'd me very politely. With Him and Mr. Allen, who had been in Rome, I had two or three hours very entertaining and instructiv[e] Conversation on paint'g and the Arts. Mr. Allen perticularly amused me with an anectdote Respect'g my Picture which you sent to the Exh[i]bition. When I have more Room I will give it to you. [*Unfinished.*]

Henry Pelham to [*Charles Reak and Samuel Okey*]

BOSTON, March 10, 1775.
GENTLEMEN,

A very Long absence from home and a consequent Hurry of Buisness upon my return With the want of a Conveni[en]t Opertunity has hitherto prevented my noticeing to you the receipt of your polite favour. I beg you would attribute my omission to those Causes and not to Neglect or Inattention. My thanks are due to Mr. Reak for his expressions of Disapo[i]ntment at not seeing me when he was in Boston. I likewise feel a real Regret in being out of the way when he did me the favour to call upon me. As you acqua[i]nt me only in General with your intentions of scraping some plates in Mezzotinto from Designs of Mr. Copley's and Mine: it is difficult for me to determin[e] in what manner I can render you any assistanc[e]. But this I can with truth assure you that I shall take a great pleasure in affording you any that is in my power and I beg you would freely communicate to me any plans in which my service will be acceptable to you. I thank you for a promise of a proof of Mr. S. Adams print. I take the Liberty of mentioning Doct. Winthrop as a Gentleman whose likeness in mezzotinto I hav[e] little doubt you would find worth your doing. He is well known at home and abroad as a Politician and a Philosopher, an emine[n]t decandant of the venerable Father of New England, and a Gentleman whose literary abilities have rendered his Name abroad an Honour to America and whose private Virtues have attracted the esteem of his numerous Friends at Home. Should you do this I would send you an exact drawing in Black and White taken from a Painting of Mr. Copley's, which is a[n] elegant Picture and a very striking likeness and would recommend its being done the same size of Doctr Franklin's, to be a match for it. I should be glad to hear from you upon the subject, and Conclude by sub-s[c]ribing myself your most Humble Sert.

HENRY PELH[A]M.

P S. The Proof I deliv[er]ed to a Gentleman sometime ago who called for them in your Names.

Copley to Henry Pelham

DEAR BROTHER,

It is a long time since I have had the pleasure of wrighting to you; the reason of this I hinted in a Letter to Your Sister, and at the same time promiss'd to be very perticular when a private conveyance offered for my letter to you, free of expence; this oppertunity now presents itself and I will fulfill my promiss with the utmost pleasure. Mr. Izard will soon leave this place on his way to London, and by him I send this. indeed the expence of postage would not have made me delay wrighting to you did not my letters to Your Sister, to whom I write very constant, furnish you with the most meterial things that concern me in my tour. I am happrehensive should I add anything further on this head you may think I am bantering you, as you have much more reason to apologise for yourself. I have not only sett you an example, as to the constant inteligence, but I leave no sircumstance however trivi[a]l unmenshoned and [un]explained, knowing by myself that it must affoard you pleasure, to be made acquainted with the smallest Incidents in the life of a near friend at a distance. I hope this hint will induce you to write more frequently and much more perticular; you should fill your paper; and improve every oppertunity to send me a letter wrote on large thin post paper, without a cover which double[s] the charge.

I have now been in this City near four months in which time I have studyed and practiced with much application although when I tell you I have only composed the Assention; painted the portraits of Mr. and Mrs. Izard in one Picture, this last not finish[ed] by a fortnight, you will think I have done but little. howeve[r] you are to reflect that it takes a great deal of time to see the Works of Art in this place. also near one month spent in Naples.

You will be glad to know in what manner an Historical composition is made, so I will give it to you, in that way I have found best myself to proceed. I have always, as you may remember, considered the Assention as one of the most Sublime Subjects in the Scripture. I considered how the Appostles would be affected at that Instant, weither they would be scattered over the Ground inattentive to the Action and converseing with one another, or weither they would croud together to hear the Charge to Peter, and when that was given weither they would not be asstonish'd at their Masters rising from the Earth and full of the Godhead Assend up into Heaven. no one who reads the Account in the first Chapter of the Acts can be at a moments loss to decide that they would be so asstonish'd, and after Crouding together to hear what Christ said to St. Peter with vast attention in their countinances, they would (keeping their places) and their attention to the Assending Christ Absorbed in holy Adoration, worship him as he rose from the Earth, and so far from speaking to one another that not one of them would reflect that he had a companion with him. no thought could at that Instant intrude it self into their minds, already fully possessed with Holy wonder. some may naturally be supposed to fall on their knees: others with hands uplifted standing worship him. Some would look steadfastly on him: others would bow their heads and in deep adoration with Eyes fixt on the Ground worship him with hands spread or on the breast but all inattentive to one another. but two Angels stood by them; and spake to them. this would naturally ingage those that were next to them, and as it were awaked from a trans, turn with surprise to hear what they said to them. it would be just to observe that the Appostolick Carracter forbids to make the expression of Asstonishment very great. it should be temperd with Love and contain Majesty of behavour acquired by many times being spectators of the Power of Christ exercised in Miracles of a Stupendious nature. This General Idea being considered, the next thing is for the Artist to Warm his Immagination by looking at some Works of Art, or Reading, or conversing; than with pen or pencil sketch no matter how incorrect his general Idea, and when he has got so far, if he can correct by his Ideas his Sketch, he should do it. but I found it necessary to keep in my Idea the effect of the Whole together, which I determined would be grand if managed in the way I here Sketch it. I determined to carry the figures in a circle which would suppose a place that Christ stood in. this I fixed before I had determined the disposition of a single figure, as I knew it would make a fine breadth of light and shadow, and give a Grand appearance to the Whole: and I am certain Raphael pursued a Method something like this. you see in his School of Athens in perticular that it has a kind of ground plan thus [1] only a little Diversified, but in general it give[s] this Idea. I have taken this kind of figure [1] supposing Christ in the Midst. you will find in the Cartoon of the Death of Annanias, if my memory is good, a figure of this sort [1] in that of Elimus, the Sorcerer, a figure not unlike that in that of the Appostle Paul Preaching this figure.[1] now I have no doubt Raphael formed this general Ground plan before he fixed the disposition of any of his figures, than place[d] them on this ground, and varyed here and there as he found it best to break any stiffness and formallity that would otherwise appear in the work. this I can say I found my advantage in fixing this Idea of the Whole. it lead me to the masses of Light and Shadow and allmost to the disposition of some of my principle Figures. I forgot to mention the Transfiguration. it is in this form,[1] I mean the Lower part of the Picture. When I had got thus far I sketched my figures, keeping the greatest simplicity with a great breadth of Light and shadow, that is I determined the Action of each figure and the manner of wraping the Drapery; than I took a Layman of about 3 feet high, and with a Table Cloath wet and rung out

---

[1] Copley has in these places drawn an outline, but not of sufficient moment to merit reproduction.

I disposed my Drapery, and Sketched it with some considerable degree of eligance, and when I was uncertain of the effect
of any figure Or groop of figure[s] I drew them of the sise on a
peace of Paper by themselves shaded them and traced them on
the Paper on which my Drawing was to appear to the Publick,
just in the way you have seen me proceed with Draperys, etc.,
in my portraits. when I had got all my out line correct and clean,
for I had traced it all from other sketch[e]s, I began to wash in
the Shades with bister. this took me about 3 Days and was a
pleasant Work as I had a correct out line and the several peaces
from which I traced that out line to Shade from. I found this
Ideal Sketching at first dificult and had recourse to the Looking
Glass for Actions and by determining the place of heads hands,
etc., as well as the propriety of the Action, which should always
be determined by feeling it yourself. you will soon dispose
your Attitudes so near the thing that you may exicute your
Picture from the life without varying from your Drawing much,
as I will explain. When I had got my Sketch in the above state
I determined to put it in Colours, so that if I should paint it I
should have nothing to alter. so I covourd my Drawing squares
and a Canvis of a Kitcat sise, and Drew all the outline. than
procured a Model to sit for some heads. from the same Model
I think I painted 5 heads varying the Colour of the hair, etc.;
tho was I to paint it large I should chuse a differant Model for
each head; but in this it was not necessary to be so correct.
From this model I Painted the heads, hands, feet the Draperys;
tho I should chuse to dispose them for a large Picture again
and use Cloath rather than linen on a Layman as large as life,
yet what I have in my Drawing is abundantly eligant for the
painting a small Picture from. I must just observe here that
although the Sketch is Ideal, yet 2 or 3 of the figures I could

not absolutely determin on without having the life. I frequently studied the works of Raphaiel, etc., and by that kept the fire of the Imagination alive and made it my object to produce a work that might stand by any others. sometimes a fortnigh[t] would pass before I could invent a single figure, and my whole Sketch was once drawn and shaded, when the alteration of one or two figures seemed necessary. on this I traced it all on another paper except those figures, and drew *them* on a paper by themselves, shaded them, and than traced them with the rest, and shaded the whole as above. I have no doubt Raphael pursued this method; it appears so by his differant drawings. I hope you will be profited by this very perticular Account of my proceedings in this my first composition. I should have been happy to have had such a plain account of the process when I was in America, and what may seem trifling to a Man who has not known the want of such information, I know to be of the last importance to one who has not had an oppertunity of knowing the manner the great Masters have pursued their Goddess with success. I hope you will procure Sir Josh: Renolds's Lectures; they are the best things that have yet appeared of the kind; I am sorry I did not send them to you when I was in London. I will just observe I think Raphael's Cartoons his best compositions; those you have, and can procure his other works in Boston from Mr. Greenleaf.

But now I have given you a minute detail of the manner of making this Composition you will be ready to ask, is it good for anything, and what is its merit? To you I can open my Heart when it would be utterly imprudent to do it to an other. we must preserve appearances and although every man judges of his own Works, yet if they have merit, and he judges justly of them, the world will severely sensure him should he let it be known he is not Ignorant of that merit the very Ignorance of which would at once rob him of the merit itself. But to you I will be open and undisguized. I believe it will support its merit in any Cumpany whatever. Mr. Hamilton is lavish in its praises, and says he never saw a finer Composition in his life, and that he knows no one who can equil it; that it is a subject the most dificult I could have ingaged in, that there is no subject but I can compose with less Dificulty. on Seeing Mr. Izard's Picture he observed, you are a perfect Master of Composition and when he saw the Colourd Sketch with 2 or 3 heads painted, he say'd he never saw finer heads; that if I produced such heads I could never want incoragement. this is very flattering, perticularly as it is the language of all who have seen those works. Sigr. Perinesi[1] and others will not allow my Colour'd Sketch to be called a Sketch but a Picture, and a finished one, tho Coloured but once. You will want to know if I intend painting it large; but to this I must reply doubtfully (although Mr. Hamilton says it will establish my reputation). Yet the time it will take me makes the Dificulty, and I could wish to accompany it with one of another kind, one of a Clasick subject, that of the Reconciliation of Achilles and Agamamnon, a very sublime Subject. if I could produce as good a composition of this subject and exicute them as well as I generally exicute my works, I should return to England with an Eclaut that would establish me in the most effectual manner, not only as a portrait but Historical Painter. but how is it possable, from the latter end of March to acomplish such a Work? it would take me 6 Months. that would be the time I aught to be just entering England. besides I am in hopes that some time or other the Assention might be apply'd for for an alter peace to some Church. if so, it would

[1] Giovanni Battista Piranesi (1721–1779).

be as large as life, and in that case I should be sorry to have painted it of a smaller sise, and to paint it as large as life would take a Canvis 24 feet by 18. so I cannot do that, unless it was bespoke for such an use. but I will do my best in all matters and trust in providence for a blessing on my affairs. I was happy to find my Reputation in England so high. Govr. Hutchinson informed me I had none to gain in that place. but my utmost vigilence to make good what I have acquired and at least [to support what I have gained]¹ shall be made use of, and I hope in this to be bless'd as I have been by the goodness of God in all my important concerns through life. could any thing be more fortunate than the time of my leaveing Boston? poor America! I hope the best but I fear the worst. yet certain I am She will finially Imerge from he[r] present Callamity and become a Mighty Empire. and it is a pleasing reflection that I shall stand amongst the first of the Artists that shall have led that Country to the Knowledge and cultivation of the fine Arts, happy in the pleasing reflection that they will one Day shine with a luster not inferior to what they have done in Greece or Rome in my Native Country.

I shall now proceed to give you some reflections on the Works of the Great Masters. I shall begin with Raphael as I think him the greatest of The Modern Painters. take his excellences altogether and they will out weigh those of any other master. yet I must joyn in the general oppinion that he has more faults than Dominicino. Raphael has studyed the life very carefully. his Transfiguration, after he had got the composition of it on the Canvis, he has painted with the same attention that I painted Mr. Mifflins portrait and his Ladys.² in that determined

---

¹ The words in brackets have been erased.
² Samuel and Rebecca Edgel Mifflin.

manner he has painted all the heads, hands, feet, Draperys, and background, with a plain simple body of Colours and great precision in his out line, and all parts of it from nature. I think his chief excellencys are, his composition, the manner in which he tells you a peace of History, and the gracefullness of his figures and force of expression. he leaves nothing unexpressed that is necessary to the Subject. I will give you two instances of this kind of expression: the first where Soloman, desides in the case of the Dead Child. the Story you know. Soloman orders the living Child to be divided, the Exicutioner hold[s] the Child and lifts the Sword to fulfill the Kings command, when the mother rushes forward to stop the blow with one hand extended, looks to the King, and with the other points to the other Woman. you see every part of the Story is expressed, and that in as simple a manner as possable. after this full and expressive manner of relating the Story what remains to be done is to give Carracter to the figures that compose the Picture. this consists chiefly in making that variety which we find in the life; and making the heads to think agreable to the subject that is before them and ingages their attention and agreable to their attitudes. this part is Ideal, tho the Variety is not. I will not contend with those that say a man may paint from his Ideas only, for I will admit it; I will admit that all men do; only I will observe that the memory of all men is not equilly retentive. one man shall see an object, and twelve months after shall have as perfect a knowledge of it as another that has seen the same object only a few Days; but yet the man who would see an object with an intention to paint it in a few Days still paints as much from Idea as the one who retains a remembrance of it a year. for all our Ideas of things is no more than a remembrance of what we have seen. so that when the

Artist has a model in his Appartment and Views it, than turns to his picture and marks whatever he wishes to express on his Picture, what is it but remembrance of what he has seen? at the same time I will allow the man whose memory is such as to retain what he has seen a year or two before as perfectly as I can one or two Seconds, is on a footing with me when he paints not having the life before him. But this I beleive no Man can do. hence we see all Ideal performances of but little merit, and those who have made the great figure in the Arts are those that have shewn more jeloussy of the goodness of their memory and refreshed it by having the life by them, by which they secured to themselves that truth of Imitation (and veriety which in Nature is Infinite) that their Works appear a kind of Second nature that delights the Spectator. But I leave this Digression, and return to the Excellencys of Raphael. the Second instance in which Raphael has shewn his refined way of thinking is in his Cartoon of Paul and Barnabus. but as Webb[1] has menshoned this perticularly, I shall refer you to his discription of it. so very desireous was Raphael of making his story understood at first sight, that when he painted Joseph relating his Dreams to his bretheren, as there was nothing that could lead to the explination of the story, as he could only Paint a young lad talking to several Persons who stood round him, he has represented in the Sky the Dreams. The same where Joseph interprets the Dream of Pharoh, he has put against the Wall of the appartment two round tablets on which he has painted the Dreams, so that any one must instantly know the Story (if he is not quite stupid) as soon as he casts his eye upon it. this is a kind of merit not confin'd to the gen-

---

[1] Daniel Webb (1719?–1798). The reference is to *An Inquiry into the Beauties of Painting*.

ious of the Painter only, but open to the acquirement of all
men of Sense; and a man who has not the least knowledge of
the Art may, nevertheless, point out the best way of expressing the Subject, or rather the means to make it understood.
I wish I could convey to you a just Idea of Raphael's Painting,
but I am at a loss how to do it unless I could recollect some one
Picture that I could refer you to; but I cannot think of any one.
I will refer you than [to] the Coppy at Smibert's of the Holy
Family, which although a Coppy from Raphael, is notwithstanding very diferent from his Painting. I will explain to you
in what it differs; the Original, which is at Florance, I have seen,
and find it has nothing of the olive tint you see in the Copy,
the read not so bricky in the faces, the whole Picture finished
in a more rich and correct manner. you remem[ber] the hands
of the Virgin and of the St. John, they are very incorrect in the
one you have seen, but in the original they are correctly
finished and the whole Picture has the Softness and general
hew of Crayons, with a Perlly tint throughout. thus I have
indeavoured to give you such a discription of Raphael's works
as may be useful to you; but before I take leave of him I must
just observe that by making use of a Model for the heads you
will naturally vary your faces agreable to your Models, and
though I would not make the heads like the model, that is, not
such a likeness as I would make in a portrait, yet should they be
like to the greatest degree I should not think it a matter to be
objected to. you will take notice in the Transfiguration Raphael
has painted warts on some of the faces by thus painting from
the life. Chusing such Models as are most agreable to the several carracters you mean to paint, you will procure that
variety in your Works that is so much admired in the first
Works of Art; as to the expression you will find it effected

by small deviations from tranquility. it is what I cannot discribe, but would wish you in the persuit of it, to endeavour to feel what you would express and mark what you feel in your Picture. it is an undiscribeable somthing for which th[e]re is no rule. you will be assisted in this by prints; tho they are very imperfect, yet you will find till you have some thing better than even the Laocoon you have will furnish somthing towards it. And here I must advise you to procure an anatomical figure and lern the mussels, so that you would be able to draw a tolerable figure with all the museles from your Knowledge of the parts.[1] But I must leave this Digression and Raphael: and proceed to Titiano, whose excellencys are very great at the same time of a different kind from those of Raphael.

I immagine by reflecting on the Ideas I had imbibed from the Discription of writers before I had seen any of Titianos Works, that you may be utterly unacquainted with his manner of Painting. taking it for granted that my Ideas and yours being grounded on the same information must be nearly the same, those who have wrote on the subject seem always to suppose their Readers to have the Works of the Great Masters before them; hence they are very defective and convey little or no Idea, at least no just Idea, of their Works. my business has been to convey to you such an account of the Works of Art as will give you the best you can have till you see them with your own eyes. I neither Study Stile nor precision, nor have I time to be even correct; for my first thoughts as I set them Down you must have without any alteration, and if you meet frequent repetitions it is because I have omitted somthing I wish

[1] The Department of Prints and Drawings of the British Museum has an early sketch-book by Copley containing nine anatomical studies, in black and red crayons, signed and dated 1756. They are done with great care and the muscles are named.

to convey to you, being much more solicitious to inform your Mind than write an Eligant treatise on the Art. at the same time it would give me much pleasure to form somthing correct and Eligant from these lose though[t]s, unconnected, though I think not undegested. for my great Affection for You and Solicitude on that Account has made me very carefull not to mislead you in any thing; and if I have not always been so Clear or explicit as was necessary let me know it and in what you wish to be informed, and I shall take a pleasure in gratifi- ing you. But to return.

Before I saw the Works of Titiano, I [s]uposed them Painted in a Body of Oyl Colours with great precision, smooth, Glossy and Delicate, somthing like Enamil wrought up with care and great attention to the smallest parts, with a rich brilliantcy that would astonish at first sight. but I found them otherwise. the writers of his Life tell you he had three manners. his first being indiferant I shall take no notice of it, but remark on his second and third as they are boath very good. I shall begin with his second in order. He seems to me to have had his Cloath first Passed over (with Whiting, White Lead, or Plaster of Paris, mixed with sise) with a Brush, and no other prepara- tion or Priming; perhaps not even pumissed: only the Cloath pretty even thread[ed] and fine. this done he painted his Picture with a broad light and very little shadow, so that I think they somtimes Want foarce. his lights are Scarcely pre- dominant and where ever you see shade, it is only a little below the general tint. so that you see it flesh throughout the light and shade is what you see in thee Street, nothing black or heavy in the shade, nothing White or stairing in the lights, the flesh of a full tint rather rather brown or Read than Pale or Cold. at the same time his Pictures are generally rather Grave,

Dark, and Warm than faint or Chalkey. with respect to light and shade you see the Prints of his Venus and Danea. they have little shade. the Danea has the most. over her face it is very warm and transparent, and all flesh, his tints very Clear and Perlly but never muddy or Gray. I can refer you no where for an example, but recollect you have been at Philadelphia and you have no doubt seen Mr. West's Coppy. tho that will give you the best Idea of it, yet I beleave was you to see them together you would think the Coppy less broken and varigated in the tints of Flesh than the original. I think it has more of the look of Putty or leather, and I am inclined to think Plain oyl Colours will not produce the effect of Titianos Colouring. there is somthing too Dauby in it. as soon as I can spare a few Days I shall try an experiment or two. I will tell you what I propose; first to prepare my Cloath as above, than Dead Colour my Picture. the Ground will imbibe the Oyl. When it is Dry Pass over it with some Gum Mastick Dissolved in Turpentine, which I shall let Dry, than finish my Picture with Glasing boath in the lights and shades. The Gum is to prevent the Dead Colour imbibeing the Oyle, so it will appear through the last Glasings with great Brilliancy. another method I shall try is to lay in the Dead Colours with Turpintine and than apply the Gum before the finishing: which should be by Glasings only. but when I have made the experiment I shall let you know its success. Titiano is no ways minute, but sacrifices all the small parts to the General effect. his hands and feet are hardly made out till you see them at a Distance.

But I must here break off as I am ingaged to Drink Tea with Mr. Izard and he setts out earley in the morn'g. I wish every blessing to attend you, and be assured nothing that can contrabute to your happyness that shall be in my power, but you may be assured of My Affectionate Love and Duty. give my Dear Mother and acc[e]pt my tenderest Love yourself, Giveing Love and compliments to all friends and take care of your health. let nothing Depress your Spirits and Beleave me most Affectionately Disposed to do everything for your happyness as for my own. I am, Dear Brother, Yours Most Affectionately,

JOHN SINGLETON COPLEY.

Mr. Izard['s] Portrait will be a very fine one.

ROME, 14. of March, 1775.

Charles Reak and Samuel Okey to Henry Pelham

NEWPORT, March 16, 1775.

S'R,

Yours by Mr. Tyler came to hand last Night and I take the early opertunaty of the next Morning to answer your Obliging and Polite Letter and aquaint you that I receiv'd yours with great Pleasure as it may posibly bring on A Connection of Business both Beneficial and in some measure a little improving these parts of the Polite Arts in this New World. wee shall publish in About a Month a Poster sized Plate of Mr. Sam Addams from A Picture I had of Mr. Mitchels Painting. wee have copied it well enouf and are not affraid of the Sucsess of it; but A plate done Properly shoud be from A good Picture. It was the best I cou'd get when last in Boston and I don't on any Account mean to disparage that Young Gent'n, or wish that this may go any farther than to you. I have A Letter now on my Desk Just Receiv'd from him wherein he kindly tels mee his Portrait of Mr. Hancock is at my service. And now for that Matter, the Moment wee have done Mr. Addams, Do'r Coopers from Mr. Copely will be in hand. when that is done, as it will be in about Two Months, and I am shure it will be much superior to Addams, Intirely owing to the superioraty of Mr. Copelys Pencil. If Mr. Hancock woud be so obliging on your aplycation as to let us have his faviorate Picture, it shall be taken the greatest Care of Imaginable, and restored in just the same state as Receiv'd, and shou'd be put in a Case and delivered to the Care of Mr. Peter Mumford our Post. wee have many subjects that Offer, but none that wee shoud wish to do sooner than that as it will be a proper Companion for Mr. Addams; and as in his wee have been Obliged cheafly to consult Profit, *so from the fine Picture of Mr. Hancock that I have already had the Pleasure to see wee shal consult Honour.* Mr. Mumford informs mee he will get that Picture, but I shoud be happy in owing that Obligation to Mr. Pelham's Friendship. Do'r Winthrop as a gent'n of that distinguishing Merrit you represent might be a proper subject, and particular[ly] as A Companion to the Ingenious and Learned Dr. Franklin. I remember the size of the Plate as I may well do, as laying the Ground on it in London for that scraped by Fisher.[1] I think it sold for five Shillings Ster'g . Que[ry] whether these high Priced Prints may be agreable to the Generality. only shoud be glad if youd Consult a few of Do'r Winthrop Friends and let mee have there and your Opinion how many Impresions wee may probably expect to sell. at the first set of the drawing I dare say will do very well to execute from. I must stop Short as the Post is this Minute setting out, so no further at Present but to beg you'l accept our best respects, and that you will add to the favior of your last by writing to us again by the first opertunaty, which will greatly Oblige your Most hum'e Serts.

CHAS REAK and SAM OKEY.

[1] Edward Fisher (1730–1785?).

Sir, the Post went without this at last, so it retards this another Week. if Do. Winthrop woud take the Value of Quarter of a Hundred for the Use of his Friends; but in Interim should be glad of Mr Hancocks Portrait.

C. R.

Henry Pelham to Copley

BOSTON, April 3d, 1775.

MY DEAR BROTHER,

Just meeting an Opertunity I cant omitt writing a few lines just to let you know that We are, thank God, in pretty good health. As my time is short and this will have a very circuitous Passage before it getts to Rome, I shall not be able to write you so long a letter as you might perhaps expect, or I could Wish, To assure you we have been for this long time past anxiously solicitous of Receiving a line from you. it seems, and indeed it is, almost an age sinc[e] we heard from you. the last intelligence was your letter to Our hon'd Mamma of the 5 of Nov'r. Indeed we console ourselves that there has been no opertunity except by the Pacquet, and I now beg that you would direct you[r] Correspondent in England to forward your Letters by the very first Opertunitys, weither the packet or otherwise, as we shall not at all value a few Shillings when it procures us the Happyness of a Letter from you. I am pleased when I can inform you that our hon'd Mamma, my dear Sister, and my dear little Cousins are well. My Mamma has had a very tolerable Winter. She desires me to present you with her kindest Love and Blessing and thanks for your letter to her. She would have wrote you a few lines, but as I thought it would worry her I diswaded her from it. so you must place the Omission to my acc't, and I am assured of your excuse knowing your willingness to forego any pleasure reather than give her trouble.

Little did I think a month go that my next Letter would carry such unwelcome news as I have now to Communicate. but alas! how precarious are all sublunary injoyments, how uncertain is human Life! with malencholy Regret I inform you that our very worthy Friends, the once amiable and engaging Mrs. Oliver,[1] Our onc[e] gay facetious and respectable Nei[gh]bour Mr. Chardon and Mr. Winslow, very late the man of Buisness, are now no more. Death regardless of Worth and Virtue, Youth and Gayety, with ruthless hand snaps the slender Th[r]ead of Life and Leavs the tender husband, the amiable and affectionate Wife, the Dutifull and the infant Children, to mou[r]n the[i]r fri[e]nds departure, and to feel the loss of there indearing Offices of Benevolence and Love, which with the hopes of a Happy immortallity smooth the rugged Path of Life and render more than tolerable that journey so thickly strowed with disapointment and Vexations. Let it be the consolation of our sorrows to Remember and Imitate their Virtues. Let us improve this Righteous providenc[e] of God in th[e]ir Removal to our profit. let it imprint on our minds the uncertanty of this world's best injoyments. Convinced that this is but a passage to Eternity, let us be with the hope and fortitude of Christians always prepared to meet that stroke however sudden which shall reunite Us to our departed Fr[i]ends, with them to enjoy the Endless Rewards of a Virtuous and good Life. A few perticulars of our Fri[e]nds' dec[e]ase you will doubtless expect. Judge Olivers Lady was seised with a Fit of the Palsey on the 17 of March. She continued sinking away till the 25th, when she died and was buried the 30 from My Sister's with all the Respect due to her Rank and amiable Virtues. Mr Chardon was taken not a month ago with a Mortification in his

[1] Mary, daughter of William Clarke.

Bowels, of which he languish'd 4 Days. Mr. Joshua Winslow, Commodore Loring's Son-in-Law was abroad the 16 of Last Month, and on the 23d was an inhabitant of the silent Tomb.[1]

My Brother Pelham is now confined with a very severe fitt of the Gout with which he has been for some time past afflicted. My Sister Pelham I am fearfull is in a declineing Way. Your Enquiries after Snap he takes Very kind. He de[s]ires his duty to you. I with pleasure inform you that he had been ever sinc[e] you left us a very good Boy.

You doubtless expect I should write you the present State of the political Contest, but this I must omitt for want of time and Room till my next, assuring you in the mean time that our Fr[i]ends here live very quietly, and ther[e] is but little danger I think of their not continuing so to do, let the dispute be as it will. in Boston we are too strong to meet with the lea[s]t disturbance. I am happy to inform you that I am very fully imployed, but People are very backwa[r]d in paying, there being now no law to Oblig[e] them to it. It would be too great a Tax upon you to enumerate all the Fr[i]ends who desire there Compliments to you, But I cant excuse myself from mention'g My Hon'd Mamma, Sister C, Brother and S. P., Judge O. Mr. Clar[k]e, Isaac, Miss Lucy, Mr. and Mrs. Bromfield and my amiabl[e] young fr[i]ends with them, as repeatedly desireing to have their k[i]nd love and Regards presented to you. I am proud of uniteing myself with so respectable a list of Friends in sincere[s]t good Wishes and Prayers for your Health and Happyness. I subscribe myself your very affectionate Brother and Humble Servant,

H. P.

---

[1] A merchant of Boston, who married Hannah, daughter of Nathaniel Loring. See *Massachusetts Gazette*, March 23, 1775.

Joshua Wentworth to Henry Pelham

PORTSMO., April 7th, 1775.

SIR,

Your favor of 14th March I rec'd 5th Inst. per post. Observe Mr. Copely's Bill for Mrs. Wentworth's portrait which, if compleat, shou'd with great pleasure discharge the demand, and as ready pay a like sum for mine. Mr. Copely, on my determination, of hav'g those portraits taken, Engag'd with me no other's shou'd impeed the excecution of them. After Mrs Wentworth had set many days, and myself one, he agreed and finish'd a Portrait for a Mrs Babcock, wch exceedingly disapointed my Intentions, and my business cal'g me hither, was oblig'd to leave Boston, without a finish of either Portrait.

I cannot determine when Mrs Wentworth will [be] in Boston; her present Curcumstances will not admit her Visit'g it for some months.

I purpose to ride thither in May, if the hurry of Govement at home does not oblige the Inhabitants to abandon their Houses for a more agreeable retreat, from the Clamours of War.

I shall wait on you when I go to Boston, in the Interim am, Sir, Your mt. obt. Servt.

JOSH. WENTWORTH.[1]

Henry Pelham to Charles Startin

BOSTON, May 3d, 1775.

DEAR SIR,

My Fr[i]end Mr Nichols with his Family returning to Philadel[phia] Induces me to trouble you with a Line, the

---

[1] Joshua (1742–1809), son of Daniel and Elizabeth Wentworth, merchant, married Sally Peirce.

Principle Purport of which is to request you to add to the many obligations I am already under by favouring me with Letters to some of your Friends in England. I feel a Regrett in being so troublesome, but know'g your willingness to Oblige I flatter myself I shall obtain you[r] Pardon.

The very Malencholly Event which has lately happend here forces me with the multitude to abandon my Nativ[e] Land, and seek that bread at a Distanc[e], which by the Vicicetudes of Fortune I am denied at Home. Mrs. Copley with the children I expect will sail in one of the first Vessels for London, Where I purpose following in a few Weeks, and where I flatter myself it will not be long before I have the pleasure of see'g you and Mrs. Startin.[1]

I must Refer you to Mr. Nichols for the Perticulars of the situation of this distress[ed] Town. It is impossable for me to describe the unhappy tran[s]actions of that fatal day and the consequent Misery to which it has reduced [the] Inhabitants [of] this once flourishing and happy Town. Consternation is pictured in every face, every Cheek grows Pale, every lip trembles at the Recital of the Horrid tale.[2]

Our very amiable Frie[n]d Miss Sally Bromfield and my self had a very providential Escape from being in the midst of the Battle. When I found[?] that there was a disturbance in the Country I took a Horse and Chaise determined to go to My Brothers at Newton and perswade them to come to Boston as a

---

[1] Erased: "Mr Copley in some of his late Letters desires his Love and best Wishes might be perticularly present'd to his Philadelphia Friends. I beg to unite with him in proper Regards to yourself and Mrs. Startin and I Conclude with Wishing you all Health and Peace. I am, Dear Sir, your much Obliged and most Humble Sert.

"HENRY PELHAM."

[2] The affair of Lexington and Concord.

place of Safety. I went to the ferry, where I was refused a passage, under pretence of the Winds being too high, tho a Chais[e] went over in the very boat befor[e]. anxious for my Frie[n]ds (as the Country was then in the utmost Confusion) I thought this a great Disapo[i]ntment, and was very angry with the Ferrymen, as I lost an hour, being obliged to go ove[r] the neck. This I so perticularly mention as it tu[r]nd out a very lucky Circumstanc[e]. Find'g my Brother unable to move, being confind with the gout, I directly turnd my attention to Miss Bromfield who was at Cambridg[e], where I immed[iat]ely went and took her into my Chaise. I went to Cambrid[g]e B[r]idg[e] and fou[n]d it taken up. deterrd by former unsuccess from attempting the ferry I went by the way of Water Town Bridge and safely reach'd Home. Mr. Harry Bromfield went the same afternoon to Cambridge to fetch his Sister Down. finding her just gone with me, he returned to the Ferry, when he fou[n]d the boats stopped by Order of the General, the Armies fast approach'g to Charl[e]stown, and that being a very unsafe place he but just escaped over Charlestow[n] Neck before the retreat'g Army enter'd it. He has Rem[aine]d 13 days in the Country unable to see his Frie[n]ds, or they him till to day, when he obtain'd a Pass from the Gen'l and retu[r]nd home. This I take a pleasure in Relating as a[m]ids[t] the Horrors of that of that dreadfull Day, I feel myself exceed'g happy in rescue'g my lov[e]ly Frie[n]d from such a Scene of Distress and Danger, and have from the fortunate Disapo[i]ntment at the Ferry lear[n]t much usefull Philosophy, not to make myself uneasy at what I cant avoid, and in all the gloomy Prospects of Life to think with Pope, Whatever is, is right.

I am just begining a Minature Port[r]ait of Mr. Clarke which I shall send by the first Opertunity to Mrs. Startin.

I conclude with sincer[e]ly Wish'g that Health and Peace may ever attend you and Mr[s] Startin.

I am, Dear Sir, your much obliged and Very Hm St.

[*Unsigned.*]

Henry Pelham to Copley[1]

[May —, 1775.]

The People in the Country have made it a Rule for a long time Past to brand every one with the Name of Tory and consider them as Inimical to the Liberties of America who are not will'g to go every length with them in their Scheems however mad or who show the least doubt of the justice and Humanity of all their measures, or even entertain an Idea that they may not produce those salutary effects they profess to have in View. This conduct has rendered My Brother P—— very uneasy. they have long looked askew at him; his being a Churchman is considered as a suspicious Circumstanc[e]. in short he has for some time meditated a Retreat from his present place of abode and has depended upon me for Intellegenc[e] of any movement in this town which might effect a threatned attack upon the tories.

My Sister Copley and myself proposed going to Newton the very day of the battle but in the Morn'g finding a disturbance in the Country we alterd our plan and with your horse and Chaise I went alone to alarm my Brother and perswade him and my Sister to come to town as a place of safety. I went to the ferry. The ferrymen refused to carry me over, the Wind being high tho there was then a Chais[e] passing over. This I consider'd as a great disapo[i]ntment and scolded at the Ferrymen who I thot acting out of their line of Duty. I here lost an

---

[1] Possibly another draft or a part of the letter on p. 322, *infra*.

hour, being obliged to Return thro the town and go over the Neck. This in the sequel will appear a very fortunate Circumstance, as it detered [me] from attempting to return the same way. I found my brother unable to move being confined with the Gout. Anxious for my Fri[e]nds, as the Country was now in the utmost Confusion, my attention was drawn to our Amiable Fri[e]nd Miss Sally Bromfield, who was then at Cambridge. I went and took her into my Chaise. The people hav'g taken up Cambridge Bridge to stop the Troops in their Retreat, and fear'g another disapo'ntment at Charlestown, I thot it most prudent to Return home by the Way of Watertown, tho it was 13 Miles, which I happyly effected by Sunsett, after hav'g Rid post a Circuit of 30 Miles. Had we Returnd thro Charleston we should have been in the midst of the Battle and have remain'd a fortnight involuntary exiles from our Fri[e]nds who as it was were very uneasy for us. This is evident, Mr Harry B. having gone the same afternoon to fetch his Sister down but finding she had ju[s]t left her Uncles with me hastned immediatly back to the Ferry where he found the boats stopp'd by Order of the Gen'l. The Armies fast approach'g and that being a very unsafe place he had but just time to escape over Charleston Neck before the retreat'g army entered it. He was forced to Rem[a]in 13 days in the Country unable to see his Fr[i]ends before he could obtain a pass to Return home. amidst the Horrors of that fatal Day, I feel myself peculiarly happy in being instrumental in rescuing my very lovely Fri[e]nd from such a Scene of Distress and Danger. The other Circumstance was this: finding I should have no busness here, my self and frie[n]ds thought it advisable for me to go to Philada. I had agreed for my Passage and was pack'g up my things expecting to sail the next Mon'g, when in the Night the Capt. fear'g some detention went off and left all his Passengers behind. This has turn'd out very lucky, as advices have just arrived that New-york and Philad. are in almost as much trouble and Confusion as we are and there is an armed force going there. This with the other disapointm't at Charlestow[n] Ferry have fully taught me that present disapointment——

[You] will doubtless be surprised to find this transmitted to London by my dear Sister, who sails in Capt. Callahan[1] to-morrow with her little Family. the perticulars she will give you. the times are such as must preclude all thots of your return'g.

Henry Pelham to John Singleton

Boston, May 16, 1775.

Dear and Hon'd Uncle,

To give you a short account of the situation of your Friends here, and to remove from your minds and that of my other dear Relations in your part of the World, Aprenhensions which must arrise for our safety in this time of Distress and difficulty, is the motive for my addressing you now. It will be needless for me to give a detail of the Causes leading to the unhappy event, which has recently thrown us into the greatest Confu-sion, and has involved this Country in all the Horrors of a Civil War. You must be fully acquainted with [the] Contest which for some year[s] past has subsisted between this Continent and Great Britain. I shall therefore pass it without any Remark, saving that it has been productive of mutual je[a]lo[u]sy and

---

[1] Erased: "tomorrow or next. In a few days." Callahan, captain of the Minerva, did not sail until May 27, and then went from Marblehead. On April 27, the British general had given leave for all persons who should choose to do so to leave Boston with their effects, and large numbers seized the oppor-tunity. A year earlier, June 1, 1774, Governor Hutchinson had left America in the same vessel, then also commanded by Callahan.

mistrust, unnatural heartburn'g, hatred and Malice, among those whose Duty and interest it was to dwell together in Peace, mutually love'g and Cherishing each other. A Conduct which would be infinitely more agreable to the design of Providenc[e] in forming us Social Beings, and mak'g us dependant on those around us more consonant to the dictates of that boasted Reason which so eminently destinguishes Man from all the other Works of Creation, and unquestionably more agreable to the express Commands of that Prince of Peace, whose Holy Religion we all profess to make the Rule of our Lives and Conduct. But alas! The last ten years is but an additional Confirmation of that Mallencholly truth taught us by the experienc[e] of ages that neither the light of Natural Religion, the dictates of Reason, the positive Commands of Christianity, nor even a Regard to present Happyness are effectual to curb the licentious Ambition, the Pride and Averice of Man, or smoth those aspiraties of the Mind which too frequently break the ties of benevolence and Virtue, and render Man his own greatest Enemy. Whatever disagrement there may be respecting a parlimentary Right to tax us, or about American opposition, we must all agree in this that a Civill War is the most dreadfull Evill that can befall a People, as it is subversive of that friendly intercourse that can so greatly heighten our Joys, gives such a cha[r]m to our innocent pleasu[res], and aleviates the Sorrows of Life.

Among other preperations of defence which the People of this provinc[e] have for some months past been very industriously making they had formed some Magazines of Provisions and Milatary Stores, one perticula[r]ly at Concord 18 Miles from Boston. The Granodiers and light Infantry Companies belonging to the Kings Troop in this town, making about 600

Men, were ordered to destroy this Magazine (they began their March from town about 12 o Clock in the night of the 18 of April), which after a small Skirmish they effected. By day-break there was a very general Rising in the Country. all were in motion, alarm Guns having been fired and expresses sent to every town. About 10 o Clock the 19 of April Gen'l G[age], having rec'd advice that the troops were attack'd as they were going to Concord, ordered out a Reinforcement of 4 Regiments under the command of L[ord] P[ercy], with 2 field Peices, the whole with the first party Makeing 1800 Men. This reinforc[e]-ment joined the others just time eno to prevent their being entirely cut to peices, they having nearly expended all their amunition. By this time a great Number of People were assembled fully equipp'd, who lined the Woods and Houses along the Road thro which the troops mu[s]t pass in returning to Boston. A general Battle ensued, whi[c]h was supported by an almost incessant fire on both sides for 7 Hours, when the troops made good their retreat with the loss of 57 Killed, above 100 Wounded, amongst whom were two Off[i]cers who have since died and severall Missing. It is impossable to ascertain the loss on the part of the Country People. they acknowledge the loss of 40 Killed on the spot, but this I apprehend must fall vastly short of the true number. A Fr[i]end of mine says he saw between 70 and 80, and the Gentlemen who were spectators of the Scene universally agree that there could not be less than 150 or 200. they lost three of their Captans. Thus you have the most perticular account of this unhappy affair that I am capable of give'g you. Words are wanting to discribe the Misery this affair has produced among the Inhabitants of this Town. Thousands are reduced to absolute Poverty who before lived in Credit. Buisness of any kind is entirely Stop'd. The Town invested by 8000 or 10,000 Men, who prevent all supplies of fresh Provision from coming in, so that we are now reduced to have recource to the stores which those of us who were provident foreseeing a political Storm had lain in. We find it disagreable living entirely upon salt Meat. it is especially so to my honord Mother, whose ill state of Health renders her less able to bear it. My Brother Jack has been near a year past making the Tour of France and Italy. My Sister Copley is just embarking with her little Family for London, where she expects soon to meet him. She is the bearer of this to England. As for myself I dont know what to say. this last Maneuvour has entierly stopp'd all my buisness, and annialated all my Property, the fruits of 4 or 5 years Labor. I find it impossable to collect any Monies that are due to me, so that I am forced to find out some other place where I may at least make a living. my present purposed plan is to remove to Great Britain where I shall be able to look about me, and where I shall have an Opertunity of consulting my Friends respecting my future pursuits. Should I be able to purswade my hon'd Mamma to undertake this Voyage, Which I sometimes flatter myself I shall, I would leave this place in 6 or 8 Weeks. With her love and sincer[e]st affections I beg leave to tender you and my Aunt Singleton my most dutifull Respects and beg your blessing. Be kind eno to present my duty to my Uncle and aunt Cooper, and Love to all my Cousins. I am, Dear Sir, with the sincer[e]st affection and Respect your most dutifull Nephew,

H. P.

PS. I should take it as a great kindness if you would favour me with a line as often as Conven[ien]t. Please to dir[e]ct to the Car[e] of Mrs. Copley in London, who will forward them to me.[1]

---

[1] This letter was sent to Anthony King, of Dublin, Pelham's cousin.

Henry Pelham to Copley

BOSTON, May 16, 1775.

MY DEAR BROTHER,

Before you rec. this you will doubtless have heard alarming Reports of a late most unhappy Event which has taken place here. I have hitherto declined giving you any account of the State of Politicks since you left us, thinking it a theme which could afford you no amusement. I now reluctantly find my self obliged to give you a detail of one of the most extraordinary and unhappy transactions which can possably disgrace the Records of Mankind. Alass! My dear Brother where shall I find Words sufficiently expressive of the Distractions and Distresses of this once flourish'g and Happy People. The Disorders of which we were lately such anxious Spectators have produced those effects which every dispas[s]ionate Mind foresaw, and every humane and feeling Heart wished to avoid: My hand trembles while I inform you that [the] Sword of Civil War is now unsheathd. For some months past the People of this Province, impelled by the most surprizing Enthusi[as]m which ever seized the mind of Man, have been industriou[s]ly making every preperation for Carrying on a War and had formed some considerable Magazines. Gen'l Gage to embarrass them and Retard their Plans, determind to break up a Magazine of Provision[s] and Milatary Stores they had collected at Concord, 18 Miles from Town. To effect this about 600 Men embarked from the Bottom of the Common in Longboats and landed at Phipps farm about 1 o Clock in the Morn'g of the 19 of April: from thence proceeded to Concord, where they destroy a quantity of Provision, a Number of Harness and some Guns. At 10 o Clock, 4 Regiments, making with the first Party 1800

Men, with 2 Field Pieces, march'd as a Reinforcement under
the Command of Lord Percy. This movement caused an universal Tumult thro the Country. Alarm Guns were fired,
Expresses sent to every town, and in a few Hours a Very large
Body of People were assembled under Arms from all Parts,
who lined the Woods, Roads, and Houses. A[n] obstinate and
Bloody Battle was the consequenc[e], when an incessant fire
and general Battle ensued and an incessant fire was supported
on both sid[e]s for 7 Hours, till sunsett, during which time the
Regulars made a Retreat which does Honor to the Bravest and
best Disciplin[e]d troops that ever Europe Bred. The fatigues
and conduct of this little Army, is not to be parrelleled in
History. They marchd that day not less than 50 Miles, were
constan[t]ly under Arms, part of them at least from 10 o Clock
at Night till an hour after Sunsett the next Even'g, the whole
of the time without any Refreshm[e]nt, attack'd by an Enemy
they could not see, for they skulk'd behind trees, stone Walls,
etc., and surround[ed] by not less than 10000 Men who most
vigirou[s]ly assaulted them with fresh Men. In short considering the Circumstances it was almost a Maricle that they were
not entirely distroy[ed]. When the battle ended they had not
near a Charge a Man. The Kings troops had 57 Killed, above
106 Wound[ed], among them 2 Officers, who are since dead
and several missing. The Rebels loss is not assertained, as
there has been scarce any communication between town and
Country since. They aknowledge they had 40 of their People
killed, but this must fall Vastly short of the true number.
Doct. Spring of Watertown says he saw betwe[e]n 70 and 80.
The Officers in general agree they could not loose less than 150
or 200, among whom are 3 of the[i]r Captains. Thus I give
You the perticulars of this most shock'g affair. I must now

discribe the State of this town. It is intirely invested by an Army of about 8000 Provincials who prevent all supply.s and Communication from the Country. The Gen'l is fortifying the Town in all Parts, has bui[l]t a Number of Battery[s] at the Neck, at the bottom of the Common, round the beach to Newboston, on fox Hill, Beacon Hill, and all along from your land entirely to Mr. Wm. Vassells, on Fort Hill and Cops Hill at Bartons Point. So that the threatned assault upon the town now gives us very little disturbance. The Ge[n]'] has entirely disarmed the Inhabitants and has permitted Numbers to move out with their Eff[e]cts. We have been obliged to live intirely upon salt provisions and what stores we have in the house, and I thi[n]k we are very fortunate. foreseeing a political Storm we had been for some time collecting provisions of all sorts and have just furnish'd eno to last our family 6 Months. Mr Clarke has done the same. It is inconc[e]ivable the Distress and Ruin this unnatural dispute has caused to this town and its inhabitants. Almost every shop and store is shut. No buisness of any kind going on. You will here wish to know how it is With me. I can only say that I am with the multitude rendered very unhappy; the little I had collected, entirely lost. the Cloaths upon my back and a few Dollers in my pocket are now the only property which I have the least Command of. What is due to me I cant get and have now an hundred guineas worth of business begun which will never afford me an hundred farthings.

I cant but think myself very unfortunate thus to have lost so much of the best part of Life, to have my Bus[i]ness, upon which my happyness greatly depends, so abruptly cut short, all my bright prospects anialated, the little Property I had acquired rendered useless, myself doomed either to stay at home and starve, or leave my Country my Fri[e]nds, forced to give up those flattering expectations of domestic felicity which I once fon[d]ly hoped to realise: to seek that Bread among strangers which I am thus crually deprived of at Home.

This I long foresaw would be the case. The expectation of this dist[r]essing Scene was the cause of that illness which sent me to Philadelph[i]a last fall: When I think of my present Situation, it requires all my Philosophy to keep up my spirits under this acumula[te]d Load of uneasiness. I can't help relating two Circumstances, which amidst all my distress Afford me real pleasure and have tended greatly to Relieve my anxiety, and it has fully taught me that present disapo[i]ntment may be productive of future good, and that we are indispensably obliged after we have conscientiously done what appears to us our Duty to leave the issue to that Almighty being, whose Fiat created and whose Providenc[e] Govern[s] the World: and weither Adversity depress or Prosperity chear us, we are equally bound humbly to adore his Wisdom and patiently submitt to his all righteous Dispensations. [*Unfinished.*]

Henry Pelham to Charles Pelham

BOSTON, June 5, 1775.
DEAR BROTHER,

Your letter of the 31st ultimo I duly rece[i]vd, and am pleased that it was in my Power to transmitt what You there requested by my very worthy Namesake Mr. Henry Bromfield Junr. I should have sent it sooner but could get no safe Conveyance. however hope it came in season to be serviceable. By him I likewise sent a letter I took out of the Post office for which paid 2/5, which with 11 Johan, and 15/ in Change is I think the sum of your account. Harry doub[t]less gave you more intellegence respecting your Friends in this Town than I can in the Compass of a Letter, and I suppose inform'd you of my return to town the day I was last at your House: Sister Copley sailed saturday sivnigh[t] with her little Family for England. She desired her kindest Love to you and My Sister Pelham, is very sor[r]y she could not make out to see you before she left the Place which was very sudden. I cant but say I am glad they are gone. I propose going there myself with my Mother, if I can prevail upon her to undertake the Voyage, which I am somewhat fearful I shall not be able to do. if not, I will endeavour to get her Consent for my spending the Winter there, which all my other fri[e]nds strongly urge, as I shall have nothing to do at home, and have no doubt but I shall be able at least to bear my expences there. This is a plan I don't allow myself to think I shall not execute. I shall in that case beg it as a favour that you would give me an introductory Letter to our Aunt whom I shall make it a point to Visitt. But before I go can't you contrive for me having an interview at the Lines? I want it much and beg if possible it may be soon. if you can appo[i]nt a time I will get there, but let it bee soon in the Mon'g and give timly Notice.

The inclosed Letter I am desired to forward you as soon as I can, and must be answerd as soon as possable. I have been for near a fortnight past much affected with a violent ague in my face, which I hope is now going off. I pray God to bless all my dear Friends at Newton. beg to be kindly Remembered to them an[d] am with affection and esteem dear Sir you[r] ever affe[c]tion[ate] Brother.

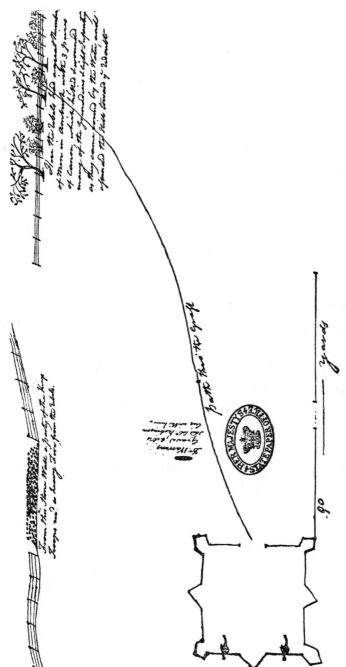

PELHAM'S SKETCH OF THE REDOUBT ON BUNKER HILL

Copley to his Mother

PARMA, June the 25, 1775.

MY EVER DEAR AND HON'D MOTHER,

By this oppertunity I have the happiness to inform you of my safe arrival in this place. I left Rome the 4th Instant and had a very agreable Journey to this place, stoping at Florance 4 Days, and two at Belogna in my way. I have been blessed with the most perfect health since I left Boston, and trust in that God who has preserved and blessed me for a continuance of his Mercy to me in the contin[u]ance of the injoyments of not only my own health, but that of my dear friends and all other blessings he has been pleased to bestow on me in his abundant goodness. The being seperated from friends I so tenderly love is exceedingly painfull to me, and my angsiety is greatly increased by the unhappy state of America. I pray God preserve and keep you all from the Miserys of War. by the last post I had a letter from Mr. Greenwood in London, and am exceedingly distressed to find there is no prospect of any thing less distressing than a Civil War sp[r]eading itself over that once happy Country. he writes me it has began already with the spiling of the blood of an hundred and fifty or two hundred persons. I hope it is not so distressing, but I cannot divest myself of the most ancious apprehentions for my Country and Friends.

While I was in Rome I saw the English Papers twice a Week, but in this place I have not the least oppertunity of hearing but by letters from my friends which I am very ancious to receive. I have began my copy of the very fine Corregio, for which I have a commission from an English Nobleman. I have half Dead Colour'd my copy, tho I have been here only one Week. I hope to be able with great diligence to finish it in about two months, when I shall hasten to England by the way of Flanders. You can have no Idea how easy it is to travil in this Country, and none of those dangers or dificultys attend it which are immagined by People that have not been in Europe. it is only passing from one Town to another, as from Boston to Roxbury, and the whole way houses, and People ready to do what ever you may want. Roberys are very rarely known to be perpitrated, and so much security from things of this kind that people travil much more by night than Day in the warm weither. it is not so in England. The great dificultys that attend traviling here is that the people will impose on one if it is possable for them to do it; for there is no regulations for the Inns, and they will make the most of their Gests. so that it is necessary to agree for every thing one wants on the Road, and in every place I find Englishmen to associate with. even in this place, which I think a little obscure place after being so long in Rome and other Great Citys, there is at this time two English persons, and one other who has resided so long in England that I must consider him as such. I don't recollect being in any place since I left London but what I met some English to associate with, which is very different from what I expected. I am now five hundred and twenty miles nearer London that I was at the extreeme part of my Tour, which was Pestum, an ancient City, about sixty miles beyand Naples. there is to be seen of this City the Walls, and the Vestiges of three or four Temples, and an Amphitheater. this is all that remains to be seen at this Day. the Ground for Ages has been plowed and so little has this place been known that it is not menshoned by any Auther, tho a place of as much curiossity as any I have seen, except Pompei and Herculaneam. from its antiquety and singular Stile of Architecture it derives its curiosity, it being older than Rome and it[s] Architecture that of the first dawning of that Science among the Greeks. I think the Walls of this City are about 4 or 5 and twenty feet thick. it lays on the Seacoast in a fine Bay, and the Ground is very level within the Walls, which are in circumferance about four miles. this place I am glad to have seen, though I should not have extended my Tour so far, had not Mr. Izard invited me to accumpany him their from Naples. we performed this Tour, stayed at Pestum 3 hours, and got back to Naples in three Days. Mr. Izard has been very much my friend on this Tour, and from Naples to Rome he would pay all my expences, and has shewn the greatest desire possable to render me every service in his power. I received a letter from him by the last Post from London, where he and his Lady are safe arrived. he is a native of Carolina and his Lady of New York and of the De Lancy Family, and a very fine Woman.[1] I had no acquaintance with him in America, but at Florance he inquired for me and called to see me and I have found him a very Valuable Friend. Mr. Boylston[2] has been within a few weeks past at Leghorn after his return from Turkey. We exchanged three or four Letters, but he is now gone on to Paris, and has perfectly recouvered his health. he writes me he is impatient to get to England, being worn out with continual traviling, having traviled 14000 miles, and that chiefly by land. I dont wonder he is tired of traviling. I am happy to hear Brother Harry has recovered his health. I hope he will long injoy that Blessing with all others that are reasonable to expect. I hope he continues to be imploy'd. I intend writing him by this oppertunity, but should be glad to hear oftener from him. I think he

[1] Alice, daughter of Peter de Lancey.
[2] Ward Nicholas Boylston (1749–1828).

might write to me by every oppertunity and that he might write more on one sheat of Paper than he does. I set him a good example I am sure. I think there is nothing, when he has read one of my letters, he would wish to ask me, so perticular I am in my desires to gratify and instruct him. I wish he would consider that the smallest surcumstances are rendered interesting from the distance I am at and I wish to ask him a thousand questions. I am not sattisfyed with a few lines containing a few formal sentiments. I want [news] of everything about his works, the Farm, the Publick, etc., etc. In his last Letter he informed me he had painted a miniature and sent it to the Exibition, but as I did not find it in the Cattalogues I conclude it arrived too late. I shall wish to see somthing next year exibited by him. his process in Miniature is I beleive very right, only Mr. Humphreys tells me he uses no Shugar Candy in his colours; that he tints them at first exceeding faint, and so brings on their effect by degrees. I wish when I get back to England to see the Picture he sent, but for this he must send me a direction. I wish also to have a direction to write to My Uncle Singleton, and Aunt Cooper; also a Direction to the Gentleman that transacts his Aunts Pelham's Business, for my attention to this shall be immediately on my arrival in London.

I think I shall be able to pay the expences of my Tour by what I shall have done in this Country, or near it; although it has not been in my power to do a couple of Pictures that [were] bespoke. one was a Madonna and Child by Guido in Rome. this there was no possability of geting leave to Copy. the other the Madonna at Florance by Raphael, the same that used to hang over my Chimney. this I could not stay to do without hazarding my place at Parma being taken by some other

Artists, as there was several prepairing for that purpose, and it was too important an object to miss. the Copy, if done as I hope to do it, will be a very valuable thing and I shall be paid accordingly for it, not being limmited in price. I have procured the copy of Guido's Aurora for Mr. Palmer. it is in Warter colours and will be in England by the time I get there, with my other things. the original is a very fine thing indeed and I doubt not you will be much pleased with the Copy when you see it. I have seen a letter from Rome by which find menshon is made of a Skirmish having been at Lexington, and that numbers were killed on boath sides. I am exceeding uneasy not knowing to what you may be exposed in a Country that is now become the seat of War. this is the evil I greatly dreaded while I was in America. sure I am the breach cannot now be healled, and that country will be torn in peices, first by the quarrel with Great Briton till it is a distinct Government, and than with Civil discord till time has settled it into some permanant form of Government. what that will be no Man Can tell. weither it will be a free or Dispotick is beyand the reach of human wisdom to deside. in the mean time we must pursue that which is our Duty and to Providence look up for a blessing on what we do. I hope you dont think I neglect you in not writing oftner to you, but I let no private oppertunity escape me without improveing it. I wish they were more frequent. by the Post I write very constantly to my Dear Wife, by which you have every thing meterial and I think it is pity to pay postage for Letters to more than one. I pray God keep and preserve you from every evil, and am, My Dear Madam, Your Most Affec-tionate and Dutyfull Son

JOHN SINGLETON COPLEY.

PARMA, the 1st of July, 1775.

Copley to Henry Pelham

PARMA, the 25 of June, 1775.

DEAR HARRY,

It is now a considerable time since I wrote you, not having a private conveyance of a Letter to you; but at this time an English Artist is going to London and I imbrace with the greatest pleasure every oppertunity of instructing you and testifying that sincere Love I bear you. I think I have given you the best Idea I am capable of in writing of the Works of the great Artists. I think I began with Vandyke's Works in England, than Rubens's at the Luximburg, Raphael's and Titiano's at Rome. But I think I have not yet finish'd with Titiano. his last manner is that which I have dwelt upon. I shall now endeavour to convey to you his first and best manner, and shall keep in my eye his Venus at Florance, as I think it is the finest thing he has produced. it differs from his last manner in its being more finished, and in all parts having a greater degree of precision in boath Colour and Contour. you have seen the Print, and I presume Mr West's Copy. I shall indeavour to build on them my discription. in them you have the Light and Shadow, and outline, and disposition; so what remains for me to give is the colouring, and penciling. you doubtless thought Mr. West's Copy finely Coloured; but if I remember it right it has more of an Inamil'd look than the original. indeed all Pictures compaired to Titianos have this look, that is more white, read, black, blew, etc. if you put your hand to the flesh of this Venus you will find it the same Colour. if you put your hand on any other you will find the Paint has more of the dauby, smooth or pasety look, blacker than the flesh, at the same time whiter, boath paler and reader. If you

examin the knee and part of the thigh of the little Jesus in the
Madonna's lap at Mr. Chardons, you will find that compaires
very well with the flesh, if you put your hand to it, but yet it is
not exactly Titian. I recommend to you to take some spirits of
Turpentine and mix up a flesh tint and put it on a peace of
linen cloath; than mix another with oyl of Poppy or nuts, and
put that on the linen by the side of the other, and you will see a
briliancy and Strength in that mixt with turpentine, and the
other will look Dark, cold, and greasy. the same differance you
find between those tints, you find between the Pictures of Titian
and those of other masters. I must indeed allow that the Vene-
cian Masters in general seem to have the same colouring that
Titian has, only not carried to that perfection. I have formed
in my mind from the most attentive consideration of Titiano,
a process which I think will produce somthing like his Colouring. it is as Follows: Take a good Cloath, pass over it with
Spanish'd White mix'd with size, so rubed into the Cloath that
all the pores are filled. let it dry. than with your pencil draw
your outline with Dark colour. this done, set your Pallet with
Colours ground in oyl, as you get them from the Colour shop.
They will be very stiff. dilute them with spirits of Turpentine,
and paint your Picture with a good body in the lights and very
thin in the shades, and in this way bring your Picture to as
great a degree of perfection as you can. when you can do no
more, pass over your Picture (which will be intirely sunk in)
with mastick Varnish. let it dry and your Picture will appear
very brilliant, and have an even gloss. this done, take retouching Varnish and anoint the picture, not all over at once but by
peace meal, for instance an head, hand, etc., or what ever you
mean to improve, and finish your Picture by glaizeings with
Colours first ground in oyl and than diluted with the retouching

Varnish, and if necessary add a little oyl. by glaizeings I mean not only glaizeing in the Shadows, but Scumbling all over the lights with Virgin tints, makeing some parts reader, some lighter, some blewer, etc., and giving a greater breadth to some parts by making a number of minute tints harmonise by one general Scumble of fine flesh Colour. your Picture, when dry, Varnish with Mastick Varnish, or Spirit Varnish if it will bear it; but I should think without trying it, it would tear up the Colours. I think Titian has managed somthing in this way, and many of his shades are given only by the glaizeings. for instance the thighs of his Venus were laid in without the divition between them being marked. and when he came to glaize, he has run over with a tint through which you see the flesh and marked this division in this way. you must conceive that the flesh tints are preserved throughout every part. you must have a perfect Idea of what I mean. I think the method is very simple, and if you have a mind to try it, it wont cost you much time, for I would not have you spend much time in experiments. if you should do some little thing, I dont mean a finish'd Picture, send it me and I shall give you my opinion on it. You are to remember after all that the eye and Judgment is to be acqu[i]red by diligence for the produceing fine things; without those no receipt will avail. the receipt is only to inable a man to effect what his Judgment informs him aught to be done. The receipt for the Varnishes are as follows: to make Mastick Varnish: Take of the whitest Gum Mastick 6 Ounces, Spirits of Turpentine 7 Ounces; put them into a bottle well corked, put the bottle into a Pot of Warter over the fire, not leting the bottle touch the bottum of the Pot. Shake the bottle every quarter of an hour till the Gum is dissolved. let it stand by the fire and in the hot warter till it is settled, and than it is fit for use.

Retouching Varnish: Take of Gum Mastick 2 Ounces,[1] Shugar of lead 1 Ounce, or some thing less, grind them very fine on a Clean stone; than Put Nut or Poppy Oyl as much as is sufficient to liquify them; put this into a vessel with a little Oyl over it to keep it from Drying, but let no warter be put on it. this Varnish looks as it lays on the Pallet like Jelly. The same process that I have discribed above one Mr. Dean, a good Landscape Painter, pursues in his lanscapes, with this differance only, that his Cloaths are primed with Oyl Colour and he dead colours with Oyl of Poppy; that is he Paints as you do, only when he has done as much as he can with a body of Colours he Varnishes with Mastick, and than after that is dry he anoints out his Picture with retouching Varnish with a brush. than with another dry one he drys his Picture as much as possable, and then Glaizes all parts of his Picture, even his Sky, with White and Ultramarine. his Colours ar[e] diluted with retoching Varnish. A method to purify Oyl: take 1 Pint of Nut or Poppy Oyl, one Pint of warter; Put them together into a bottle or flask and put the flask into the Sun, and shake it four or five times a Day for a bout a fortnight. pound very fine some white Marble and put it into the flask; at the last shaking this will fine it. Sand will do, if you cannot easily get marble.

The Gum you may purify in the following manner: put it on a Paper, lay the Paper on a plate of Iron over a moderate heat till the Gum is soft; than press the Gum with your finger and thumb and the Clear will press out, leaving all the gross parts behind.

Mr. Wests Receipt for retouching Varnish is differant from

---

[1] On the margin is written: "You will find it dificult to grind the Gum; it being apt to cake under the Muller. You had best Grind it by it self."

the above, and is as follows: Take about one Ounce of Gum Mastick, Dissolve it in Spirits of Turpentine, and while it is warm add about a Table spoonfull of Nut or Poppy Oyl, and add about half a Table spoonfull of Spermicity to break the texture of the Gum. this you apply to your Picture with a brush. it will never change or leave any stain. The quantity of Turpentine should be so much that when the Gum is dissolved it will be of the consistancy of Honey. it may be about 1 Ounce of Gum to an Ounce of Spirits of Turpentine. Another Receipt: Take of Gum Mastick somthing more than a Table spoonfull, and put it into a Gill of Spirits of Turpentine. put also into it half as much Spermacity as Gum, and when dissolved apply it to your Picture with a brush. A method to give richness to your Colours: Take of Gum Mastick as much as a Table spoon will hold, put it into a Gill of Poppy Oyl, warm it over the fire till the Gum dissolves, and than Mix it with your Colours.[1]

You will see all these receipts are very nearly the same, only Mr. West puts Spermiceity in his, which I think cannot be any advantage, if the Colours can be used without it, as I suppose they may, and are by other Artists. these are the Varnishes used among Painters. my spirit Varnish is unknown to them and I think if these Varnishes would bear the Spirit at last it would be very well. I have never yet try'd any of these, but as they are in such general use I think there is no Danger in useing them. Mr. West has sometimes put Copeall Varnish in his Colours. he mixes as much of it with Poppy Oyl as will

---

[1] There is a bracket opposite this paragraph with the words, "from Mr. West." On the margin is written: "You must observe than when you have put the retouching Varnish on your Picture that you wipe it off as clean as you can with a little Cotton Wool, or Peice of Woolin Cloath."

consist with the free use of the Pencil in applying the Colours to the Canvis. he says it gives great richness to the Colours. I find the Picture I am now Copying so remarkably rich in the tints and Clear at the same time, that I am convinced Corregio must have use'd Varnish or somthing of that sort in his Colours; but weither it is best, if Gum is used, to dissolve it in Oyl, as Mr. West does, or Grind and mix it with the Oyl, as in my first method, I dont know, as I have not try'd either method. And the more I reflect on the effect of Gum being mixed with the Colours, the more I am incouraged to beleive it will have a tendancy to keep the Colours from changeing, and at first give them brilliancy. but I could like to finish then with Spirit Varnish, that is when my Picture was intirely done Varnish with it, and if the Spermicity is not used in the retouching Varnish, I think it would do very well, and Spermaceity is use'd by Mr. West only and not by other Artists. But your great object is to acquire thourough Mastery of the principals and exicution of Your Art, and these Delicasy's of Art must come in as ornaments to those. In about one week from this time you will receive my letters by Mr. Izard. I have there been perticular, But I must renew my injun[c]tions to you to be diligent. I would have you get an Anatomycal figure; it may be had at Smibert's and with a book learn the mussels with their uses and incertions. dont go below the external Mussels. The length of the bones you have in the Book of the Antique Statues publish'd with their measures. When you know the Mussels (by the way you must begin with the Bones before the external Mussels), You may sketch any figure from Idea well anough for an historical composition. I mean the first sketch. it is an amasing advantage in the pursuit of any Study to know one is right, and one-half is in a confidence that one can do what they wish. A man in this must have as much faith that he can do what he undertakes as a Christian must have in the truth of his religion. When you know the bones and Mussels, which you will very soon, you will have acquired one very necessary thing, and if you should than (as I would have you) sketch any Historical Subject, the first thing you will do will be to fix on the disposition of your figures, and if you should find yourself at a loss for the appearance of any of the figures as you may in Certan attitudes, so that you cannot sketch them near anough, and as you cannot have recou[r]se to the life except that you may try the Attitude before a Glass, you have some good Accademy figures that will help you in this. but observe by this I dont mean to draw you from your portraits, for that is the most advantageous at least at present. only I don't think a Man a perfect Artist who on occation cannot Paint History, and who knows but you may have a talent in history like Raphael till you try; and if you have, your fortune is secure in this Life. but not to dwell on this proceed as I have directed, and when you have master'd what I have menshoned, send me a sketch. you have as good or a better layman than any I have seen since I left America for your Draperys. the best Drapery for history is Cloath, flaniel or Linnen, Wet and rung out. Mind always to get a breadth of Light and Shadow as one great thing assential in Art. And dont be discouraged if you should make two or three sketches and they dont please; for Mr. West told me he beleived he had made fifty at least for his return of Regulus; and Mr. Hamilton[1] has had a sketch in Colours on his easel ever since I came to Rome, and how much longer I know not, and every now and than altering some part of it, and had not done it when I left Rome.

[1] Gavin Hamilton (1730–1797).

it is the Parting of Hector and his wife. but when you have got your general Idea fixed and so that you wish to shade, I mean with any degree of accuracy, I recommend as in my last letter that you do this figure by figure. When I was at Modena I saw an original Drawing of the figure in the Transfiguration that points up to the Mount shaded, cut off by the out line of the parts of the other figures. I was pleased because confirmed in this method of proceeding. but portrait painting I shall pursue, unless tempted to some things in history by any that may wish to imploy me in that way. Mr. Hamilton observed just before I left Rome that I was better establish'd than Mr. West, because he could not paint such portraits as those of Mr Izard and Lady, and portraits are always in demand. I am happy in the reflection that you have made a progress I think equil to most of your Age that are in Europe, and certain I am if you apply with Vigour you will succeed very well. I have no doubt you will greatly profit by what I write you, and I shall be happy to see somthing of yours better than any thing you had done when I was in Boston. You are to remember that the works of the great Masters are but Pictures, and when a man can go but a very little beyond his cotemporarys he becomes a great Man. the differance between Raphael, Titiano, Angelo and the common run of moderately good Artists, is not so great as one would Imagin from the Praises bestow'd on those Great men. but they are the first Artists and they merit the Most elaborate Praises from the World. The Picture of a Naked Venus and Cupid at Smibert's is Copy'd from one of Titiano's in the possession of the Great Duke of Tuskany, which hangs over the Celebrated Titian Venus, but is by no means equil to it. the little head of St. John that hangs by the side of the window in your little Painting Room is copied from a St.

John in an holy Family by Titiano in the same appartment, and in its general effect just what Titianos is. perhaps it may have been an original sketch by Titian for that Picture. I know you are happy in this acqui[si]tion and you may wonder in my account of Titian's works I had not refered to this; but I don't know weither it is like Titian in the smaller beautys of Painting, tho in the Whole, as well as I remember, it is very just. if at Philadelphia you saw in Mr. Allens house A Picture containing three figures very Dark, one of them playing on a harpsicord with the head much turned to one Shoulder, you will be glad to know it is a Copy of Georgione. one observation more on Titian and I think I have left nothing unexplaind to the utmost of my power. it is this, that his shades are light on his flesh. tho other parts of his Picture have very Dark masses, but I am not sure if in a body of Oyl Colours the Shade were made light as his it would not look faint. as you see in Crayons the shades are much fainter or lighter than in Oyl, yet they look foarceable anough. for Titian's Pictures have somthing of the look of strong tinted Crayon Pictures, that kind of Dry look yet not meally. but as I think a Picture would look painted as above discribed, for it would be intirely sunk in as Dead as Crayons and the Varnishing over this would by no means destroy this appearance, some that have indeavoured to imitate Titian have painted first in Warter Colours, than Glaized with Oyl. Mr. West has done this, and produced somthing like Titian; but I conceived by puting Oyl on, the Picture becomes Oyl Painting, which my process does not from the Varnish laying over this Dry Colour, which prevents the Oyl entering in to the Colours, and of consiquence the under Colours cannot change. And if the Varnish should, you will always see those bright Colours through the Varnish.

but one tryal will determin the point, at least it would with me
who have seen Titian's Pictures. I shall Try an head the first
oppertunity I can get for that purpose, but I shall not perplex
myself with striveing to investigate the manner of any Painter,
only in one or two experiments that wont cost me many hours.
Indeed Sr. Jos: Renolds, Mr. West, and many others, say I
should be very rong to alter my manner. indeed it is the same
with that of the Roman School in which they have produced
the finest Pictures in the World. Before I leave Rome I should
give you my remarks on Michael Angelo's Works, but I shall
go a little out of that regular way of proceeding and Take up
Corregio first, as I am before him, and strive to inform you of
his excellencys In the best manner possable. but I must suspend this till another oppertunity, and hope you will excuse the
inaccurac[i]es in this Letter, for I have no time to write it over
on other Paper, and I only aim to be understood. if I am my
aim is answered. I should have sent you the receipts for
Varnishes sooner, but it was my intention to have try'd them
first myself; but I have not been able to do it. Some Persons
make their Varnish much Stronger of the Gum, and make no
differance between retouching Varnish and Other. they put 3
Ounces of Gum to one Ounce of Spirits of Turpentine, and
when they would paint over a head the second time or third,
with a brush rub this Varnish over the head and paint on it.
Mr. Hamilton uses none for retouch[ing] his Pictures but a little
Oyl as I used to do. On the whole I think the first Varnishes
I have menshoned seem to me to have the advantage, and
they are what I shall try first, and shall let you know my
oppinion of them on the tryal, and which if you should do any
thing you would be very perticular in your remarks on it. But
I must bid you Adieu for the present. remember me to all

friends and beleive me with sincere Love your Affectionate Brother,

JOHN SINGLETON COPLEY.

PARMA, the 2d of July, 1775.

This Day will dead Colour all my Picture of St. Jerome.

Copley to Henry Pelham

[PARMA, July 15, 1775.][1]

DEAR HARRY,

The deplorable state of Boston is such that I dont know what you may be called to in so critical a conjunctor. it may be (for my fears suggest many terrable things) that you are called to Arm yourself. But if you should be, it is my injuntion that You do not comply with such a requi[si]tion if this does not come too late which I pray God it may not. I trust an injuntion from me will have its Weit intirely. my reasons when I am happy to see you I will give you, and if y[ou] find it a requi[si]tion that is submitted to by all Orders of People you need not be backward to give my desire as a reason. let it have its full weit, and if you Love me in the least, let the desire be from whom it may comply not. I have this exceedingly at heart and trust you will implicitly oblige me in this way. I conjure you to do as I desire. for God Sake, dont think this a

---

[1] This note was sent to Pelham in Boston enclosed in Mrs. Copley's letter of September 18, 1775. Upon the margin, Mrs. Copley wrote: "P.S. this letter is dated the 15 of July." Copley's letter of the same date to Mrs. Copley, from Parma, is printed in Amory's *Life of John Singleton Copley*, 60–61. On July 22, 1775, Copley again wrote Mrs. Copley: —

"I would here renew my instructions to Harry not to suffer himself, for any person, or on any account whatever, to take part in the present dispute. I doubt not he will comply with my wishes; my reasons are very important." *Ib.*, 63. The note to Pelham above bears the postmarks, "Lu[glio] 29; Inglitterre; 1/ —."

Triffling thing. my reasons are very important. you Must follow my directions and be neuter at all events. if I could say more to bind you I would, but I know this is sufficient, and I depend upon you. Adieu, my Dear Brother, Adieu, may God preserve y[ou]. All Duty to our Dear Mother.

J. S. COPLEY.

[Addressed:] To Mr. Henry Pelham To the Care of Mr. Thos Bromfield Mercht at the New England Coffee House, London To be forwarded to Boston by the first oppertunity.

Henry Pelham to Susanna Copley[1]

BOSTON, July 23, 1775.

MY DEAR MADAM,

I should ill deserve that friendship and Regards with which you have hitherto honour'd me and which I am ambitious, ever to possess, was I longer to omitt congratulating your departure from this land of Ruin and Distress, and expressing my hopes that long ere this you are happyly arrived at a more friendly and peacefull shore, where I sincerely pray you may long enjoy every blessing that can fall to the lot of Human Nature. You had scarc[e]ly left us before we began to experience all the inconveniences attending A seige, and behold the desolations ever consequential upon a War. As you have doubtless had the perticulars of the destruction of property at Noddle Isle, of the Govenou[r]s proclimation declaring Adams and Hancock with their Abetters and aiders traitors and Rebels, of the suspension of all Civil Law and Courts, and the establishment of the

---

[1] This draft was written in red ink on absorbent paper, with corrections in black ink. The letter actually sent was dated July 26. See *Mrs. Copley to Pelham,* September 18, 1775.

Martial Law and the important Battle and Victory at Charlestown and distruction of that Town, of all which I had with my Telescope a very perfect, but very malencholly View, I shall forbear reciting an account which cannot fail of renewing Sensations which would be painful to a mind as yours susceptable of the finest feelings of Humanity Benevolence and Compassion. Its retrospect for a few Years back compared With the present Contest cant but be a matter of uncommon surprize to the most inattentive Observer. Within the few years which indulgent Providence has permitted to rool over my head, I well remember the Inhabitants of this Town and adjacent Country put into the greatest consternation and uneasiness upon a vague report of the approach of a small Army of French, and this at a time too when they had added to their own Strength the Victorious Arms of the most powerfull Nation in Europe Drawn in their Defence. Now we see this very Country arming themselves and unsupported by any foreign Power ungenerously Waging War against their great Benefactors, and endeavouring to Ruin that State to whom they owe their being, Whose Justice and Gennerosity has fostered them to the[i]r late flourishing and Happy Condition, and whose arms has protected them in the uninterupted Enjoyment of all the blessings of Peace.

We are at present invested by an army of about 14000 Men, whose almost Continual Firing of Shot has in a gr[ea]t degree reconciled us to Noise of Cannon; and we are daily spectators of the Operations of War. since the last Vessel sailed from this 500 Men in whale boats attacked and, I am sorry to say it, within sight of the British Flag, carried of from long Island just below the Castle 13 Men, who had fled to this Town from the Country and Miss Lydia Ward, Doct'r Perkin's Neice, who was there for her Health. they have not since been hea[r]d off.

likewise a Number of sheep and cattle, and returned the next day and burnt all the buildings with a Quantity of Hay. A few days ago they distroyed the light House at Noonday, with in a quarter of a Mile of a Man of War.[1]

I with pleasure inform you that your Friends here are as happy if not more so than could be expected considering the narrow limmitts to which we are confined, and our being entirely cutt off from all supplies, except what our Friends in Europe will let us have.

I was in hopes I should have had the Happyness of seeing you in England this fall, but now give over all thoughts of it, as I cant at present prevail upon My honoured Mother to undertake the Voyage, and should be very unneasy at leaving her during this scene of Confusion. Your Son is a fine boy in goo[d] Health. My buisness is entir[e]ly ceased. I have not now a single day's buisness. But to fill up time I have begun a Survey of Charlestown, for which I have permission from Gen'l Gage and Gen'l Howe, who were polite eno to grant me a general Pass directed to all Officers commanding Guards for going to and returning from Charlestown. Gen'l How[e], to assist me in the labori[o]us part of Measuring, has kindly put a Sarjant and his[2] Men under my Comm[an]d. This Plan when finished will give a good Idea[3] of the late battle and I propose sending Home a Coppy to be engraved, together with a View of it as it appears in its present Ruins, with the encampment on the Hills behind it. I have often passed Doct Warren's Grave. I felt a disagreab[le] Sensation, thus to see a Townsman an old Acquaintance led by unbounded Ambition to an untimely

---

[1] See *Mass. Hist. Soc. Proceedings,* xiv. 290.
[2] Possibly "two", or "ten"; but probably "two" changed to "his."
[3] Possibly "view."

Head Quarters Boston 28th August 1775

The Bearer Mr Henry Pelham has his Excellencys
Commander in Chief permission to take a
plan of the Town's of Boston & Charlestown and
of the Rebel works round those places, in doing
of which he is not to be obstructed or impeded
but has leave to pass & repass to & from the advanced
and Lines, the Camp, the Heights of Charlestown
& all other places necessary for completing his said
work, ... of the Kings
works &c .... he goes .

Ja: Urquhart
Town Major

To
all concerned

death and thus early to realise that Ruin which a lust of Power and Dominion has brought upon himself and partly through his means upon this unhappy Country. I would wish to forget his principles to Lament his Fate. I almost forgot to tell you that Mr. T. Mifflin of Philadela is aid de Camp to Gen'l Lee, and that the Continental Congress have taken the entire direction of the War, have erected themselves into an Independant body, are addressed by the title of Excellenceys and call themselfs the states General of the united american provinces, and this Army the grand Confederate Army. They have appointed Mr. Washington of Virginia Lieutenant Gen'l, and Ward, Putnam, and Lee Major Gen'ls. they are all now at Cambridge. They have been very industrious in constructing fortifications all round this Town, and it is said as far back as Worcester. What the Result of this Contest will be God only knows. I have not heard a Word of Brother Pelham since you left us. I wonder much at not having a single line from Brother Copley since one dated the 26th of last Sept., now near a twelve month. Mrs. Cordis, Capt. Ruggles' Neice and a near Neighbour at Chun,[1] whom you have some knowledge off, obligeingly promises to deliver you this. My hon'd Mamma desires her kindest Love and Blessing to you, My dear Brother and my little amiable and lov[e]ly Friends. Accept my Love and best Wishes which ever atte[nd] you and them, and beleive [me] sincerely Dear Madam your very affectionate Brother and Humbl[e] Servant.

[*Unsigned.*]

P.S we are extremly anxious to hear from you, mu[s]t beg of you to write often. I much wish to know where My brother is.

---

[1] Charlestown? Probably Rebecca Russell, wife of Joseph Cordis, of Charlestown is intended.

Copley to Henry Pelham

PARMA, the 6 of Augst., 1775.

MY DEAR BROTHER,

My principal design in writing to you at this time is to give you my oppinion and advice relitive to your present unhappy situation, which although you have had in other Letters, for I have wrote to you two or thre[e] times lately on the subject, yet not in so full and possitive a manner as I now think it best to do. The flame of Civil War is now broke out in America, and I have not the least doubt it will rage with a Violence equil to what it has ever done in any other Country at any time. You are sensable also by this time of the determin'd Resolutions of Government to persevere in Vigorous measures, and what will keep them firm in this determination, is that they Act as (at least) 4-fifths of the people would have them, they so Resent the outrage offered to them in the destruction of the Tea. you must think I aught to have many friends and thanks for the pains I took to prevent so violent and rash a peice of conduct. I was sure it would produce the consiquences that have followed and are only the faint beginings of More fatal and terrable evils than have yet taken place. You must also know I think that the people have gone too far to retract and that they will adopt the proverb, which says, when the Sword of Rebellion is Drawn the Sheath should be thrown away; and the Americans have it in their power to baffle all that England can do against them. I dont mean to ward off the evils attendant on Civil War, but so far as never to be subdued, so that Ocians of blood will be shed to humble a people which they never will subdue, and the Americans from the Id[ea] that England would not act against them have tempted its Power

My Dear Brother   Parma the 6 of Augt. 1775 —

          My principals design in writing to you at this time is to
give you my oppinion and advice rettive to your present unhappy situation
which although you have had in other Letters for I have wrote to you two or three
times lately on the subject yet not in so full and positive a manner as I
now think it best to do, / The flame of Civil War is now broke out in America
and I have not the least doubt it will rage with a Violence equel to that it
has ever done in any other Country at any time, you are sensible also by this
time of the determin'd resolutions of Government to persevere in vigorus measures
[   ] will keep them steady firm in this determination, is that they act at least
[least] 4 or 5 fifths of the people would have them / they so resent the outrage offered
to them, in the destruction of the Tea you must think I aught to have many friends and thanks for
the pains I took to prevent so violent a measures and such a peice of conduct I
was sure its would produce the consequences that have followed & are only the
faint begining of More fatals and terrable evils than have yet taken place
you must also know I think that the people have gone too far to retract & that they
will adopt the proverb, which says when the sword of Rebellion is Drawn the [   ]
shoud be thrown away and, the Americans have it in their power to baffle all
that England can do against them, I dont mean to ward off the evils attendent on
Civil war but so far as never to be subdue, is that oceans of blood will be
spilled to a people which they never will subdue and the Americans from [   ]
that England would not act against them have temp'd Power to the extreem
all its weight rage upon them, and after they have with various success deluged
the country in Blood the Issue will be that the Americans will be a free independent
people this may be the result of a struggle of many years, Thus I have stated what
appears to me to be the naturals course of the present contest, and in its course
the different Towns will have at different times to incounter all the misorys of [   ]
sword faming & perhaps pestelence as that is generally an attendent of War [   ]
I now would ask our Dear Mother if you wether a months Voyage is by any means
an evil to be compaired to the evils above menshoned if not why she will hisitate
one moment, I am surprized she did not come with your Sister, by your Letter
you seemed determined but I write this lest my Dear Mother should still deliberate
you are to consider if things should come to that extremity that would fix her
determination it may be out of her power than to leave the place I shall be
very glad to find you have imbarqed, but if it should be otherway I think
you cannot prevails with our Mother to come but when this reaches you it will be
late perhaps yet where as the latter end of May or the begining of June is the
time to have short & smooth passages at the same time, however it may be that
even a January passage would be more Mijeable than to stay in Boston this you will
judge best of yourself, you can have no Idea of my Anxiety for you while you remain
that place I therefore request you will bring Dear [   ] Mother if [   ] me Yours Affectio. J. S. Copley

to the extreem and dr[awn] all its weight [of] rage upon them, and after they have with various success deludged the Country in Blood the Issue will be that the Americans will be a free independant people. this may be the result of a Struggle of many years. Thus I have Stated what appears to me to be the natural course of the present contest, and in its course the different Towns will have at different times to incounter all the miserys of War, Sword, famin, and perhaps pestalence, as that is generally an attendant on War and so is famin. I now would ask our Dear Mother by you, weither a month's Voyage is by any means an evil to be compaired to the evils above menshoned? if not, why she will hisitate one moment. I am surprized she did not come with Your Sister. by your Letter you seemed determined, but I write this lest my Dear Mother should still deliberate. you are to consider if things should come to that extremity that would fix her determination, it may be out of her power than to leave the place. I shall be very glad to find you have imbarked, but if it should be otherways, I think you must prevail with our Mother to come; but when this reaches you it will be late, perhaps Octr., whereas the latter end of May or the begining of June is the time to have short and smooth passages. at the same time, however, it may be that even a January passage would be more eligiable than to stay in Boston. this you will Judge best of yourself, you can have no Idea of my Anxiety for you while you remain in that place. I therefore request you will bring Our hond. Mother, and beleive me Yours Affect'y

J. S. COPLEY.

Give my Affectionate love and Duty to all friends, perticularly My Dear Mother and let me expect to see her in England as soon as possable.

Johnson to Henry Pelham

[1775?]

SIR,

I have seen Mr. Robertson the Engeneer, who Consents to show you his draughts of ours and the enemys Works. If you'll be so good to perfect the draught you are makeing of this town and the enverons and insert these in it, before the Admiral Sails, youl oblige me by letting me have the draught.

If you call at Capt Robertson's tomorrow morning early youl find him at home. he lives in the Street where Mr. Hallowell the Commissioner dwells,[1] ten or twelve houses nearer Concert hall[2] on the other side of the Street. I am, Sir, your obt. Servt.

JAMES[?] JOHNSON.

[Addressed:] To Mr. Pelham New Boston.

Henry Pelham to Copley

BOSTON, August 19, 1774 [1775].

MY DEAR BROTHER,

It was my intention to have wrote you a long Letter to have accompanyed a plan which I have almost this moment finished, proposing to have exhibited to the Publick as perfect an Idea as was possable upon Paper of the late most important and glorious action, which I was an anxious Spectator of, and to which under God I attribute my present capacity for writing, and I hope will be our future security.

---

[1] Benjamin Hallowell occupied land on Hanover Street which was sold under the confiscation act and later became the property of the Hanover Street Church.

[2] Concert Hall was at the corner of Hanover and Queen (Court) Street.

I was disapointed in my expectations. this morning upon waiting on Gen'l Gage, he acquainted me that it would not be altogether proper to publish a plan of Charlestown in its present state, as it would furnish those without with a knowledge of the fortification[s] erected there and in a polite manner desired I would postpone the sending it at present. Mrs. Copley desired we would write word when we met with fresh Meat. You will form some Idea of our present disagreable Situation when I tell you that last Monday, I eat at Gen'l Howe's Table at Charlestown Camp, the only bit of fresh Meat I have tasted for very near four Months past. And then not with a good Conscience, considering the many Persons who in sickness are wanting that and most of the Convenency[s] of Life. The usual pleas now made by those who beg a little Bacon or Saltfish is that its for a sick person.

Mr. Clarke says he has inclosed you Copies of some late intercepted Letters. by them you will find what those who stile themselves patriots are after, and where there Schems will drive us. Independency [is] what alone will content those who have insinuated themselves into the good Opinion of (generally speaking) a well meaning but credulous people. Upon the supposition that this Country was totally independent on the Parent State, in the Name of Common Sence what one advantage could accrue? Should we be free from Taxes? We know we could not support a goverment for ten times the expence. Should we be Safer from forreign insults? Reason tells us that we should be exposed to every Inconven[ien]ce that a defenceless and impoverish'd People ever experienced. Would our internal Peace and Happyness be greater? Here alass! We may look back to those Days of Felicity and Peace which we enjoyed under the fostering Care and indulgent Protection of Britain, and contemplate ourselves as having once been the happiest people in the Empire; and on this View I am sure every un-prejudiced Person will execrate those distructive Schems, and that unbounded Ambition whi[c]h from the pinacle of Ease has plunged us into the depths of Distress and Ruin. Judge Sewall,[1] who kindly takes the Care of this, just setting out on his Voyage obliges me to conclude abruptly acquaint'g you that we are all as Well as the times will permitt. with wishing My dear Sister and family ever[y] possable felicity, I am, my dearest Brother, your

[*Unsigned.*]

P. S. I write this in your house in the Common where the Company unite with me in good Wishes. Our hon'd Mam[ma] desires her kind Love to you all. I must beg when you write me, to be carefull what you say, as all letter[s] that come into the[i]r hands are prise. I beleive there is one or more of your Letters at Cambridge. I almost hope ther[e] is, as I should be grieved to find you had not wrote to me. when you write send your letters [di]rectly to this Place.

Copley to Henry Pelham

PARMA, Augst 22d., 1775.

MY DEAR BROTHER,

I take this oppertunity to write to you, although I dont know weither you are still in America or on your Voyage to England. if you are in Boston I ám sensable you must want every conso-lation that can be affoard'd you in so unhappy a situation. this induces me to address you at this time, that you may have the small comfort my letters can affoard you, which is all that is

---

[1] Jonathan Sewall, Attorney-General of Massachusetts.

in my power while you remain in that unhappy place. I really hope to hear of your safe arrival in England with our Dear Mother. I cannot but be very thankfull to that beneficient being for all his mercy to me through life, but in a very perticular maner for the course of my affairs (which has removed me from that place of distress just at the time it did), being so overuled as to have preserved me from much distress anxiety and dificulty; and I trust that, although I may by this unhappy struggle be reduced to a state of poverty, I shall have my health and meet with that incouragement in England which will enable me to provide for my family, and in a decent manner bring these Dear Children up which God has blessed me with. I am just now on the point of finishing my Tour, which I should have found it very dificult to have taken if I had stayd in America longer than I did, and if I had left it sooner, it would have been doing more violence boath to myself and Dear Wife to have fix'd in England. but now there is no choice left; and my business is so near accomplish'd that my family could not have done better than to have come to England when they did. how short a way do we penetrate into the secrets of Futurity! did you think when I left Boston such a sceene would have taken Place? that I was leaving so much distress? and that my choice was so undoubtedly the most eligiable? and what ere long I should have been obliged to have adopted? and than it would have been to a much greater disadvantage. I now have the hope that my happiness will be made still more compleat by meeting you and my dear mother in England. I shall (if it pleases God to spare my life) be there in Octr., as I am near done in this place, and shall make the best of my way there as soon as I have finished my Copy of the Corregio, which I am about at this time.

Here you will wish (if your troubles do not ingage your thoughts to other things that more nearly concern life) to have a very perticular Account of this Picture; but as I expect to see you when I get to London, I shall suspend my remarks on it till I see you; or if my expectations are not fulfilled, than I will send them to you in wrighting, with my process in making the Copy and an account of the Copy. in the mean time, let not your Spirits be the least dejected, for as we cannot perceive what is before us, weither it is good or evil, so we aught to resolve all into an intire submission to the dispensations of providence, after we have done all in our own power. this we should be carefull to do, and by pursuing our duty we shall always feel an happiness within ourselves that the World cannot rob us of. We even should not entertain a doubt of the goodness of God to us, even to the blessing us in this life with what is good and comfortable. you are now young and a sufferer with the multitude; but now let me ask you if you are so great a sufferer as I am? yet I am not dejected in the least, and was not my impatience to get to England greater than I can express, and my anxiety for you and my other friends in America very distressing to me, I say was it not for these considerations, I could say my spirits were never better than at this time. yet I have lost perhaps my all, as you have; but I have a family, you are single; you are much younger too. these are things that throws the balance much in your favour, very much in your favour. aught you than to be over ancious? in your last Letter by your Sister from two Incidents you drew a very just conclution, and I would have you never lose sight of it. you may say perhaps that my prospects in England gives me an advantage above you, but dont think that, for if I am successfull there you will be a sharer of it; and I assure you your own Works have as much merrit in them as most of the Artists of your Standing, and much more than three quarters of them. even those who have Study'd in Italy don't in general produce better things than you are capable of produceing. go on with your Studys, and let those fight that chuse to fight. at all events do somthing for the exibition the next year, send it to me. if it is what I could wish, it shall have a place; if not, I will not expose it. not that I doubt of your abillity to [do] it well, but I would have somthing that should make some figure, that should be singled out among the others, and should prefer delaying a year or two rather than be undistinguishd in the Crowd; and it generally happens that those are overloo[ke]d that have not somthing to distinguish them more than the bare merrit of the exicution. beauty for instance, if it is singular, it will with good exicution draw the attention of the publick. that I was singularly happy in in my first exibition. if I can think of any thing within your reach, I mean as to a model, I will menshon it in my next, and wish you to do somthing, if you still stay in America; but I shall be greatly disappointed if you do not prevail with our dear Mother to leave it.

I propose going from this to Venice and through the Tirole, Germany, and Flanders, which is the shortest way to England and a different Rout from that I took in coming to Italy. I shall not return to Parris as I intended, When I gave my perticular rout in a former Letter to your Sister, because that would be going out of my Way. do continue to send me the perticulars of the proceedings from America. I am uneasy for our Brother Pelham and Family. I am also apprehensive that in the Winter, if the Frost should be severe and the Harbour froze, that the Town of Boston will be exposed to an attack; and if it should be taken all that have remained in the town will be consider'd as enimys to the Country and ill treated or exposed to great distress; for I think the King's ships [are] what at present secures the town from assalt; but when they are lockd up in Ice, the Provincials may find means to set them on fire, and will surely do it, if it is a possable thing, which I think it is. And than how will it be possable for the army to defend a Town, exposed as that will be from every side to be penetrated? I pray God to keep and preserve you all from any additional callamitys; but I have a thousand fears continually crouding into my mind. give my most effectionate Love and Duty to my Dear Mother, to My Father, Brothers, Sisters, Uncles, Aunts, and all Friends, and beleive me, Dear Harry, your most Affectionate Brother,

JOHN SINGLETON COPLEY.

A Plan of Charlestown

A Plan of Charlestown in New England, with part of Boston &c. exhibiting the Redoubt stormed June 1775, with the Works, since erected by his Majestys Troops. Surveyed and Drawn with the General's permission by Henry Pelham.

August, 1775.

Proposed Dedication

To the Honorable Major General Howe —

Animated by whose Conduct and Valour the national Ardour and Bravery of two thousand British Officers and Soldiers, after having been obstructed in their march by a Number of Rail Fences and flanked by a hot fire from dwelling Houses, gained a Victory On the Heights of Charles-Town, June 17, 1775, over the Enthusiasm of above four Thousand Rebels who were entrenched in a strong R[edoub]t[1] Mounted with Cannon,

---

[1] The letters in brackets have been erased.

defended by an extensive Breast Work and concealed behind
a close prepared Hedge supported with Cannon also;
    This View of the Scene of Action is respectfully inscribed by
                    his most Obedient
                                    Humble Servant.[1]

                Mrs. Copley to Henry Pelham

                            Islington, September [t]he 18, 1775.
Dear Brother,
    I have Long been looking out for an oppertunity to forward
Letters I have receive'd from your Brother and my Dear
Husband. I am out of the way of knowing when the Transports
Sail. I was much disapointed to find Mr. Huges had saild for
Boston, that I mist the oppertunity of letting my Friends hear
from me, as I had letters wrote and did not know of the Vessel
Sailing. you will see Mr. Copley's great anxieaty to prevail on
our Mama to leave America. I was much disapointed to find
by your kind Letter of the 26 of July, that you had giveen over
all thoughts of comeing to England this fall. I have been looking out for you every arival till My Papa's Letter of the 18 of
July, which inform'd me your Mama could not detirmin to
come. you can have no Idea of My distress for my Friends in
Boston. the accounts we continuly have are so distressing,
that I am supprised that our Mama or any that can leave
America should hesitate one moment about it. could I add any
Arguments to Mr. Copley more persuasive I should not be
wanting, but would beg lea[ve] to tell our Mama through you

---

[1] This plan was afterwards embodied in a large map of Boston and the
surrounding country, well known for its execution. It was published in London, June 2, 1777, and, doubtless for political reasons, was dedicated to Lord
George Germain.

that I should be happy to have in my power to contribute to her comfort. for I think we are so made for each outher that we cannot be happy when we have reason to think our Friends are exposed to distress. my distance is great, but my Thoughts are most continuly in the circle of my Friends. I think how happy should I be to be able to administer any Balm to heal the wou[n]ds of there distress. but hope you and the rest of them will indeavour to keep up your Spirits. for the greater our trials are the greater cause have we to exert all our resolution and fortitude. I have often thought with pleasure on some Sermons Mr. Parker preached not long before I left Boston, from these words: The Lord Raineth. the great uncertainty where my Friends would be has prevented my writing to them so frequently as I should outher wise have don. for I should be loath to have my Letters read in Congress, for I should not expect so much cander as I hope for from my Friends. I am daly hopeing to hear of my Papa's dietermination to leave Boston, and Brother and Sister Bromfield. a report has pre-vail'd here for some time that the Troops are to remove from Boston to some outher place; but there is no depending uppon common report. we hear Captain Robertson is arived in the Downs in 24 Days from Boston, and that Mrs. Gage is come with him. I am in continual expecttation of hearing from my Friends, and please my Self I shall hear of there dietermination to Leave America, as it appears as if the troubles would daly increase. the last accounts I have from Mr. Copley is the 5 of this Month. he tells me he expects to be in England in Octor. you will find you[r] Letters where [were] wrote on the same Sheet with mine. Some of them where by private hands so that they have arive'd about the same time. in His last he says he expects to Meet you and his Mama here when he arives.

Scence I have been in England I have been in Mr. Bromfields Family, where I have Meet with the greatest frindship, and should have been very happy, was it not for my great uneasyness for my absent Friends. as to England you must not expect from me any accou[nt] of it at present, for my thoughts are so intent uppon America that at times I can scarcely realize my Self to be out of it. I have not had the least inclination to Vissit any of the publick places of Entertainment. you will think me much wanting in taste, but I expect a double pleasure in seeing what may fall to my lot, when Mr. Copley returns. Mr. and Mrs. West's Servilitys called me to return a Visit to them. I was much entertained with his works, which are very great and must have cost him much Study and labor. I shall omit giveing you any particuler account, as I hope before long you will have an oppertunity of Viewing them your Self. the Americans Muster very thick in England. Mr. Vassall and Family, and Mr. Thomas Brattel, Mr. Geair,[1] arive'd here last week; and we hear Captain Foldger is to bring a Hundred passengers, but cannot learn who they are. I shall be happy to have my Friends amongst the Number. I hope to find our Mama and you have altered your resolution.

[Sept.] 21 Scence writing the above, I have receiv'd your Letter of the 19 of Aut: to Mr. Copley, with one from my Papa and Sister Lucy. every account increases my distress. I pray Heaven to prepair me for all events. I am much disapointed to find my Friends had not ditermind to leave a Country which is involved in the greatest Miserys, but think before this they must have ditermind to leave it. I have not the least Thought that this Letter will meet you or any of my Friends in Boston. I pray God to direct you to those Measures which will be for

---

[1] Geyer.

your Safty. I am very anxious for my poor Babe, but am happy it is under the care of those who will do the best for it. I desire to be resind to the all wise will of the great disposeer of all things, neither to dispise his chastenings, nor to faint when I am rebuke'd of him.

Through the goodness of God there has been a plentifull Hearvest in England, and every kind of thing that can be sent, will be, to the releaf of those who are sufering in a Land of plenty for want of the comforts of Life.

Should this meet you and any of my Friends with you, please to remember me to them with tender Affection, and let them know that my self and Children are well. Should I find they remain in America, which I much hope they will not, I shall write to them soon. pray present my Duty to our Mama, and except of my best wishes for your Happyness, and beleave me to be your Affectinate Sister

SUSANNA COPLEY.

P S the inclosed letters are all I have received from Mr. Copley scence my arival. he mentions haveing Sent a large packet by Mr. Izard, but I have not seen it.

Henry Pelham to Copley

BOSTON, Octr. 10, 1775.

MY DEAR BROTHER,

The Secretary's politeness affords me an Oppertunity of writing a few Lines, which I hope will meet you happyly situated agreable to your most sanguine Wishes once more in London. Every Day affords fresh instances and adds distressing confirmation of the inconstancy of Fortune, of the uncertainty of Life, and the Vanity of all worldly prospects. The variagated Callamities with which this life is checkered, forces the mind to look forward to another and teaches us to adore that Almighty Being, whose unbounded Goodness assures us of an happy Immortallity, being the certain Reward of a Life of integrity and Virtue. The distressing Circumstances of this Country; The perticular Situation I am now in, The Abscence of many very worthy and dear Friends, and the diminution by Death of the very few that remaind, make me feel very unhappy. The recent and unexpected Death of Miss Lucy Clarke, is what I much deplore, as she was a very valuable and worthy Friend, whose conversation I always found as sensible, as her Behaviour was polite and Friendly: I most sincerely condole with you and Mrs. Copley upon this Event. Her real worth, Benevolence and Piety, as they attracted the Respect and Esteem of her Friends while Living, will ever endear her Memory to them now Dead. I have lost another very agreable Acquaintance in young Lady Pepperell, who died this Morng of a Bilious Fever, after a severe illness of 3 Weeks.[1] I find myself extreemly perplexed. I am entirely at a loss to know what to Do. The Total Stoppage of Buisness forbids ny remaining here, and how to leave the place I dont know. My hon'd Mother not inclining to undertake a Voyage and to leave her in so very disagreable a Situation would make me very uneasy. I now much want your advice, but the Distance precludes me that advantage. I am unfortunate in having but few friends here who are sufficiently informed to give me that advice which would regulate my Motions. It is now a twelve month since I have done any Buisness worth nameing. What Money I had oweing to me I cant get a farthing off, and what Buisness I had in hand the Cruelty of the times has rendered unprofitable.

[1] Elizabeth, daughter of Isaac Royall. Stark, *Loyalists of Massachusetts*, 208, states that she died on the passage to London.

It requires the full exertion of all my Philosophy, to support my Spirits under the many Disapointments I have experienced for near two Years past. I then fondly flattered myself (from my Buisness which at that time began to increase) that I should be enabled at some future Period, to avow with Reputation and Propriety, a tender attachment for one of the most lovely and amiable of my Female Friends. An Honorable and sincere Affection for female Virtue and Accomplishments is what never can justly raise a Blush in any Face. Sure I am you'll think it need not in mine, when I mention Miss Sally Bromfield as the Object of my highest Esteem and Regard.[1]

As it was ever my intention to act agreable to the strictest Rules of Justice and Honour, I have hitherto kept this a Secret in my own Breast, thinking it totally unbecoming a generous Mind, under such circumstances as mine, to disturb a Lady's repose by soliciting a Return of that Regard and attention which my present situation forbids me to expect. To a Brother's sympathiszing Friendship do I now first trust this Secret of my Soul. I should not now have done it had I not wanted that advice which your good Judgement and knowledge of the World so well quallifies you to give, and the many and Continued Marks I have experienced of your kindness and disinterested Friendship, prompts me to ask. The Confusions which commenced upon the fatal Era of the Tea's arrival, at once blasted all my fondest hopes. I at once saw all my prospects vanish, and then first felt the corroding Anguish of Disapointment.[2] My Sperits sunk and I found myself obliged to take a

[1] Sarah Bromfield (1757–1831) married Eliphalet Pearson in 1786. She was daughter of Henry and Margaret (Fayerweather) Bromfield.

[2] First draft: "Foreseeing that if one spark of British Spir[i]t Still an[i]mated the Councills of the Nation she would resent the Outrage and insult offer'd her Laws and Commerce, my Spir[i]ts sunk, etc."

journey to recover my health, which a constant Succession of new Scenes, with a change of Air and Exercise by the blessing of Heaven, in a few months effected. Soon after my Return from Philadelphia, increasing Buisness, again flattered my ardent Wishes. But Alass! a few Weeks soon cut short my glimmering prospect and entirely dissipated every remaining Hope. Those events which I long foresaw have taken place and Civil War with all its Horrors, Now blasts every tender Connection, every Social Tie upon which the happyness of mankind so materially depends. We are now unhappyly a float in one common Ruin[1] and have only left us the Mortifying Remembrance, of those halcyon days of ease and peace, which we now in vain, wish to reinjoy. From this State of my mind you will be the better enabled to direct my future destination. I propose remaining here this Winter in hopes you will favour me with your early advice, as that delivered with freedom, will greatly determine my Conduct. I congratulate you and Mrs. Copley, upon her safe arrival with my dear little Fri[e]nds in London, My hon'd Mamma joins me in this and in tender Regards and good Wishes for you my Sister and the little Family. I cant conclude without expressing my uneasiness at your long Silence. when I returned from the southward near a year ago I rec'd 8 Letters which had arrived during my absence; since which I have not had a line from you. I speak sincerely when I say this long Silence hurts me much. Your affectionate Conduct forbids my thinking it any want of Regard. Upon the strictest Review I cant find the cause originateing in myself, Nor yet can I attribute it to the accidental loss of Letters, as 8 in six Months and none in twelve hold no possable proportion.

---

[1] First draft: "The Ambition of some and the intemperate and misguided Zeal of others has most unhappyly overwhelm'd us in one common Ruin."

You will do me a kindness if you would explain the Cause. I am, my Dear Friend, your most affectionate Brother and humble Sert.

H.

Henry Pelham to Copley

Boston, Jany. 27, 1776.

My dear Brother,

One or two Vessels have slipped away without my writeing to you. sorry I am that in reassuming the Pen after so long an Omission, I am called upon to condole with you and my dear Sister upon the death of your little Son, who died the 19th Instant of a consumption with which he has been declining for some months past. As Mrs. Bromfield has very lately given my Sister an Account of the Progress of his disorder till within a few days of his death I shall omitt it. Being confind with a Cold I had not seen him for several days, till Nurse sent to aquaint me he was very ill and that she thought he could not live. upon my going down I found him very near his end, lying seemingly insensable with every symptom of an approaching dissolution which in a few Hours took place. Soul and Body perhaps never parted with less pain than those of my amiable and lovely little Friend's. Not a groan or a Struggle discomposed his innocent and chearfull face. His remains were deposited in Mr. Clarke's tomb. The funeral was from Mr. Bromfield's. Mr. Parker[1] read the burial Service. Thus early has our little Friend paid the great Debt of Nature and left the Vice and Miseries of this life for the unchan[g]able joys and Happyness of blessd Eternity. Tho' Affection may call forth a tear yet Reason and Humanity forbid our mour[n]ing his departure. When we take a Retrospective View of past Life

---

[1] Samuel Parker, of Trinity Church.

and recollect the innumerable troubles and Disapointments, The Cares and Anxieties which have tarnishd our happyest Hours; when we see the distress and Danger in which the greatest part of our fellow mortals are involved, and reflect upon the various ills attendant upon the happyest in this Mortal State, We cant view Death without his Horrors. But when we turn our eyes to the bright scenes which lie beyond the grave, the unclouded and serene Happyness, the virtuous and good there, find Death instead of appearing the King of Terrors to them will assum[e] the milder aspect of a Messenger of Peace and Comfort.

I should do injustice was I not to mention the great care and faithfulness with which nurse discharged her Duty by the infant. Her whole attention and time was devoted to its comfort and welfare: and she appeared to have a real affection for her charge.

I have before incidentally mentioned the receipt of your very agreable favour of March the 14, 1775, tho it was above Nine Months before it came to hand. I found it in the post Office: Somebody had Curiosity eno' to open it. This is a liberty now very frequently taken: However they had manners eno' to seal it again, which I thank them for: I mention this to give you a caution both as to the subject on which you write and to the manner in which you send your Letters. You are to recollect that I now live under a military goverm[e]nt, where the will of the commander in Chief is the Law and the good of the service is the rule of Action: The Army was perhaps never governed by a better sett of general Officers than the present, weither we consider them as Soldiers, as Men, or as Gentlemen. Genel. Howe's and Lord Percy's Character as Soldiers are establishd by their Bravery and good Conduct since they have been in America. Their generosity and Virtues in private Life are universally known and acknowledged: But I am sorry to say the secrescy that attends military operations affords innumerable Opertunities to the Envious, the Revengefull, the mischeviously wicked, to blast, undiscoverd and unknown, the Characters and Reputation of those who are infinitely better Subjects and better Men than themselves. several Instances of this kind have lately taken place. I have hitherto avoided every cause of Blame, on the contrary, am considered as what I really am, a faithfull and loyal Subject to the most amiable and Injured of soveriegns, and am hon'd with the Civilities and Notice of some of the first Characters in America, yet I have had and possably may now have Enemies who would improve even an innocent peice of prudential advice to my disadvantage. I could therefore wish you to exclude all political Observations from your Letters, and leave me to scrable thro this turbulent and Dangerous Contest as well as I can. For you[r] Observations, tho intended for my Benefit, may eventually prove detrimental, the Events of war being precarious, and it being entirely uncertain into whose hands your letters may fall, both sides now opening all they meet with: The men of war are the safest Conveyances, the transport and provision Vessells too frequently becoming prize to the privatiers which have for some time and still Continue to infest these Seas: I have been more perticular and lengthey on this head, as it will reach your hands unexamined, Sir Wm. Pepperell taking the care of it: I am much grieved at the disagreable diference that subsists between you and him, for I must consider him as a very amiable and Worthy man. I wish something might take place to remove it, as I think it founded intirely on Missapprehension and Mistake: As to News we seldom have any. We still continue in the same State as when Mr. Clarke left us.[1] Both side[s] strengthing their Works, and preventing the other from receiv'g supplies. Pork and peas, and little eno of that, still continues to be our Diet: a baked Rice pudding without butter milk or Eggs, or a little salt fish without Butter, we think luxurious living. Lamenting our most disagreable Situation is the only them[e] of our discourse. Contriving ways and means to gett a pound of Butter, a quart of peas to eat, or 3 or 4 rotten boards the ruins of some old barn to burn, our only buisness; and the recollection of our having some friends at a Distance from this scene of Anarchy and Confusion almost our only Happyness.

Our hond. Mamma gives her kind Love and Blessing to you my Sister and the Lovely little ones: she is in great trouble on the death of her little grandson. desires sincerely to condole with you on the Event. her Health is nearly the same as when you saw her, rather injured by the very poor living we have. She, as well as myself, are rendered very happy upon hearing of you or my Sister. if you knew what joy it gives us I am certain no opertunity would escape unimproved. I intended to have observed upon some parts of your very improv'g Letter, but defer it till my next, having already I fear tired your patienc[e], tho I have not yet done. You desire me to be very perticular. I will so, without observing order or Method. My next perhaps will be accompan[i]ed with a plan of Boston and Charlestown which I have been surveying with the Country for three or four miles round this town in this plan I lay down all the works which are erec[t]ed to confine the Troops and Torrys to the narrow limitts we now range in: I dont think if I had Liberty I could find the way to Cambridge, tho I am so well

[1] The Clarke family arrived in London, December 24, 1774, twenty-one days from Boston.

aqua[i]nted with the Road. not a Hillock 6 feet High but
What is entrench'd, not a pass where a man could go but what
is defended by Cannon; fences pulled down, houses removed,
Woods grubed up, Fields cut into trenches and molded into
Ramparts, are but a part of the Changes the country has gone
thro. Nor has Boston been free from the Effects of War. An
hundred places you might be brought to and you not know
where you were. I doubt if you would know the town at
all. Charlestown I am sure you would not. there not a Tree,
not an house, not even so much as a stick of wood as large
as your hand remains. The very Hills seem to have altered
ther form. In Boston almost all the fences: a great Number of Wooden Houses, perhaps 150, have been pull'd down
to serve for fewel. in this ruin you[r] Estate has escaped,
no Injury being done it; Dr. Byles', Dr. Cooper's, Dr.
Ma[t]hew's Meeting Houses turned into Barracks. Dr. Sew-
ells' into a Riding School, Fanuel Hall into a Theatre. The
old North pulled down and burnt. Every rising fortified. in
short nothing but an actual sight of the town can give an Idea
of its situation. My Brother Pelham and family I have not
hea[r]d any thing of for 8 Months, nor dont know with[e]r they
are dead or alive: Mr. and Mrs. Bromfield are well. I there
frequ[ently] spend some of my agreable Hours: Betzey is well;
she and little Ned were lately inoculated; they are both recovered. he was finely pepered off with it: In the natural Way it
has been very fatal 1 in 3 dying. by innoculati[o]n in gener[a]l
it was very favourable. By a letter Mr. Bromfield has lately
rec'd from Harry I was made very happy to find that himself
with Miss Nabby[1] and my very amiable and lovely fr[i]end were
well. Miss Sally spend[s] the Winter at Andover; Nabby at

---

[1] Abigail Bromfield (1753–1791) married Daniel Denison Rogers.

Salem. I have amused myself for some hours past with viewing 4 fine prints I bought yesterday at Vendue. 3 of them please me very much. they are the portraits of Lady Middleton, half length, after Sir P. Lely; the Dutches of Ancaster, whole length, after Hudson; and Lady Campbell, the duke of Argyle's Daughter, whole leng[th], after Ramsay. all three good impression[s] from McArdells plates.[1] There is a Report in Town that the Rebels have mett with a consider'ble defeat at Quebeck, that their general Montgomery with 200 of his Men are killed, and that Coll. Arnold with 300 more are prisoners. This report seem[s] generally believ[e]d. We hope soon to hear of you[r] and Mr. Clarkes arrival in E. be kind eno to present My Mamas and my respectfull Compli[ments] to him. my kindest Love and good wi[s]hes attend you, my Sister, and the young family. I wish you to remember that in Boston you have a sincerely affectionate Brother, who thanks you for all your favours and is your very hum. Sert.

H. P.

Henry Pelham to [Henry Bromfield, Jr.]

BOSTON, Feb. 4, [1776.]

the[2] design of this is to invite you to meet me at the lines on Tuesd[ay] the 20th. Some things of a domestick kind I wish a Conferenc[e] upon. The Friends[h]ip that Subsists between us I hope will be a stimulus in your part as it will be on mine to let nothing but unavoidable accidents disapo[i]nt the pleasure I anticipate. in this Interview. Should you be prevented on that day come the Tuesday Following: I wish you would come down with my Brother Pelham I have wrote to him desiring it, but

[1] James MacArdell (1729?-1765).
[2] Erased: "I have the generals leave to meet."

for fear my Letter should not come to his hands I beg you to write him a line as soon as you receive this acqua[i]nting him with its contents, and my earnest desire to see him.

Your Fr[i]ends are all will. Give my kind Love to the Ladys and believe me to be with sincere affection my Dear Fr[i]end, your very hum sert.

HENRY PELHAM.

Henry Bromfield, Jr. to Henry Pelham

MY DEAR FRIEND,

Your Letter of 27th Decem'r I did not receive till my Return from Eastward abo't a Fortnight past: I believe I need not assure you it mett with a most cordial Reception. The Sensations it produced are not easy to be described; let your own Feelings declare them.

It serv'd to recall to my Imagination the pleasing past; when surrounded by the sweet Circle of Peace, blest with the Smiles of Lenient Heaven, we enjoy'd the Social Converse of Relations, Connections and Friends, which temper'd the Business of the Day, and while it tended to our mutual Comfort and Pleasure, rendered even the Fatigues of it agreable. How happy then our Lot. None could be more so. But, Alas! How chang'd is the Scene. The Reflection on our past Happiness serves but to make the Sense of our present Deprivation the more painful. Hapless Boston I often see at a Distance, but am at a Loss to call a Neighbour and take a friendly Walk. How different was our Situation at our last Meeting from what we can each recollect, on that very Spot, where, engag'd in friendly Intercourse, our Feet have often Stray'd.

Our Interview was very short, and from the Contents of your last Letter, which came to Hand since, I have Reason to think you did not communicate all you intended. I shall apply for Leave to accompany the next Flag, in Hopes of meeting my Father. Shall be happy to meet you again before you embark.

The Motive you are pleas'd to ascribe to me is really flattering, which I will overlook, considering it was dictated by the Partiality of a Friend. Mr. Babcock's Acco't with the Order on him I left sometime ago with Mr. Webb of Wethersfield; whether he has recd the Money he has not yet acquainted me, but I expect to hear from him Soon. The Letter you mention as inclos'd I have not Seen. The Post Master assures me it is forwarded to New Haven.

I have desir'd my Father to pay you £10.12.8 Lawf. My., being the Amo't of Sale of your Horse and Carriage. I wish it was more, but is the most I could obtain. Letters from my Uncle in London, as late as 2d Novr. mention Mrs. Copley being still with him; that her little Family had pass'd thro' the small pox; and they were all well. From his Saying nothing of Mr. Copley I conclude he was not arriv'd there. The Ladies are well and beg their Compliments. Please to make mine to such as enquire after me, and should I be disapointed of the Happiness of Seeing my Father, present my Duty to him and my Mother. O! How moving is it to be so near and yet debarr'd so great a Pleasure. Surely this Separation of Friends is to be deplor'd as the greatest Misery of these most distressing Times. Favor them with as much of your Company as your Convenience will admit of: it was always priz'd, and I know will be particularly now.

I trust a Separation of our Persons will never tend to lessen our mutual Regard, and assure you, that whatever my Situation be,

I am most Sincerely and affectionately your's

HENRY BROMFIELD, JUN.

ANDOVER, Feby. 25th, 1776.

Dr. Henry Caner[1] to Copley

[No date.]

DEAR SIR,

I am surprized that what Rubens says of Da Vinci's peice should incline you to think of that in my Possession as incompatible with his Description. I confess it has further confirm'd me in the opinion that it can be no other than the Production of that great Master. If it be allow'd that Rubens and Webb are describing the same Peice, I do not see how this Conclusion can be avoided, since Rubens's description is fairly reconcileable, and Webb's is undeniably particular. In the present Peice our Saviour is in the midst, as free and unencumber'd as the truth of the history will admit; His attitude is grave; his Arms quite free, one of them easily extended, the other hand lightly resting upon the Shoulder of the beloved Disciple. The Apostles have suitable places assigned them, and appear agitated agreeable to the Occasion.

I fancy if you and I were to consult the Peice together once more with Rubens's and Webb's Description before us, we should not only concurr in Opinion, but pronounce in favour of this Peice as the Production of da Vinci. I am, Sir, Your most humble Servant,

H. CANER.

FRIDAY 10 o'Clock.

[1] Dr. Caner was rector of King's Chapel, 1747–1776.

To all People to whom these presents shall come greeting Know ye that I Henry Pelham of Boston in the County of Suffolk and Province of Massachusetts Bay in New England Portrait Painter have constituted and appointed Henry Bromfield Esq. of Boston aforesaid to be my true and lawful Attorney for me and in my Name and to my use to ask demand sue for recover and receive and on Receipt thereof give discharges for all sums of Money Debts Accounts Reckonings, Claims and demands of every nature and kind whereof I have cause of suit or Action in the aforementioned Province and suit in Law or Equity for recovering thereof to commence and persue hereby impowering him my said Attorney, to appoint Attorneys and Substitutes under him And I hereby covenant to Ratify and confirm whatever he my said attorney shall do or cause to be done in the Premises by Virtue hereof. In Witness whereof I have hereunto set my hand and Seal this Ninth Day of March Anno Domini One Thousand Seven Hundred and seventy Six and in the sixteenth year of his Majestys Reign

Signed sealed and delivered
in pursuance of us
Byfield Lyde
Sarah Lyde

Henry Pelham

Copley to Henry Pelham

[No date.]

DEAR HARRY,

the weither being very damp and I have somthing of a Cold so thought proper to stay at home to Day should be glad to know how our Mamma is and Snap is. I am engaged to paint Mr. Taylors[1] Face tomorrow at 9 o'Clock therefore beg you will set my Pallet in the morn'g accordingly pray give my Affectionate Duty to our Hon'd Mamma, and accept my Love

J. S. COPLEY.

Sunday Even'g.

[1] See page 77, *supra.*

London Decr 10 1783 Recd of John
Adams Esqur one hundred Guineas
in full for him drawn by me

J. S. Copley

Philadelphia August 7th 1866

Recd of Mrs Adams one hundred dollars
in payment for a portrait painted by my

Index

Index

Abbot, Samuel, 107.
Adams, Abigail, 185 *n.*; portrait, 374.
Adams, John, 122 *n.*; portrait, 374.
Adams, Samuel, 107, 210, 264 *n.*, 288, 344; portrait, 294, 308.
Ainslie, Thomas, portrait, 23, 30.
Algarotti, Francesco, *Count*, 51.
Allen, William, 163, 272, 293, 341.
Amory, John, 107.
Anderson, James, on Free-Masons, 185.
Andrews, Benjamin, portrait, 197.
Antonio, 177.
Apthorp, Charles Ward, 128.
Apthorp, Trecothick and, 88.
Apthorp, snow, 30.
Arms, coat of, 89.
Arnold, Benedict, 369.
Association, Continental Congress, 274.
Auchmuty, Samuel, 166, 198, 292.
Austen, Henry, 180.
Avery, John, 107.

Babcock, Adam, 267, 371; letter, 281.
Babcock, *Mrs.*, 313.
Baker, ———, 13 *n.*; death, 15, 16.
Balch, ———, 125.
Balston, Nathaniel, 107.
Bambridge, ———, 208.
Bannister, John, 146.
Bannister, Samuel, 131 *n.*
Bannister, Thomas, 131, 178, 184.
Barbados, 38.
Barber, Nathaniel, 95.
Barber, Wilkes, 95, 98.
Barnard, John, 85, 86.
Barrell, Joseph, 162.
Barrett, John, 107.
Barrett, *Mrs.*, 168 *n.*
Barrett, *Miss*, 167.
Barrow, ———, 114.
Barry, Henry, 288 *n.*
Bayard, ———, 126, 129, 134, 292.
Bernard, Francis, Jr., 96.

Billings, *Mrs.*, 183.
Bingham, William, 206.
Bliss, Moses, 291.
Bossley, ———, 278.
Boston, fire, 1760, 23; smallpox, 29, 276, 368; stamp office, 36; massacre plate, 83; powder house, 106; disturbances, 201, 211, 218, 232, 267, 288, 290, 312, 344; besieged, 324, 365; map, 350, 367.
Botetourt, *Baron*, 96.
Bours, John, 281.
Bowdoin, James, letter, 185.
Bowen, Jabez, 281.
Bowes, Nicholas, 107.
Box, John, 29, 107.
"Boy with the Squirrel," 35, 37, 48, 50, 59; Reynolds on, 41; West, 43.
Boydell, John, 82.
Boylston, Nicholas, 107, 136, 149.
Boylston, *Mrs.* Thomas, 213 *n.*, 215.
Boylston, Ward Nicholas, 330.
Brattle Street Church, Copley's designs, 185, 186.
Brattle, Thomas, 107, 186, 359.
Brimmer, Herman, 107.
Brimmer, Martin, 107.
Britannia, 6.
Bromfield, Abigail, 368.
Bromfield, Hannah (Clarke), 115 *n.*
Bromfield, Henry, Sr., 115, 362 *n.*
Bromfield, Henry, Jr., 315, 317, 325, 358, 368, 369; letter, 370.
Bromfield, Margaret (Fayerweather), 362 *n.*
Bromfield, Sarah, 314, 317, 362, 368.
Bromfield, Thomas, 115, 140, 344, 359, 371.
Bruce, R. G., 34, 35, 37, 44, 48, 49, 68; letters, 41, 55, 58.
Buccleugh, *Duchess of*, 6 *n.*
Bulfinch, Thomas, 149.
Bunker Hill, 345.
Burbeck, ———, 263.
Butler, ———, 183.
Byers, James, 204, 205.